THOMAS HORN
— THE —
EARLY YEARS
Two Books In One

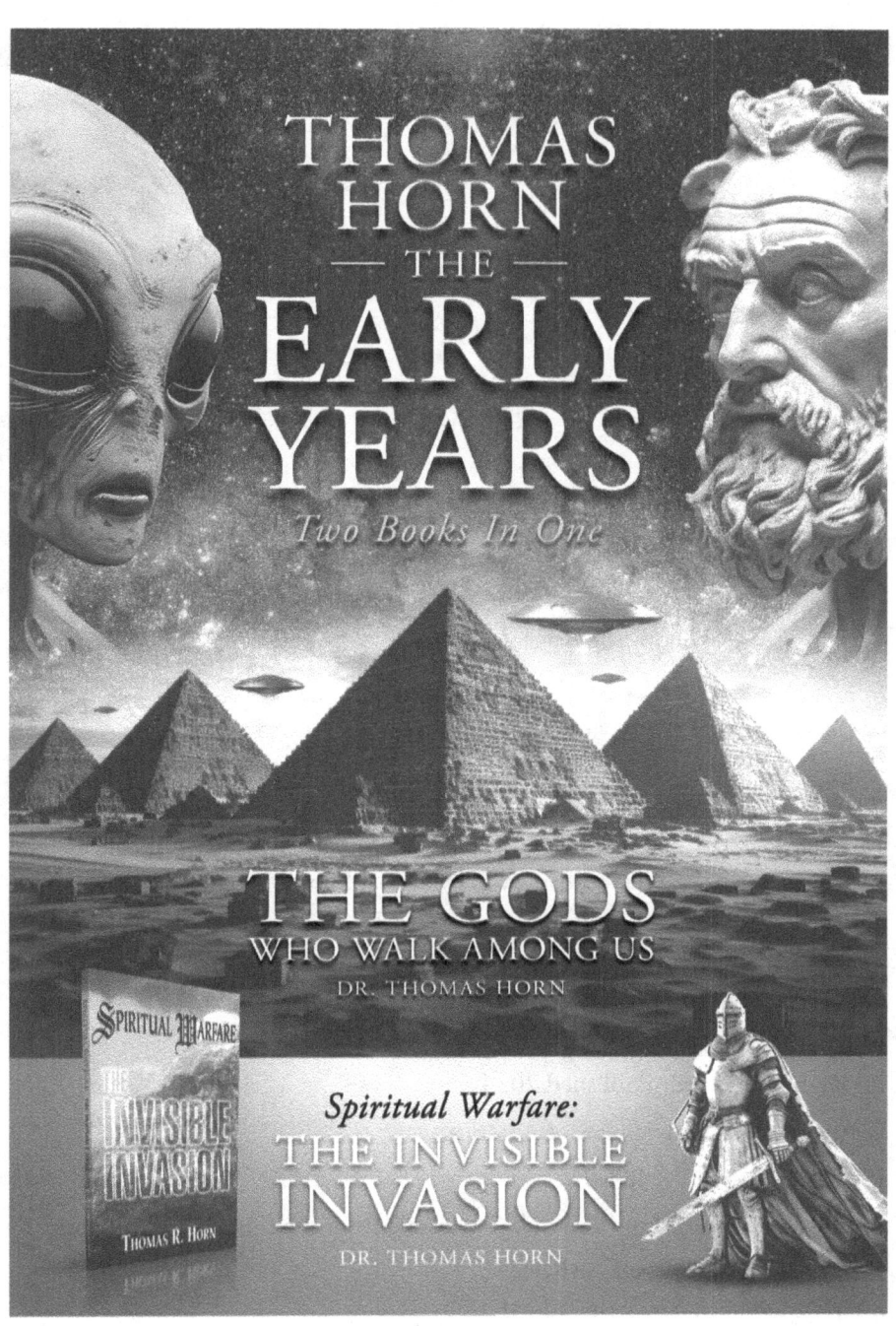

DEFENDER
CRANE, MO

THOMAS HORN—THE EARLY YEARS:
Spiritual Warfare: The Invisible Invasion and *The Gods Who Walk Among Us*
By Thomas Horn; collaborative work by Donald Jones in *The Gods Who Walk Among Us*

Defender Publishing
Crane, MO 65633

© 2024 Defender Publishing
All Rights Reserved. Published 2024.

Printed in the United States of America.

ISBN: 978-1-9480-1483-0

A CIP catalog record of this book is available from the Library of Congress.

Cover design by Jeffrey Mardis
Interior design by Katherine Lloyd

Unless otherwise indicated, all Scripture quotations are from the King James Version of the Bible.

CONTENTS

SPIRITUAL WARFARE: THE INVISIBLE INVASION

Acknowledgments 5

Foreword 7

One: THE ENEMY'S STRATEGY OF SIEGING CITIES IN AMERICA 9

Two: THE ENEMY'S SECRET FORCES 31

Three: EVIDENCE OF INVASION AND FIRST RESISTANCE ...51

Four: THE VICTORS' MASTER WEAPONS...............75

THE GODS WHO WALK AMONG US

Foreword 139

Acknowledgments 141

One: THE ORIGIN OF THE GODS.....................143

Two: THE GODS WHO WALKED AMONG THE EGYPTIANS...................161

Three: THE GODS WHO WALKED AMONG THE GREEKS...197

Four: THE OLD GODS OF THE NEW AGE...............227

Five: THE NEW AGE OF THE GOD KING...............253

Notes 273

Spiritual Warfare:
THE INVISIBLE
INVASION

By Thomas Horn

*To my wonderful wife, Juanita,
and to the future of our children—
Althia, Joe, and Donna.*

ACKNOWLEDGMENTS

I wish to acknowledge Judy Vorfeld for all of her tireless assistance. Without her input and inspiration, this book would not have been possible.

FOREWORD

America is facing one of her most crucial hours. Our major cities, and possibly our minor ones, are in the grips of Satan. Inner-city problems have now reached the suburbs. Since that which begins in the city eventually saturates the country, the solution to our nation's problems involves changing the city. Therein lies the dilemma. How do you deal with big city problems? There is only one answer—engage in spiritual warfare for your city.

One of my concerns over the Church's current affinity with spiritual warfare, however, is that it seems to be overlooking a major factor: its own relationship with the Lord. We've slowed down in our pursuit of God. We are guilty of putting our glory in church buildings and programs while God sits on the sidelines. It is time to glory in our God once again.

Though the battle is obvious our strategy may not be. *Spiritual Warfare* is a call back to the basics of Christianity. It's a strong call to humble ourselves, to pray, to fast, and to return to righteous living. Those things alone will deal a death blow to the enemy's effectiveness in any community.

Spiritual Warfare is a well-written, well-documented account of Satan's tactics in controlling a community. It addresses current issues and shows us the hope we have in Christ. Thomas Horn not only presents the dilemma faced by the Church today, he also prescribes the solution.

—Reverend Ron Auch

— Chapter One —

THE ENEMY'S STRATEGY OF SIEGING CITIES IN AMERICA

On 5 April 1991, network television broadcasted an exorcism when Catholic authorities granted ABC's *20/20* permission to televise this ancient ritual. This was a first for network programming. Regardless of one's particular religion, it illustrated the contemporary presence of demons.

I wondered: If individual demon possession exists, could nations also come under siege to dominant demonic powers? If people who preside over legislative bodies abandon the moral laws of God, would they thereby espouse a social system that invites a regional increase in the influence of supernatural evil? Is there a cause and effect connection between an invisible invasion of demons and the disintegration of a society?

After several years of analysis, I have come to believe that demons play an active social role in every age of history. While their activity has frequently been overlooked, their close collaboration with certain unregenerate architects of society has at times allowed evil forces to control the machine of municipal government. When the powers of evil discover a society that has become a force for moral good, they set about through a sophisticated network of both visible and invisible principalities to bring that society down one city at a time.

Countless multitudes without the light of divine revelation never see beyond "flesh and blood" (Eph. 6:12). Therefore, dictators, conquerors, presidents, governors, legislators, and such human beings appear, to some, to be the only real characters upon the stage of human history. Unenlightened into the truths of the Scriptures, many are unaware of the unseen presence of "principalities...powers...rulers of darkness...and spiritual wickedness in high places" (Eph. 6:12). When facing social and moral collapse brought on by submission to evil, they cannot perceive a divine social purpose; and, because they are "blinded by the god of this world" (2 Cor. 4:4), they are not aware that the once godly and great foundations of their society are swept away.

Enter the 1990s. The United States leads the world in terms of science and industry. Wall Street bustles with business majors seeking quick fortunes and entrepreneurs deluding investors with hopes of favorable returns. Space shuttles and satellites push forward the frontiers of space exploration, while medical science scrambles to keep up with unprecedented daily discoveries. But while the marvels of American development advance with staggering success, something sinister seems to struggle against the moral character of American cities, eroding our social and cultural strength from within.

At a time when the United States is considered the most advanced, civilized, high-tech nation in the world, spiritual regression and moral decay abound. Idolatry, drug abuse, alcoholism, violence, Satanism, deviant sexuality, interest in New Age religions, and various forms of psychic phenomena exist in every facet of our culture. Socialism looms above us as liberalism permeates the mainstream of American philosophy. Every institution once considered sacred is under an all-out assault. The populace is ravaged by sexual disease while the rate of illegitimacy—perhaps the single most important bellwether of future social disintegration—has risen to 30 percent of all births. In some cities the figure is more than 80 percent.

What's happened to the Christian traditions of America? How can such an intellectual country permit spiritual and social decadence not seen since medieval times? I believe an objective evaluation of our moral

THE ENEMY'S STRATEGY OF SIEGING CITIES IN AMERICA

dilemma must take into account not only the visible agents of city or state governments, but the unending interaction between spiritual and human personalities. This unseen realm of demonic powers energizes and motivates ever-present and sometimes vocal human counterparts. What we see happening in America's cities illustrates a present darkness operating with evil intentions concerning our nation's future.

There are three sources of spiritual power that can influence a nation: 1) divine influence, proceeding forth from the domain of God; 2) satanic influence, coming from the sphere of Satan; and 3) human influence. This third influence, being neutral, has the potential to influence society for good or evil as it submits to divine or satanic control.

There have been times in history when people submitted to God's influence, cleansing the legislative halls and social policies of demonism. This spoiled the strategies of Satan and made possible the salvation of the lost, the renewal of the righteous, and the healing of the nation.

Conversely, there have been historic times when nations turned their back on God, opening the door for "evil angels" (Ps. 78:49) to invade that society. These were times when Satan's voice dominated the mindset of the majority, and systems of government and philosophy were influenced by a destructive spirit capable of blinding men and women to their individual need of Jesus Christ.

To the ancient city of Corinth, a city known for its pride, ostentation, hypersexuality, and lasciviousness (which not only was tolerated, but consecrated through the worship of Venus), Paul informed the saints, "...the god of this world [Satan] hath blinded the minds of them which believe not, lest the light of the glorious Gospel of Christ, who is the image of God, should shine unto them" (2 Cor. 4:4).[1] The Oxford Dictionary defines *hypersexualization* as "the attribution of sexual or erotic characteristics to someone or something to an extreme or inappropriate degree."

Archons ruling from the air above Corinth blinded the minds of

SPIRITUAL WARFARE: THE INVISIBLE INVASION

many Corinthians until the latter were incapable of perceiving their horrid sinful estate and need of Jesus Christ.

It's interesting that the apostle would send this warning to the city of Corinth—a Greek prototype of America's wealth, military strength, and great mental activity.[2] Outwardly, one would have thought these educated Gnostics were wellequipped intellectually to understand the spiritual truths and social significance contained within the Gospel. Yet, Paul said their minds had been blinded by the god of this world. Their superior human knowledge, though impressive to intelligentsia, had not protected the Corinthians from the subtle influences filling the atmosphere above them. Drunk on fleshly pleasures they became a nation under demonic siege. It is within this unseen arena of evil supernaturalism that unregenerate men are organized. Under demonic influence, they are orchestrated within a great evil system (or empire) described in various scriptural passages as a satanic order. In more than thirty important biblical passages, the Greek New Testament employs the term *kosmos*, which describes an invisible order or government. In such *kosmos*, unredeemed men—separated from God—are hostile to the ways of God, and are organized as a resisting system or federation under Satan.

At Satan's desire, archons command this invisible, geopolitical sphere, dominating *kosmokrators* (rulers of darkness who work in and through human political counterparts). These, in turn, command spirits of lesser rank until every level of earthly government is touched by this influence. In Ephesians 6:12, the apostle says that it is this dominion, not flesh and blood, that are at odds with the communities of the world. Our primary problem is not with evil men who govern or philosophize, but with the unseen forces that puppet them. With vivid testimony to this, Satan offered to our Lord all the power and the glory of the governments of this world. Satan said, "This power [control] will I give thee, and the glory of them [earthly cities]: for that is delivered unto me [at the Fall of Man]: and to whomsoever I will I give it. If thou therefore wilt worship me, all shall be thine" (Luke 4:6–7, brackets added).

THE ENEMY'S STRATEGY OF SIEGING CITIES IN AMERICA

This is a picture of a world system out of step with God; a fallen planet under Satan's dominion. In short, a place in need of redemption. If we could see through the veil into the invisible world that inhabits planet earth, we would find a world alive with good against evil. It's a place where the prize is the souls of men, and where legions war for control of its cities and people.

It Begins in the City

While we cannot see Satan's demonic forces with human eyes, their desire to stand in the place of God and rule the nations is defined in Scripture. What we *do* see with our eyes indicates for us those places within society where Satan's troops have first landed.

Every earthly war is won or lost one city at a time. In the spirit world it is the same. If Satan conquers a nation, he does so one city at a time. It is his modus operandi first to invade individual cities of social and political significance and then to expand his agenda outward from there. Satan's agenda includes the ultimate removal or perversion of the Gospel of Christ; the introduction of occult practices; the devaluation of human life; the obstruction of moral law; the glorification of the debased; and so on. Thus, if an invasion of demonism were occurring in the United States, we would see Satan's agenda gradually introduced, and finally accepted, among the trend-setting cities of America. The government would enact laws allowing the expansion and exercise of these immoral deeds, while restricting any imposed moral prohibitions against them based upon the laws of God.

This process has been illustrated many times throughout the Old and New Testaments. Let's consider what we can learn from a few of the biblical examples of influential cities used by Satan.

Biblical Example #1: Pergamum

> "And to the angel of the church in Pergamos write; These things saith he which hath the sharp sword with two edges; I know thy works, and where thou dwellest, even where Satan's seat is: and

thou holdest fast my name, and has not denied my faith, even in those days wherein Antipas was my faithful martyr, who was slain among you, where Satan dwelleth" (Rev. 2:12–13).

In the letter to the church in Pergamos (Pergamum), verse 13 says, "I know…where thou dwellest, even where Satan's seat is." The Greek verse reads *Satanos thronos esti*, literally, "Where a throne to Satan is." The city of Pergamum was an influential city used by Satan to affect the whole nation.

At the writing of Revelation, chapter 2, in the Hellenistic kingdoms of Asia Minor—twenty miles from the Aegean Sea and forty miles north of Smyrna—stood the most impressive surviving city built during the conquests of Alexander the Great: Pergamum. Named from the Latin, *pergamentum* (parchment), this was a city known for its great library, massive royal palace, museums, and temples dedicated to the Greek and Roman gods—Zeus, Apollo, Athena, and especially Asclepius.[3] A theater seating ten thousand people sloped down to the *stoa*, a column-lined promenade that looked out over the plains below. Ancient Pergamum claimed Galen, a man gifted in the field of medicine who was second only to Hippocrates in fame, but not in deed. It was this same Galen who gathered all the medical knowledge of antiquity into his writings, and who remained the supreme authority in medical science for more than a thousand years.[4]

But Pergamum, while advanced, was a city under demonic design. The principal stronghold, according to the Christian world, centered around the worship of the god Asclepius. At the base of Pergamum's hill stood the shrine of Asclepius, equipped with its own library, theater, sleeping chambers used in healing rituals, and long underground tunnels joining various other shrines to which pagans journeyed to receive the healing powers of Apollo's favorite son. The Christian church considered these mystical powers as demonic, for the worship of Asclepius focused on the image of a serpent, sometimes called Glycon.[5] This idol was an enormous serpent-figure some historians see as the origin for the modern symbol of healing—a serpent winding about a pole.[6] Asclepius carried the lofty title, "the hero god of healing."[7]

In Numbers, chapter 21, Moses designed the brazen serpent on a pole that was used by God as an oracle of healing. Seven hundred fortythree years later, in 2 Kings 18:4, we find that Israel had begun to worship the brazen serpent with offerings and incense. From here the image was adopted into Greek mythology where it became the symbol of Asclepius, the Greek god of healing.

Asclepius was reported to have cured untold numbers from every conceivable disease—even raising a man from the dead. This caused Apollo through his oracle at Delphi to declare, "Oh Asclepius!, thou who art born a great joy to all mortals, whom lovely Coronis bare to me, the child of love, at rocky Epidaurus."[8] Such a healer was he reported to be, that Pluto, god of Hades, complained to Zeus that hardly anyone was dying anymore, and so Zeus destroyed Asclepius with a thunderbolt. Afterward, Apollo pleaded with Zeus to restore his son, and this intercession so moved Zeus that he not only brought Asclepius back to life, but immortalized him as the god of medicine. First at Thessaly, and finally throughout the Greek and Roman worlds, Asclepius was worshiped as the saviour god of healing.[9] At Pergamum he was hailed as *pergameus deus,* the god of the city of Pergamum.[10]

Aristophanes described how long, tame snakes were incorporated into the worship of Asclepius, and how they glided between the sleepers at night in the sleeping chambers in Pergamum.[11] On Attic reliefs of the fourth century B.C., we see snakes licking the patients who slept in the healing chambers of Asclepius's shrine, and cures on display referred to the virtues of this licking.[12]

To the newly formed Christian community in Pergamum, Asclepius was reminiscent of the serpent in the Garden of Eden, and the snakehandling methods used in worshiping him were considered as idolatry and demon worship. These convictions were so strong that Christian stonecutters who worked in the quarries around Pergamum refused a commission to fashion a large statue of Asclepius, and for this refusal they were put to death. Antipas, the Lord's faithful servant mentioned in Revelation 2:13 as dying a martyr's death "where Satan dwelleth," is reported by some to be the leader of those slain for resisting Asclepiunism.[13]

Christians in Pergamum understood the local history that lured the pagan community into the serpentine idolatries of Asclepius, and considered it demonic. Delphi with its surrounding area, in which the famous oracle ordained and approved the worship of Asclepius, was earlier known by the name Pytho, a chief city of Phocis.[14] In Greek mythology, Python—the namesake of the city of Pytho—was the great serpent or demon who dwelt in the mountains of Parnassus, menacing the area as the chief guardian of the famous oracle at Delphi.

In Acts 16:16, the demoniac woman who troubled Paul was possessed with a spirit of divination. In Greek this means a spirit of python (a seeress of Delphi, a pythoness). This reflects not only accepted Jewish belief, but the scriptural revelation that the worship of Asclepius and other such idolatries were, as Paul would later articulate in 1 Corinthians 10:20, the worship of demons.

In Acts 7:41–42 (Jerusalem Bible), we find that when men serve idols they are worshiping "the army of heaven." Psalm 96:5 says, "For all the gods of the nations are idols" (*'elilim*, LXX *daimonia* [demons]). Many other biblical references indicate evil supernaturalism as the true dynamic of idolatry and reveal that idols of stone, flesh, or other imagery are simply *'elilim* (empty, nothing, vanity); but, they also show that behind these images exist the true objects of heathen adoration—i.e., demons. Thus we see the presence of idolatry wherever cities come under demonic siege. Such was the case with Asclepius of Pergamum.

While the city of Pergamum was magnificent—and natural man would have been impressed with its commerce, organized religion, labor, trade, artistry, and excellence in education—the One who stood with a two-edged sword by which He pierced the veil and discerned all truth, Jesus the Omniscient, saw things in Pergamum that the human eye could not see. Our Lord revealed that Pergamum was the geographic center from which Satan influenced that region. It was *Satanos thronos esti,* a place dominated by demons. When the exalted Christ looked into that city run by Roman (and later papal) authority, He saw things not only as they appeared to be, but as they were in all reality.[15] Jesus understood that the symbol of Asclepius (the caduceus, a winged-topped staff with one or two snakes winding about it, given to Hermes by Apollo, the father of Asclepius) wasn't really an oracle of healing, but rather a perversion of the brazen serpent in Numbers, chapter 21.[16] Jesus looked upon that invisible influence in the skies above Pergamum and designated Pergamum as *Satanos thronos esti,* a city under demonic siege. For Jesus to have designated Pergamum as a specific area under Satan's dominion was to have provided all Christian generations with a pictorial revelation—a lasting diagram of demonic, territorial modus operandi. Modern failure to accept the possibility that influential cities can fall under demonic influence (which then expands outward toward regional influence and finally national domination), is a direct contradiction to scriptural illustrations, including those above.

From the example of Pergamum we learn: 1) idolatry and demon worship increase when cities come under Satan's design; 2) God's revealed truth is perverted; and 3) Christians are persecuted for their convictions.

Biblical Example #2: Persia/Grecia

In the tenth chapter of Daniel, we read that the prophet had been fasting and praying for twenty-one days. He had inwardly purposed to chasten his heart before the Lord, hoping the God of Israel would see his fast and grant him a revelation of Israel's future.

On the twenty-first day of his fast, while standing on the bank of the Tigris River, the angel Gabriel appeared before Daniel in stunning splendor. Gabriel informed Daniel, "...from the first day that thou didst set thine heart to understand, and to chasten thyself before thy God, thy words were heard, and I am come for thy words" (Dan. 10:12).

If an angel had been dispatched from heaven from the first day, why did it take twenty-one days before the angel arrived? Gabriel provided the answer by explaining that a powerful Persian demon had opposed him for twenty-one days. Not until Michael, the archangel, came to assist in the battle was Gabriel free to continue his journey.

In Persian theology this opposing spirit would have been identified as Arimanius. According to Persian religion, he was the Death-dealer—the powerful and self-existing evil spirit, from whom war and all other evils had their origin.[17] He was the chief of the cacodaemons, or fallen angels, expelled from heaven for their sins. After their expulsion, the cacodaemons endeavored to settle down in various parts of the earth, but were always rejected, and out of revenge found pleasure in tormenting the inhabitants of the earth. Arimanius and his followers finally took up their abode in the space between heaven and earth and there established their domain called *Arimanabad*. From this location, the cacodaemons could intrude upon and attempt to corrupt human governments.

In Daniel, chapter 10, this opposing spirit is biblically identified as "the prince of the kingdom of Persia" (Iraq/Iran). Later, Gabriel informed Daniel that upon his departure the "prince of Grecia shall come."

These were specific geographies referred to as being ruled over—or at least greatly influenced by these demonic forces. The reference was not to an earthly prince, but to a ruler or specific territorial power—the prince of Persia. The fact that these opposing princes were not mortal but were appointed invisible emissaries from Satan, is made obvious by the inability of an earthly prince to see, or oppose, the angels of God. Thus, the conflict in this context is supernatural warfare on a territorial scale. In the seventh chapter of Daniel, God revealed four different types of kingdom influences: the Babylonian, the Medo-Persian, the Greek, and the Roman, each of which was a mere human agency under the control of supernatural powers. The principality of the MedoPersian kingdom is depicted as a warmongering spirit

THE ENEMY'S STRATEGY OF SIEGING CITIES IN AMERICA

seeking to dominate through military power, while its predecessor Babylonia is characterized by the foolishness of humanism pretending to the throne of God. Throughout the Bible, spiritual Babylon is equivalent to the world-system that is at enmity with God. The beginning of Babylon was the tower of Babel, where at the macrolevel Satan's strategy to formulate a one-world system was first attempted. In recent years, the prince of the kingdom of Persia has emerged once again as an opposing spirit seeking to conflict with the security of the nation of Israel. Having sought nuclear capability (firing the first shot in the war against Iran, and most currently invading the small country of Kuwait), Iraq has risen to the center of world concern as the prince of the kingdom of Persia. It has again risen to oppose the prophesied future of Palestine, and the hope of all believers. The most powerful weapon contemporary Persia has in its arsenal is called the Tammuz missile. According to Babylonian religion, Tammuz was the son of Nimrod by Semiramus. He was worshiped as the god of procreation, and dwelt in the regions of the underworld. In the spring he was resurrected by the weeping of his wife, Ishtar. Sexual orgies and the crying of maidens for his return accompanied this season.[18]

As the world lunges forward toward its climactic encounter with Jesus Christ, the belligerence of the prince of Persia and other underworld creatures will undoubtedly escalate. Babylon is depicted in the Scriptures as the final kingdom-spirit with whom God will do battle (Rev. 14:8; 17:5). Isaiah describes an alliance of many nations that would come up against Iraq in the end times "to destroy the whole land" (Isa. 13:4–5). And so shall the prince of Persia and his city under siege be marked for destruction.

From the example of Persia we learn: 1) the air above cities can be controlled by evil spirits; 2) evil spirits try to manipulate earthly governments; 3) evil spirits oppose our prayer life and try to keep us from discerning God's answer; 4) spiritual warfare happens on a territorial scale; and 5) the fervent prayers of the righteous will prevail against Satan.

SPIRITUAL WARFARE: THE INVISIBLE INVASION

Biblical Example #3: Gadara

"And they came over unto the other side of the sea, into the country of the Gadarenes. And when he was come out of the ship, immediately there met him out of the tombs a man with an unclean spirit.... For he said unto him, Come out of the man, thou unclean spirit. And he asked him, What is thy name? And he answered, saying, My name is Legion: for we are many" (Mark 5:1–2, 8–9).

Earlier I mentioned that any city or community provides an open invitation for an influx of destructive powers when, among other things, those in governmental authority promote the dishonoring of moral law and the open practice of spiritual rebellion. Evidently this happened in ancient Gadara.

One hundred sixty-four years before the birth of Jesus Christ, the Maccabee brothers, along with their father Mattathias, decided that Israel had been under Greek and Syrian tyranny long enough. Gathering together in a group, these military zealots determined to throw off this suppression and win back the temple and their freedom in the name of Jehovah God. With the desecrations of Antiochus Epiphanes and a general conviction that the Messiah was about to appear, the Maccabean wars began. Two historical books, First and Second Maccabees, tell the story of the Maccabee brothers and how they went to war against the empires of Greece and Syria.

The leader, Judas Maccabeus, organized a great army that rose up against Antiochus, Appolonius, Seron, and other surrounding rulers.[19] Neighboring factions quickly joined this uprising, and surprisingly this rag-tag rebellion grew in size and fame through ingenious strategy and action in battle, even succeeding to regain temporarily Israel's national zeal and independence. Then around 70 B.C., Israel again succumbed to the oppressive rule of an outside power, this time to its former ally, Rome.[20] During the Maccabean wars the city of Gadara was the bloody scene of war and conflict.[21] As a member of the Decapolis and a chief fortress lying two miles in circumference, Gadara was wiped out when infantries from Syria and later armies under Rome marched against the Jewish insurrectionists leveling Gadara to the ground.[22] The destruction of the city was so devastating that some thought Gadara would never rise again. With much of the surrounding valley of Gilead torn by war and some areas little more than ruins, more than 150 years would pass before Herod the Great appeared (about 37 B.C.).[23] While known as a scoundrel, Herod was also a great builder. He found the walls of Jerusalem down and the temple of Zerubbabel destroyed. For political reasons he raised money, relying on his friendship with the caesar of Rome, and rebuilt the walls and the temple. About this same time, Octavian presented him with the city of Gadara.[24] Herod surveyed the shambled remains of this once-beautiful city, and it appears he decided to rebuild it.

Although Pompey renovated Gadara in 63 B.C., it was probably not until the appearance of Herod that Gadara was fully restored, rising to its highest pinnacle of magnificence.[25] Two theaters were erected. A massive temple to Artemis fronted by an open temple precinct more than two thousand yards square was built. An aqueduct system of ingenious design was built to elevate and purify the waters which flowed into the city from the Sea of Galilee. Other glorious accomplishments too numerous to elaborate caused Gadara to rise from its Maccabean tragedy to a new glory.

Upon surveying the restoration, Rome, as its custom was, decided to protect its investment by placing a legion of soldiers in Gadara. The legion was to serve under Herod's regional authority, and was to provide leadership and protection for the city. Instead, corruption set in within two years.[26] Temples were looted, pillaging was rampant, and atrocities against the people were tolerated, as the Roman legion abused the Gadarenes with unwarranted examples of military chastisement and sexual perversions. Militant sexualism became the regional trademark of the Roman soldiers, as the Gadarenes were reduced to little more than slaves serving only to fulfill the degrading appetites of the deviates from Rome.

For more than fourteen years, this legion required the inhabitants of Gadara to indulge their carnal desires. On several occasions the Gadarenes tried to appeal this situation to the headship of Rome, including complaints to Agrippa, and later to Augustus Caesar in 21 B.C.[27] But, Agrippa and the emperor only confirmed the authority of the legion under Herod. The Gadarenes eventually gave up, and the delegation representing their final claims to Augustus committed mass suicide rather than return to Gadara and endure further abuse.[28]

Gadara, once beautiful, became a place people avoided. Upon landing on the coast nearby, visitors could see the cemeteries and tombs that had been dug into the mountainside to accommodate the great number of Gadarenes destroyed by the Roman legion.

The same mountainside tombs provide the historical backdrop against which Mark, chapter 5, unfolds, where Jesus of Nazareth, fifty-three years later, crossed over the sea and stepped down upon the shores of Gadara. A Gadarene demoniac—a man so possessed that neither chains nor shackles could hold him—ran from his dwelling among the tombs to greet the Master. Jesus demanded that the spirit identify itself, and it said, "We are legion, for we are many" (Mark 5:9).

The word *legion* used here in identifying this spirit is significant. It was not a Jewish term. Nor was it Grecian, Aramaic, Syrian, or any other language having an ancient history within this region. Rather, it was a Latin term given as a military title for soldiers appointed by Rome. The demons, in vocalizing their number and identity, used an interesting choice of words in stating they were a legion. Any sincere conclusion must hold that when the demons cried, "We are legion," they were in some way identifying themselves with the corrupt Roman legion that had troubled that area for years.

Because those in legislative authority were allowed to corrupt themselves, destroy moral order, and take delight in the destruction of the innocent, Gadara had become a stronghold of demonic activity. Like flies drawn to a dying carcass, principalities settled into Gadara like street gangs claiming turf. In fact, years after the Roman legion had long been dead, demons cried out of a man and said, "We are legion."

It is of further interest to note this legion pleaded with Jesus not to "send them away out of the country" (Mark 5:10). Why would demons make such a plea? Why would legions of demons oppose removal from that particular region? As a chief city of the Decapolis it had become a habitat, as Jesus said of Pergamum, a *Satanos thronos esti,* an influential city under demonic design.

Further evidence of a demonic saturation of Gadara is suggested by the multiple existence of demons dwelling in this single Gadarene, as a legion could number as many as 6,826—and this possessing a single man![29]

Because the social leadership in Gadara, and specifically the appointed Roman legion under Herod, had been allowed to dishonor God's laws and live in spiritual rebellion, Gadara had fallen under Satan's destructive plan. It had become a city even demons considered to be their own, as was illustrated by their surprise at seeing holiness and questioning, "What have I to do with thee, Jesus, thou Son of the Most High God?" As is typical with areas dominated by evil supernaturalism, the people of Gadara did not accept the One who could have delivered them from destructive powers. Ultimately at the first outbreak of the Jewish revolt, all the people were massacred and the city of Gadara was destroyed. Gadara was captured by Vespasian, and the town itself and the surrounding villages were reduced to ashes.[30] Today, ruins of a grand colonnaded street still boast the beauty of ancient Gadara, whose archaeological remains are by far the most beautiful and extensive east of the Jordan.[31]

From the example of Gadara we learn: 1) government promotion of immorality opens the door to evil; 2) governments are compromised by evil when they begin to control, rather than serve the people; 3) justice and judgment are decayed in cities under the control of spiritual darkness; 4) demons identify with evildoers; and 5) oversexualization and despair increase in such cities.

Biblical Example #4: Ephesus

Throughout the missionary journeys of the Apostle Paul, never did he encounter a greater challenge than when he entered Asia, and specifically the great city of Ephesus as he attempted to convert the populace through the preaching of the Gospel. Ephesus was to Asia what New York City is to America; it was their commerce point, their interchange city, where east met west and north met south. As such, the culture and religion of Ephesus excelled as a trend-setting community, reaching to the very grassroots of the local society.

The worship of Diana in the temple of Diana in Ephesus was the greatest single unifying religion among all pagan people up to that time. It took 220 years to build the massive temple to the goddess Diana. Stationed in the heart of Ephesus, the temple was 425 feet long, 220 feet broad, and had 127 columns of solid white marble, each standing 60 feet high.[32] The treasures of the temple were of immeasurable value. The whole of the temple was so architecturally magnificent as to be considered not only a considerable attraction for the people of the region, but one of the seven wonders of the ancient world.[33] The image of Diana as enshrined in her temple at Ephesus is believed to have been a meteorite that fell to the earth. From the semblance of a many-breasted female the ancients perceived that it was divine—a deity—that fell down from the god Jupiter.[34] So popular had the religion of Diana become that, by the time the Apostle Paul arrived, it was estimated that "all Asia and the world" (Acts 19:27) worshiped her. Into this setting came the Apostle Paul. He understood the sociological and religious influence of Diana worship, yet he came offering the truth of the living God. Later, Paul wrote to the Christians in Corinth, "I have fought with beasts at Ephesus." Paul warred with the evil principalities that held Ephesus as a city under siege, for as the Gospel was declared throughout the ancient city, "God wrought special miracles by the hands of Paul: So that from his body were brought unto the sick handkerchiefs or aprons, and the diseases departed from them, and the evil spirits went out of them" (Acts 19:11–12). Verse 13 continues the

THE ENEMY'S STRATEGY OF SIEGING CITIES IN AMERICA

portrayal of Ephesus as a center of demonic activity, noting that certain local exorcists maintained their employment through the ongoing need to call demon spirits out from the bodies of local people.

Material evidence of demonic presence was clearly witnessed in the rampancy of witchcraft and occultism, as was illustrated by the great number of occult books and paraphernalia burned as people converted to Christianity (Acts 19:19). Such occult activity indicates that Diana of Ephesus, like the Syrian goddess Ashtoreth, was worshiped with impure rites and magical mysteries.[35] Diana was worshiped in the heavens as Luna (the moon), on earth as Diana, and in the underworld as Hecate—the goddess of the sea and witchcraft.[36] Hecate's appearance was frightful with hissing serpents hanging around her shoulders. Her assistance was besought by magicians and witches who made sacrifices unto her of puppies, honey, and black female lambs. As Hecate, Diana was the mother of the wizards, Circe and Medea, and represented the darkness and terrors of night. She frequently sent terrifying demons from the lower world to encourage and teach black magic and witchcraft. Nightmares were attributed to her as she roved the night with the souls of the dead, visible only to dogs, who howled as she approached.[37] Finally, one cannot overlook that it was to the city of Ephesus that Paul most vehemently warned, "Put on the whole armour of God, that ye may be able to stand against…principalities, against powers, against the rulers of the darkness of the world, against spiritual wickedness in high places" (Eph. 6:11–12).

As local authorities directed the mainstream population into idolatry and the worship of Diana's various manifestations, Satan's kingdom seized this advantage and ruled the social and cosmic atmosphere throughout the ancient city.[38] Not until the Gospel of Jesus Christ was preached in apostolic power was this hold broken, and the eyes of men and women opened so they might see, hear, and understand their need of Jesus. Until then, Ephesus would endure the continued oppressions of the sanguinary and pitiless power of Hecate which permeated the whole of Ephesian society, as witnessed in the tumultuous outcry in Acts 19:23–41, verifying that Ephesus was a city under Satan's dictates.

From the example of Ephesus we learn: 1) witchcraft and the occult increase in cities under Satan's control; 2) bodily diseases ravage areas where immorality is allowed; 3) idolatry can be packaged, protected, and marketed within society; and 4) occult activity mixed with social policy creates a destructive cultural combination.

Pergamum, Persia, Gadara, and Ephesus illustrate how the machine of municipalities can be used of Satan to oppose the will of God and to destroy a nation. We learn by their examples that social actions have spiritual and moral consequences. Finally, the Bible warns that this phenomenon—demonic conquest of nations one city at a time—is an ongoing concern for every age.

To the Ephesians Paul wrote, "For we are not fighting against human beings but against the wicked spiritual forces in the heavenly world, the rulers, authorities, and cosmic powers of this dark age" (Eph. 6:11–12 TEV). Earlier he said, "And you hath he quickened, who were dead in trespasses and sins; Wherein in time past ye walked according to the prince of the power of the air, the spirit that now worketh in the children of disobedience" (Eph. 2:1–2). Such verses reveal that social disobedience to God's Word is the result of having walked according to the prince of the power of the air, and that to promote spiritual rebellion within society is to play into the hands of destructive powers whose goal is the demise of that society.

A Modern Day Problem?

Does modern America stand at this crossroad? Are there cities across America falling under the mesmerization of some apocalyptic invasion brought on by territorial demonic warlords? Apparently. Some cities in the United States today are like Ephesus of old. They exhibit the symptoms of having come under siege to demonic spirits who plan to use the relaxed moral attitudes of the times to dismantle the United States, city by city, and bring her to destruction.

Portland, Oregon, is my place of residence and a contemporary example of this phenomenon. Consider the following:

- The state with the highest proportion of people who do not claim a religious affiliation is Oregon,[39] with the city of Portland considered the greatest per capita mission field in the United States. Out of nearly a million people in the Portland area, less than 4 percent attend a church of any affiliation.[40]
- Portland has an inner-city gay population nearing 30 percent, and is number one per capita for lesbians in America.[41]
- Portland ranks high in gang violence and prison overcrowding, with the highest per capita crime rate of any major city in the country.[42]
- Among the worst in the nation for those suffering from stress and chronic depression, Portland has a suicide rate 25 percent higher than average American cities elsewhere.[43]
- A recent edition of the Portland *Oregonian* quoted *Psychology Today* as saying that Portland is a more stressful city than Detroit, Philadelphia, or Chicago.[44]
- The Oregon Health Division reported in November of 1990 that Oregon's children are more likely to use drugs, suffer injuries, and die at birth than children in the nation as a whole.[45]
- A recent study reported that ten out of every one hundred witches and warlocks in the United States live in the Oregon-Washington area, with the city of Portland listed as a prime location.[46]

A conspicuous indication of the presence of witchcraft and idolatry in Portland can be seen in the official female image that stands overshadowing the entrance to the city of Portland office building. The female image, holding a trident, or three-pronged spear, and fashioned out of copper, is called Portlandia. She was inspired by another female image, Lady Commerce, who appears on the official Portland City Seal.

Intentional or not, in the occult world Portland's "Lady Commerce" can be identified as a witch or sorceress, because of the trident in her right hand, and the macrocosm, or six-pointed star above her head. *The Encyclopaedia of Occultism,* written by Lewis Spence and published by University Books for university studies, explains the meaning of these symbols on pages 257 and 262:

> **The Macrocosm:** A six pointed star...represents the infinite and the absolute—that is, the most simple and complete abridgment of the science of all things. Paracelsus states that every magical figure and Kabalistic sign of the pantacles which compel spirits may be reduced to two—the Macrocosm and the Microcosm.
>
> **The Trident:** In magical rites these were considered of the utmost importance. Indispensable to the efficacy of the ceremonies were the...magic fork or trident....Witches and sorceresses are usually depicted using the trident in their infernal rites.

Two of the most important instruments used in practicing witchcraft—the macrocosm and the trident—are directly associated with the female who seems to invite all such compelled spirits to make Portland their home. The Portland City Seal has been controversial for years. Neither the city archives, nor the Oregon Historical Society can confirm the original intent of the macrocosm which, if used under Judaism, could be referred to as the Star of David, while the trident may otherwise be linked to the god Poseidon in Greek mythology or to the sea in general.[47] The significant combination of these symbols when used together has no known historical or symbological importance other than to the Greek goddess Hecate, who was at once both

THE ENEMY'S STRATEGY OF SIEGING CITIES IN AMERICA

goddess of the sea (symbolized here by trident), and witchcraft (symbolized by macrocosm).[48] One would also question why the trident changes from right hand to left hand if Portlandia is fashioned after Lady Commerce? What does this transition signify? Why is Portlandia officially referred to as a goddess? And why does her right hand appear in a relaxed, horned-hand position—a symbol of occult devotion? This could be nothing more than a fluke. But perhaps, as with the city of Ephesus, it merely reflects the unseen powers seeking to destroy the United States one city at a time. The goddess Portlandia—in symbolism and spirit—embodies the social ills eroding the city of Portland, and other U. S. cities, as they are brought under the designs of Satan.

Portland is one of many contemporary examples. The problem is growing. There is no city exempt from the same condition, especially where the church is passive and the wicked rule from places of authority. Proverbs 29:2 says, "When the righteous are in authority, the people rejoice: but when the wicked beareth rule, the people mourn [are made to be oppressed]." In Habakkuk 1:4, we read, "Therefore the law is slacked, and judgment doth never go forth: for the wicked doth compass about the righteous; therefore wrong judgment proceedeth."

City by city, American society is coming unglued. The United States is now the most violent society in the industrialized world. An unparalleled spread of lawlessness rules the hearts of a generation of American youths raised without values. Civil order has all but vanished as twenty-nine thousand citizens are murdered each year. More than six million additional violent crimes are committed annually.

Former AIDS czar Kristine Gebbie gave a speech on 20 October 1993 at a conference on teenage pregnancy.[49] Gebbie, a Clinton appointee whose job it was to stem the tide of AIDS, made no reference to abstinence. Instead, she called on teens to seek pleasure from sex in this "repressed Victorian society." She reflected the mood of the times by accusing profamily groups of spreading misinformation about sex, saying that too many Americans deny sexuality. It is a morally bankrupt people who propose dealing with society's problems

SPIRITUAL WARFARE: THE INVISIBLE INVASION

by distributing condoms, giving junkies clean needles, putting metal detectors in schools, and installing health clinics on school grounds so fourteen-year-old girls can acquire an abortion.

What's happening to America's cities? More than meets the eye, and certainly more than we will solve without God.

— *Chapter Two* —

THE ENEMY'S SECRET FORCES

> "For still our ancient Foe, Doth seek to work us woe;
> His craft and power are great, And, armed with cruel hate,
> on earth is not his equal."
> —Martin Luther

The meeting had been evangelistic in style and I was physically exhausted. I was looking forward to my easy chair and a short nap before preparing for the evening service. Of course, I had no idea what was about to occur.

I had been preaching a series of messages from Ephesians 6:12 which reads, "For we wrestle not against flesh and blood, but against principalities, against powers, against the rulers of the darkness of this world, against spiritual wickedness in high places." For several weeks my sermon discussions had included thoughts on Satan's social and cultural agenda. Having no real experience with the supernatural, I was left to muster only so much doctrinal theory when it came to the subject of evil supernaturalism. All of that was about to change.

As I walked out of the front door of the church, the friendly chatter and usual hand shaking was suddenly interrupted by a strange, young woman who seemed to come from out of nowhere and began motioning for my attention. As she ran up to me waving her hands and muttering something about her boyfriend, I thought, *Oh, great.*

This has already been a long morning, and now I've got to deal with a druggie. If it hadn't been for my self-pitying attitude, I might have noticed the terror that permeated her eyes. Making gestures for me to follow, she moved through the crowd quickly, glancing back occasionally to confirm that I was following. Later, I found out that a few of the saints had noticed what was going on, and they had been keeping an eye on us.

Suddenly, the young girl stopped and pointed toward an unknown vehicle sitting in the parking lot. She said, "He told me to turn in here and park." Unaware of the circumstances, and surrounded by dozens of believers, I put on my best pastoral face and approached the automobile. As I did, what I can only describe as a kind of unworldly or ethereal uneasiness began to fall over me like a haze. A few more steps and I surprised myself by whispering, "Lord, the battle is yours." I wasn't sure why I had said it, but somewhere deep down in my spirit, I knew that I had been prompted to do so.

I could see a mat of tangled hair as the young man sat hunched over in the passenger seat of the convertible. Cautiously, I walked up and tapped on his shoulder, intending to ask how I could be of help. I didn't get the chance. Without warning, his head jerked upward to expose a wild and beastlike snarl. The sudden reaction took me by such surprise that I gasped and jumped backward by at least a couple of feet. His face was distorted and spattered in blood, and he spoke with a growling, guttural voice, "Man of God, I'm gonna kill you!" With that, the possessed young man jumped out of the vehicle and moved towards me, shouting, "You're gonna die! I'm gonna kill you, man of God!"

Myriads of thoughts raced through my mind. I contemplated running (and to be honest, I might have done so), but before I could get my legs moving, a strange calm began to sweep over me, unlike anything I had experienced previously. "Lord, the battle is yours," is what I had whispered, and now it was like someone else was guiding my body and mind. In an instant my thoughts were clearer than they

THE ENEMY'S SECRET FORCES

had been earlier. I had more composure and was more certain of the power of the Gospel than the circumstances should have allowed. I suddenly felt like a tower of faith. Later, it was evident to me, that Christ with me, and Christ within me, had been in control of the entire situation.

As mature believers gathered around and began to pray, the next thing that happened was to become for most of us the single most supernatural event we had ever seen. Before I could move, the young man started towards me in a full run. Like some kind of ferocious animal, his eyes glaring and his teeth snarling, he leaped at me like a lion after its prey. But, he ran into something. It's hard to explain. To the human eye there was nothing there. Yet something, invisible but very real, had moved into position between me and the young man, and whatever or whoever it was had stopped his motion so completely that he propelled backward with a look of astonishment on his face. Falling to the ground, he began convulsing and thrashing wildly about. A moment later, he jumped to his feet again. This time he stood straight up, looking at me with piercing and unholy eyes. To this day I can still remember those hollow eyes, black as night. They were filled with such glaring hatred that it became immediately apparent that this was a conflict between supernatural forces—a battle for the status of a human soul.

The saints bowed to their knees around the young man, not in fear, but in awe of what they had just seen. The young man stood frozen, his jaws gritting together so hard that I could hear his teeth cracking. His eyes rolled back into their sockets, and his body began to twist and contort. It reminded me of the special effects used in making the film, *The Exorcist*. His arms turned backwards; his legs, his fingers, his neck and his head, began to twist with a grinding sound. His body writhed and trembled as blood ran out of his mouth and out of his nose. It was just as if large invisible hands had taken hold of his body and were trying to tear him apart.

Again he fell to the ground. This time with help from others, we took the opportunity to grab him in an attempt to keep him calm. Since it was already evident that he could not injure any one of us, our concern was to keep him from doing any additional harm to himself. The problem was that he had the strength of several men. I watched as burly loggers joined their arms and weight together in an attempt to hold him down. Each time they were about to gain control, a sneer would cross his lips and he would lift them off the ground. He grabbed a large, three-inch wide occult medallion that was hanging around his neck, pulling it with such force that he broke the thick metal chain. He shoved the medallion and the chain into his mouth, and was trying to swallow them both, but someone caught the chain and quickly pulled it out.

His hands beat and plucked at his head uncontrollably, tearing his face and eyes. I thought to myself, *Jesus, do something, or this kid is going to die!* I was reminded of the young demoniac in the ninth chapter of Mark, where the spirit "cast him into the fire, and into the waters, to destroy him." In the Gospels there are several accounts of demonic possessions where the spirits, upon being exorcised, attempted to destroy their hosts. Suddenly it was clear. Jesus had led the young man to our front door because the accumulative crowd at that particular service had been assembled for the Master's use. A young man, possessed by evil, wanted deliverance. Jesus was not about to let him down. We found out later that the girl had driven the car, while the possessed boy sat slouched down on the seat, giving directions without looking up at the road.

It seems the young man had decided that very morning to give up his occult activity and to convert to Christianity. That's when it happened. He had suddenly lost all control over his body. No matter how he tried, he could not regain his composure. He could not stop an involuntary attack by his own hands. He had struggled with the ongoing assault all the way to the church, until at last he had lost all remaining mental discretion. Like the wild man of Gadara who cried and cut himself with stones, the boy had no power over the destructive forces intent on destroying him. Somewhere during his lifetime, he had turned his will over to a sinister power, and now he was being torn unmercifully, flailing about on the parking lot.

Sometime during the struggle I thought I had heard an intelligible appeal. It was just a whisper, but I was sure I had heard the young man say, "Please, help me." I listened closely, and in the midst of the snarling and threatening curses, I heard it again, "Help me." It's hard to describe my emotions, but I knew the battle would be over soon. Thankfully, it was. Notwithstanding an energetic, demonic struggle, accompanied by the most visible evidence of demonic reality, a beautiful and full deliverance came through the name of Jesus Christ. The young man convulsed and then collapsed, and the demon came out of him. Mysteriously, at that very moment, a herd of horses in the field across the road from the church began kicking and neighing and running frantically in the opposite direction. Throughout the neighborhood dogs howled with an eerie howl. But, the young man's eyes opened, and with his right mind he accepted Jesus and prayed the sinners' prayer. He went on to become a regular member of the youth activities in that church.

We glorified God that day and were amazed at the power of the Gospel. But, it was just the beginning of my enlightenment. For several weeks after that event, my phone would ring in the middle of the night and a growling voice would say, "This is principality, and I know who you are!" Other manifestations followed a campaign of intimidation, and the kingdom of darkness attempted to discourage any further revelations concerning their social activity.

Space does not allow for a full disclosure of the events that gradually convinced me that I was living in a setting like ancient Gadara—a geography under Satan's control. Eventually, I discovered that a nearby area had once held one of the first and largest satanic churches on the west coast. The original building had since been purchased and burned down by a minister, but the area had long been dedicated to the powers of evil.

The Origin of Demons

Up to this point we have noted: 1) there are evil powers which, having established strongholds, control the air above certain cities and expand outward from there; 2) the precedence for this phenomenon is both historical and shown throughout the Scriptures; and 3) the human inhabitants in these areas are overtaken in idolatry, disobedience, and other sins.

The second question we shall consider is: If indeed evil spirits exist and war for control of the planet by dominating its cities and inhabitants, what is their origin? Where do they come from, and why do they conduct such a deviant battle to rule the earth and destroy mankind?

Experts in the field of demonology offer various hypotheses that they believe explain the origin and intent of such creatures. We will investigate six theories offered by modern religious authorities.

1. Superstitious Designations?

The proponents of this thought believe that demons do not exist except in the imagination. They argue that man's early habit of blaming every natural disease or catastrophe on the presence of demons illustrates a psychological fallacy, and they are quick to point out that pagans once ignorantly interpreted volcanoes, and other such natural wonders, as the manifested anger of demon gods.

A portion of this theory is not without merit. The human imagination can be persuasive. Our minds can convince us that natural wonders are the presence of ghostly beings. Some people even take medications to control their imaginations; their mental impressions are so powerful that they hear voices, and they see shadowy creatures. Others, through their use of drugs, experience similar phenomena. However, since these facts alone do not diminish the reality of demons, and since the literal existence of demons is denied by this theory, it is not considered a viable option by any serious demonologist.

2. Spirits of a Pre-Adamic Race?

Those holding to this concept believe a pre-Adamic race existed on the original earth before it became "dark and void" (Gen. 1:2). These humanlike creatures lived under the government of God, and were presided over by Lucifer, the "anointed cherub that covereth" (Ezek. 28:14). When these pre-Adamites joined Lucifer in a revolt against God, a cataclysm of darkness fell upon the earth, physically destroying its human-like inhabitants. Only the spirits of these creatures survived to roam the earth in a disembodied state. This is supposed to explain the apparent desire of demons to possess human bodies.

3. Other-Worldly Creatures?

Consider these facts:

Around the world many continents are dotted by thousands of prehistoric and colossal pictographs that presumably could not have been designed from the surface of the earth.

Thousands of years ago the ancient Mayans created and used advanced medicines, including penicillin.

Centuries before the colossus of Rome, civilizations around the world built pyramids out of stones so large and with such precision that the same engineering feats could not be repeated again, until very recently with large machines.

Fourteen hundred years before Christ, the Assyrians depicted Saturn with rings and chronicled the detailed movements of the moon. European astronomers did not make the same deductions until the seventeenth century A.D.

Not long ago, archaeologists were stunned when they uncovered evidence of brain surgeries, bone transplants, and other advanced surgical procedures conducted by the ancient Peruvians perhaps thousands of years before Columbus set sail for America.

This causes one to wonder: Where did these ancient civilizations acquire such advanced technology and information?

SPIRITUAL WARFARE: THE INVISIBLE INVASION

Since little is known about life outside the limited sphere of our planet, many contend that intelligent creatures traveled from distant worlds thousands of years ago; imparting galactic wisdom to people around the globe. Some students of theology have picked up on this concept, blending it with traditional demonology and suggesting that demons are perhaps visiting creatures from another world, whose molecular structures, like ultraviolet rays, are invisible to the human eye, but nonetheless distinct in anatomical design.

Those holding this view point to the universal consistency with which extraterrestrials and UFOs have been reported throughout history, and that continue to be reported worldwide at a rate of about six sightings per hour. Eric Von Daniken's best-selling book, *Chariot of the Gods?*, supports such a view by speculating that the earth was first visited by these creatures thousands of years ago, leaving behind archaeological evidence that gave birth to legends and mythological gods. Unlike Von Daniken, in demonology these creatures are presented as invisible and menacing, the originators of evil supernaturalism.

Sufficient historical evidence does exist to suggest an invasion of earth by heavenly creatures thousands of years ago. That these beings imparted some great knowledge to ancient civilizations is possible, if not somewhat controversial. While I believe this approach can be used to argue the location of demons (in the heavenlies), as a theory for the origin of demons it leaves many questions unexplained. Furthermore, it opens the door for certain New Age heresies, where some who are ungrounded in the Word and fascinated by the paranormal view the human race as but one of many civilizations among an ever-expanding cosmos. It would be easy to pass such people off as having seen too much *Star Trek*, if it weren't that a growing number of Christians today sincerely believe that the universe is filled with untold numbers of alien societies. As appealing as that idea might be to some, the dangers of such a "galactic-family" view are inherently anti-Christian, and should be avoided.

4. Offspring of Angels and Women?

Those holding this view point to Genesis 6:4, which says, "There were giants in the earth in those days; and also after that, when the sons of God came in unto the daughters of men, and they bare children to them, the same became mighty men which were of old, men of renown." Today's English Version (TEV) provides the ancient rendition. "When mankind had spread all over the world, and girls were being born, some of the supernatural beings saw that these girls were beautiful, so they took the ones they liked.... In those days, and even later, there were giants on the earth who were descendants of human women and the supernatural beings."

This theory says that disobedient angels (sons of God) left their angelic estate and sexually intercoursed with human females. Out of this unholy union, mutant life forms were born, half human and half demon—the cursed nepheli of ancient days. These beings had giant physical bodies, but spirits of demons. At death, the unredeemable spirits vacated their physical bodies only to roam the earth without rest, cursed creatures tormenting humanity.

Proponents of this teaching also point to the "incubae" and "succubae," or male and female manifestations of demons that reportedly are born of, or intercourse with, humans.[50]

Those who disagree with this theory point to Matthew 22:30, arguing that it proves that angels cannot marry. What this verse actually says is that the angels of God "in heaven" do not marry. In the Book of Jude we learn that some angels did not remain in heaven, and that they chose to leave their first "estate" (peri, circuit, fixed boundary). That is, they left their habitation, took on human traits, and were judged of God for doing so.

According to the Bible, angels can appear in bodily form and perform human functions. In the plains of Mamre (Gen. 18:1–8), they ate and drank and talked with Abraham. They walked and looked like men. Later, they spent the night with Lot. In Hebrews 13:2 we read, "Be not forgetful to entertain strangers: for thereby some have entertained angels unawares." While it may be rare, and in some cases forbidden for angels to perform human activities, nowhere in Scripture are we told that it would have been impossible for defiant angels to have left their expected order, and to have physical intercourse with primitive women. To the contrary, something of such great magnitude befell the original angelic realm that God ordered the unruly angels to be placed in chains under darkness, and to be preserved until the day of judgment (2 Pet. 2:4, Jude 6). The historical record surrounding this event indicates that some kind of physical intercourse occurred between angels and women, and that the subsequent offspring of this union were the half-human, half-demon creatures known as *nepheli*. More shall be said of this later.

5. Spirits of Wicked Men Deceased?

This teaching, still popular with a fragment of modern theologians, seems to have its origin in early Greek mythology. The Homeric gods, who were but supernatural men, were both good and evil. The hypothesis was that the good and powerful spirits of good men rose up to assume places of deity after experiencing physical death, while the evil spirits of deceased evil men were gods doomed to roam the earth and its interior. At death, their spirits remained in an eternal limbo, unable to perish, yet incapable of attaining the grandeur of heaven or Mount Olympus. Hollywood favors this concept, regularly producing such money-maker films as *Poltergeist*, and *Nightmare On Elm Street*. Movies sensationalizing the concept of indestructible spirits from deceased wicked men top the film-making charts as we approach the year 2000. Freddy Krueger, played by actor Robert Englund, is the maniacal slasher from the popular film series *Nightmare On Elm Street*. As the seemingly indestructible evil spirit of a deceased child molester, Freddy returns to wreak havoc on the teen progeny of Elm Street. In a film called *Childs Play*, a doll possessed by the spirit of a deceased voodoo strangler calls upon Damballa, the serpent god, to give him the power of immortality. Such characterizations reflect a growing fascination with the afterlife, and popularize the notion that demons are the spirits of wicked men deceased.

The ancient Jewish historians Philo and Josephus held this view, as did many of the early church leaders. To prove this theory, *some* have pointed to the twenty-eighth chapter of 1 Samuel, where Saul consulted with the witch of Endor in an attempt to communicate with the spirit of Samuel. Modern pagans and spiritualists have long considered the biblical woman of Endor to have been an ancient medium who conferred with a "spirit guide" in order to communicate with the dead. Thanks to television programs such as "Unsolved Mysteries," psychics have periodically transported us to "hauntings," where malevolent human spirits are supposedly lost, or stuck *between* two dimensions.

While I do not *believe* that evil spirits are derived from dead wicked men, demons do *exist*. That metaphysical phenomena occur is also beyond question. The fact is, what *some* refer to as psychic vibrations or hauntings, are often demonic manifestations.

One should also note that areas where murders, child molestations, or other very negative circumstances have occurred, have afterward *become* prime locations for "hauntings." It would *seem* that evil powers converge on locations where violence has transpired, and vulnerable people have sometimes been seduced into committing ungodly acts by nefarious powers residing in those areas.

6. Fallen Angels?

Of the six theories, this is the most popular in Christian theology. This teaching is based on the scriptural assumption that at some time in aeons past Lucifer rose up in great rebellion against the God of heaven. Somehow he successfully persuaded one-third of the angelic host to stand with him in insurrection (Rev. 12:4). At this point God cast Lucifer and his rebellious angels out of heaven, at which time they became *daemonions*, or demons. Less in form and nature than they originally were, they now brought darkness and chaos upon the virgin earth. In Ezekiel 28:13–19, the prophet gives the following description of this event:

> Thou hast been in Eden the garden of God; every precious stone was thy covering.... Thou art the anointed cherub that covereth; and I have set thee so: thou was upon the holy mountain of God; thou hast walked up and down in the midst of the stones of fire. Thou was perfect in thy ways from the day that thou was created, till iniquity was found in thee. By the multitude of thy merchandise they have filled the midst of thee with violence, and thou hast sinned: therefore I will cast thee as profane out of the mountain of God: and I will destroy thee, O covering cherub, from the midst of the stones of fire.

Isaiah 14:12–14 continues the record on Lucifer's fall:

> How art thou fallen from heaven, O Lucifer, son of the morning! How art thou cut down to the ground which didst weaken the nations! For thou has said in thine heart, I will ascend into heaven, I will exalt my throne above the stars of God: I will sit also upon the mount of the congregation, in the sides of the north: I will ascend above the heights of the clouds; I will be like the most High. Yet thou shalt be brought down to hell, to the sides of the pit.

The Apostle John records the fall of Lucifer in the Book of the Revelation (12:7–9). John also tells of other angels:

> And there was war in heaven: Michael and his angels fought against the dragon; and the dragon fought and his angels, And prevailed not; neither was their place found any more in heaven. And the great dragon was cast out, that old serpent called the Devil, and Satan, which deceiveth the whole world: he was cast out into the earth, and his angels were cast out with him.

THE ENEMY'S SECRET FORCES

SPIRITUAL RANK OF DEMONS

Regardless of the position one holds concerning the origin of demons—whether they are spirits from a pre-Adamic race, offspring of angels and women, fallen angels, or a mixture of them all—in every age of history demons have played a mysterious and militant role. Their quest is to stand in the place of God, ruling all of creation (Isa. 14:12–14). To that end demons are soldier-like. We do not read of equality among demons, but rather we see something similar to a rank and file among them. "Michael and his angels fought against the dragon and his angels," we recall from the passage in Revelation. Similar verses suggest a subordinative or military order among the sphere of demonic beings. Demons are biblically characterized as highly subversive, well-organized creatures with a mission.

As a military comparison, we have in the United States Army, privates, over which there are corporals, over which there are sergeants, etc. This rank and file continues up to the commander in chief, the president of the United States.

Satan's army is similarly subordinative. There are wicked spirits (*poneria:* the mass of common demon soldiers comprising Satan's hordes). These include seducing spirits, familiar spirits, deaf and dumb spirits, spirits of fear, etc. Over these are rulers of darkness (*kosmokrators:* martial spirits given to espionage; secret powers who seek to influence earthly governments by working in and through their human political counterparts; governing spirits described as away from, or separate from God, light).[51] Above these abide powers (*exousia:* high-ranking officials whose modes of operation are distinctly militant). Over these are the principalities or archons of Satan's army (*arche:* brigadier generals over the militant divisions of Satan's host). Finally, as supreme commander and king, Satan abides as the "prince of the powers of the air" (Eph. 2:2).

The Apostle Paul referred to the military order of evil supernaturalism as "principalities," "powers," "rulers of darkness," and "spiritual wickedness in the heavenlies." In the litanies of the witches' Sabbath,

SPIRITUAL WARFARE: THE INVISIBLE INVASION

witches sing to Astaroth, prince of thrones; Carreau, prince of powers; Perrier, prince of principalities; and Lucifer, Beelzebub, and Leviathan, the rulers of darkness.[52] The following are a few other names that various societies have attributed to the evil of darkness throughout history, and against which we must war today:

Abaddon—Hebrew, "the destroyer"
Adramelech—Samarian devil, chancellor of the infernal regions
Agathodemon—Egyptian serpent devil with a human head
Ahpuch—Mayan devil
Arimanius—Persian devil, chief of the cacodaemons (fallen angels)
Alastor—chief executioner to the monarch of Hades, a cruel demon
Aldinach—Egyptian devil
Amon—Egyptian ram-headed devil
Apollyon—Greek synonym for Satan
Asmodeus—Hebrew demon of sensuality and luxury
Astaroth—Phoenician goddess of lasciviousness
Arioch—demon of vengeance
Baalberith—Canaanite devil
Balaam—Hebrew devil of greed
Baphomet—goat-headed symbol and name for Satan
Bast—Egyptian devil of pleasure
Beelzeboul—"lord of the height," Satan as the prince of the air
Beelzebub—Satan, prince of devils, lord of flies
Behemoth—Hebrew personification of Satan as an elephant
Beherit—Syriac name for Satan
Bile'—Celtic god of hell
Bisclaveret—British demon, werewolf
Bogey—Slavonic demon, bug-a-boo, the bogeyman
Boh—Welsh spirit or magic word used to frighten children ("boo")

THE ENEMY'S SECRET FORCES

Chemosh—Moabite demon
Cimeries—African devil-riding black horse
Coyote—American Indian devil
Dagon—Philistine avenging devil of the sea
Damballa—voodoo serpent god
Demogorgon—forbidden Greek name of the devil
Diabolus—Greek fallen one
Diablo—Spanish devil
Dracula—Romanian devil, "son of Satan"
Emma-O—Japanese ruler of Hell
Euronymous—Greek prince of death
Fenriz—son of Loki, a wolf devil
Gorgo—dim. of Demogorgon
Haborym—Hebrew synonym for Satan
Hanan-Tramp—French demon who suffocates children at night
Hecate—Greek devil of the sea and witchcraft later joined to Diana
Incubus—male demon of seduction, child of nightmares
Kali—daughter of Shiva, high priestess of the Thuggees
Kelpie—Scottish demon
Kernos—Celtic oak-god of the underworld, worshiped by druids
Lilith—Hebrew female devil who presides over the succubae
Loki—Teutonic devil of mischief
Mammon—Aramaic god of wealth and power
Mandragoras—demon who possesses idols, fetishes, and voodoo dolls
Mania—Etruscan goddess of hell
Mantus—Etruscan god of hell
Marduk—god of the city of Babylon
Mastema—Hebrew synonym for Satan
Melek Taus—Yezidi devil
Mephistopheles—Greek devil who shuns light

SPIRITUAL WARFARE: THE INVISIBLE INVASION

Metztli—Aztec goddess of the night
Mictian—Aztec god of death
Midgard—son of Loki, serpent devil
Milcom—Ammonite devil
Moloch—Phoenician and Canaanite devil
Mormo—Greek king of ghouls
Naamah—Hebrew female devil of seduction
Nergal—Babylonian god of Hades
Nihasa—American Indian devil
Nija—Polish god of the underworld
O-Yama—Japanese name of Satan
Paigoel—Hindu demon
Pan—Greek god of lust, later relegated to devildom
Pluto—Greek god of the underworld
Proserpine—Greek queen of the underworld, confused with Hecate
Pwcca—Welsh name for Satan
Rahu—Hindu devil, "the tormenter"
Rakshasa—Indian demon
Red-Man—French demon of the tempests
Rimmon—Syrian devil
Sabazious—Phrygian devil
Saitan—Enochian equivalent of Satan
Samana—Aryan god, the "Grim Reaper"
Sammael—Hebrew devil, "venom of god"
Samnu—Asian demon
Sedit—American Indian devil
Seik Kassa—Burmese demon who possesses trees
Seiktha—Burmese demon
Sekhmet—Egyptian goddess of vengeance
Set—Egyptian devil
Shaitan—Arabic name for Satan
Shiva—Hindu demon of destruction

Spunkie—Scottish demon
Succubus—female demon of seduction, child of nightmares
Supay—Inca god of the underworld
Swawm—Burmese demon, vampire
T'an-mo—Chinese counterpart of Satan
Tchort—Russian name for Satan
Tezcatlipoca—Aztec god of hell
Thamuz—Sumerian god, later relegated to devildom
Thoth—Egyptian devil of magic
Tunrida—Scandinavian female devil
Typhon—Greek personification of Satan
Yaotzin—Aztec god of hell
Yen-Lo-Wang—Chinese ruler of hell

Many of these spirits are still actively called upon and unwittingly served by the earth's masses. As an example of how certain of the ancient spirits listed above can still be found subverting societies, I site the following case:[53]

The Agathodemon

Almost every city in Korea has a "guardian" god. Temples are built to these deities atop the highest local mountains, and a priesthood is established for their service. This form of worship is very old in Korea, and usually exercises great influence over the local people.

Dr. Paul Cho tells the story of when he was a young Bible school graduate, and he went into a small Korean community to start a pioneer church work. It didn't take long for the local priest to come from the temple of the guardian god, and to inquire of Cho what he was doing. When the priest understood that Cho's plans included a Christian missionary endeavor, he was infuriated. The priest adamantly insisted that Cho leave the village, but Cho refused, advising him that God had sent him there to build a church and to preach the Gospel. Angrily, the priest departed, but vowed to return.

SPIRITUAL WARFARE: THE INVISIBLE INVASION

A few days later a large crowd of people returned with the pagan priest to challenge Dr. Cho. They said, "Cho, do you really believe that Jesus Christ is the same yesterday, today and forever, and that He can still work miracles?" Cho answered, "Yes, I do." They said, "This then is our challenge. Down in the village is a woman dying with a disease. She's been bedridden for seven years and her child is also dying. If Jesus can heal her in the next thirty days, we will leave town and you can have your church. But, if she's not healed, you must leave or we will return and kill you and your followers." With that, the angry crowd departed, advising Cho with certain confidence that they would return in thirty days to kill him.

The next day Cho traveled with his mother-in-law to the little village and found the dying woman. He suggested that if the woman would pray the sinners' prayer and accept Jesus as her Savior, perhaps the Lord would heal her. But, she was very angry with God, blaming Him for her physical condition. She wanted nothing to do with God or Christianity. Dr. Cho tried repeatedly to bring her to conversion, but every attempt ended in defeat. Finally, Cho decided that prayer would be his only approach.

Over the next few weeks Dr. Cho prayed in earnest that the woman and her baby would be healed. Nothing happened. Finally, on the evening of the thirtieth (last) day, Cho began to worry. He reminded God that the people would be coming from the temple of the guardian god, and that a miracle had to occur by morning or the mob was going to destroy his tent and kill him and his followers. He prayed with passion for several hours. Then, at 2:00 A.M., he received a powerful vision.

As Cho looked, he saw the front door of his home opening slowly. As it did, an eerie oriental music began seeping in through the entrance, coming in from somewhere outside. Suddenly, a large snakelike creature appeared in the doorway. It had the body of a serpent and the head of a man, and it swayed back and forth to the melodious rhythm. Moving through the door with a dancing action, the creature spoke, "Cho, if you don't leave this town, you are a dead man. I have been

THE ENEMY'S SECRET FORCES

ruling this area for all of these years, and who are you to come here and disturb my nest?"

With that the serpent-like being sprang through the doorway landing on Dr. Cho. At once, a fierce battle erupted, with the fiendish creature overpowering him. Slithering around his waist with a quick, diabolical movement, the creature began trying to asphyxiate Cho. He twisted and contorted his reptilian body, moving back and forth with a jeering smile; his cold, dead eyes peering down laughingly at Cho.

Growing stronger, he tightened his grip around Cho's body, constricting his waist and arms. Cho could feel his bodily sensations leaving and his hands and feet growing numb. He thought, *Jesus, I'm dying!* Then Cho noticed something. The creature's eyes had changed at the moment he had thought on the name of Jesus. Cho thought it *again, Jesus.* This time the serpent cringed and his grip began to weaken. With all of the strength he could muster, Cho opened his mouth and whispered, "Jesus." Like a thunderbolt of two-edged steel, the name of Jesus discharged from his mouth like a sword, driving deep into the heart of the creature. The being jerked back and, with its eyes filled with terror, fell to the floor wailing with an unworldly moan. Dr. Cho lifted his leg and crushed the creature's head beneath his foot.

Picking up the creature's dead carcass, Cho walked to the front door intending to throw the lifeless being outside. As he did, he observed that all of the village people had gathered together in the front of his home. Holding the snake-man over his head, he threw it down in front of them, saying, "This is the god that you have served all of these years, but now you must turn and serve the true and living God."

With that, Dr. Cho awoke to find that it had been a dream/vision. The hour was 4:00 A.M., the time for early morning prayer meeting at the tent.

When Dr. Cho arrived at the tent-church to join the others for prayer, he had scarcely walked through the doorway when a Korean layman ran up to him shouting, "Pastor, come quickly!" Glancing out the tent door, Cho could see what appeared to be the entire city coming up the valley walls. He thought, *Oh Jesus, the priest is coming from the temple of the guardian god, and he's brought a mob to kill me!* Cho wanted to run and hide. He might have, but then he noticed something curious. The people had an odd look on their faces. Instead of an angry throng led by sinister forces, the people appeared to be happy. As Cho walked out of the tent, his eyes were drawn to a woman at the front of the crowd. He thought, *It couldn't be.* But, it was. Leading the group, with her baby in her arms, was the formerly paralyzed woman. She ran up to Dr. Cho and said, "Oh Brother Cho, thank you so much for coming and praying for me last night. The Lord heard your prayer and I'm healed!" Cho answered, "I did not come to your house and pray for you last night." But, the woman insisted, "Oh yes, you came at two o'clock this morning and stood outside my window. You said loudly, 'Woman, be healed in the name of Jesus Christ,' and I arose and found that I was healed, and my baby is healed."

With that, Dr. Cho remembered that it had been at 2:00 A.M. when he had seen the vision and the serpent-creature had been destroyed.

Subsequently, all of the village was converted to Christianity. The temple of the guardian god was destroyed and the property was donated to Dr. Cho. He built a church on it.

Today, Dr. Cho pastors the largest church in the history of the world. It all began in a city under siege to a hideous evil spirit, known in ancient Egypt as an Agathodemon, a serpentlike demon with a human head.

By whatever name they may otherwise be called, some of America's modern cities have fallen prey to principalities and powers. Can we, like Cho, win in the battle against such ancient foes? Is there a way we can identify and destroy their strongholds? Can the church in modern America reclaim our city streets before it is too late? That is the topic of the next two chapters, and the most important words in this book.

— *Chapter Three* —

EVIDENCE OF INVASION AND FIRST RESISTANCE

Rush Limbaugh, the popular radio personality, in an article entitled "America Needs More God," said, "We have been on the receiving end of a vast experiment: what will happen to a culture if we remove the underpinnings of morality?...you get anarchy...and menace...you get a nation of citizens unable to exit their homes.... I, for one, am convinced that America needs more God."

Rush Limbaugh is right. The great social need in America today is a moral regeneration produced through a spiritual awakening.

The reason spiritual awakening is so important in light of a demonic conquest of America, is that among the benefits of revival exists divine energy to overcome the government of Satan. During revival, believers are "awakened" to their duty. That is, their eyes are opened and they see the need for spiritual warfare, their responsibility for doing something about it, and the mighty weapons available within the kingdom of God. As the U.S. military has used its superpower status to unseat oppressive dictators and liberate native peoples, so spiritual awakening moves the mystical Body of Christ, with its angelic beings and saintly intercessions, to exercise its superpower status against the darkness of this world, unseating invisible tyrants.

Jesus said in Luke 11:21–22, "When a strong man armed keepeth his palace, his goods are in peace: But when a stronger than he shall come upon him, and overcome him, he taketh from him all his armour wherein he trusted, and divideth his spoils." This points out the potential that is ours as believers, and mandates a certain responsibility for the righteous within society to act aggressively against Satan's social goals. It is our Christian duty to equip ourselves and confront the strong man in order to save our society. We must stand against moral relativism. We must oppose the modern age's worship of self. It is our responsibility to invade the heavens and drive away evil forces so that the light of the Gospel may shine with increased brightness. In the letter to the church at Ephesus, Paul states the responsibility of the church in this matter, concluding this was by divine intention. "His intent was that now, through the church, the manifold wisdom of God should be made known to the rulers and authorities in the heavenly realms" (Eph. 3:10 NIV). It is our duty to make the city-liberating power of the Gospel known to the rulers of the kosmos.

Thankfully, God does not give responsibility without also providing the necessary dynamics for the task. For the purpose of spiritual warfare, God has provided the believer with access to both power and authority over Satan's kingdom. Jesus has been seated in "heavenly places, far above all rule and authority and power and dominion, and every name that is named, not only in this age, but also in the one to come" (Eph. 1:20–21 NASB). Everything is now subject to Jesus, and Jesus is the head of the Church (Eph. 1:22–23). Since God hasn't given the keys to the kingdom of heaven to lobbyists, but rather to His Body, the great hope of every lost generation and community is a repentant and powerful church whose weapons of warfare "are not carnal, but mighty through God to the pulling down of strongholds; casting down imaginations, and every high thing [proud or contentious spirit] that exalteth itself against the knowledge of God, bringing into captivity every thought to the obedience of Christ" (2 Cor. 10:4–5).

Qualifying for Authority to Turn Back Satan's Invasion

In Luke 11:20 Jesus said, "If I with the finger of God cast out devils, no doubt the kingdom of God is come upon you." This verse reveals

EVIDENCE OF INVASION AND FIRST RESISTANCE

that kingdom authority is required to turn back demonic powers. Do believers inherently possess kingdom authority? No, but it's available. God reveals the criterion that is necessary for Christians to experience kingdom authority. The secret is found in 2 Chronicles 7:14, where we read, "If my people, which are called by my name, shall humble themselves, and pray, and seek my face, and turn from their wicked ways; then will I hear from heaven, and will forgive their sin, and will heal their land."

The use of the word *if* in 2 Chronicles, chapter 7, suggests that the necessary action on the part of believers is not assumed. At the same time, the word *if* qualifies God's response based on our actions. If we will humble ourselves, pray, seek His face, and turn from wickedness, God will in turn hear our prayers, forgive our sins, and heal our cities. We stand in sufficient authority against an invasion of evil if we are people of humility, prayer, and uprightness. The New Testament weapons of warfare listed in Ephesians 6:14–17, are the end result of these attitudinal dispositions.

In either case, the word *if* remains, and it is an important word. We do not stand with God's authority just because we've joined a Christian coalition or a political action group or even a prayer meeting where loud, teeth-gritting, mad commands are directed toward Satan. True spiritual authority is given by God to whom He qualifies. His criteria are clear. It is the humble, the repentant, the praying righteous, that He anoints with both power and authority. All Christians have the resident power of Christ within them, but not every Christian has the authority to use it. As a locomotive has great physical power but no inherent authority, and must first come under the guidance of a higher intelligence in order to operate using that power, modern believers, if they are to be effective, must align themselves with God's standards and be guided by His spiritual wisdom and insight.

This is not to suggest political disengagement for the church, but true spiritual victories such as America needs, cannot be won by means of legislation or political influence alone. All of the political action in the world will not cleanse one stain of sin from our beleaguered nation. This is where some city prayer gatherings miss the point. Though politically enthused, they often fail to recognize that the first step in confronting spiritual strongholds is to deal with Satan's corresponding inroads within the church. Only as we, through repentance, first pull down Satan's strongholds within our own lives are we prepared to confront him on a territorial level. Jesus was more concerned with establishing His presence among the disciples than He was with confronting Satan, because when His lordship is established among us, it is the nature and authority of Christ speaking through us that penetrates the kosmos and turns back Satan's power.

But, a problem remains—many churchgoers would rather hear about how much power they have than to hear about their need for discipline or repentance. A recent poll indicated that the message of repentance is a flat subject among churchgoers today. If that's true, what should we expect in the nineties if God's people, especially those living in a city under demonic siege, merely posture, neglecting real repentance and prayer? Historically, when the godly covet righteousness and hunger for intimacy with God, the kingdom of heaven overcomes social disintegration through revival. But, when God's people grow inwardly cold, darkness, lawlessness, and an invasion of demonism prevail within society. When Israel forgot the Lord in the Book of Judges, idolatry and other forms of social evil thrived. But, when Israel remembered the Lord, harlotry, drunkenness, and idolatry were put out of the land.

Consequently, if the modern church possesses no intimate hunger for God, if there is absence of real convictions guiding the pilgrims' progress, if passion for God takes second place to religious pleasure, we then have programs without social power, and Christianity without community impact. Our commands to Satan are futile.

Let's Be Honest

Social revival is the antidote for demonism. That is the kind of spiritual awakening that rejuvenates believers and alters the course of society.

EVIDENCE OF INVASION AND FIRST RESISTANCE

Are we experiencing that kind of revival across America today? Not yet. Social indicators and statistical evidence suggest that our culture is getting worse. On our present course, America is headed, city by city, toward destruction.

The late Jamie Buckingham, award-winning columnist, in a *Charisma & Christian Life* article entitled "Buckle Up for the 90's" said: "I do not expect the tide of evil and immorality in America to ebb. We are cycling, as cultures and civilizations have always cycled, and are now on the down side of glory. Our once great and godly nation, having crested the hill of God's grace, has begun a slow descent into the abyss of self-destruction."[54]

Was Buckingham's observation justified? Is America losing the battle against principalities and powers? Satan wants to destroy the United States for many reasons: our support of Israel, our evangelistic attitude, our economic ability to help the world, etc. But, if Satan will succeed, he must first establish a generation raised on situational ethics who are denied a biblical education in youth. Then he can produce a society without a consciousness of God, without moral absolutes, and without a sense of social responsibility. Such a generation could not escape calamity; that is a historical fact. Such a generation would embrace a spirit of antichrist. That is Satan's plan.

Is this plan succeeding? Is demonic social engineering overtaking this generation? Let us look at key social indicators that point to a growing demonic invasion of the United States.

INVASION INDICATORS

1. Sexual Immorality

Since 1950 there has been a 65 percent increase in America's population. Compared to this there has been:

- a 243 percent increase in homicide
- a 100 percent increase in suicide
- a 426 percent increase in illegitimate births

- a 212 percent increase in divorce
- a 2,317 percent increase in child abuse
- a 230 percent increase in rape.[55]

Concerning the dramatic increase in incidents of rape (the fastest growing crime in the U.S.), a recent study by John Court, published in his book *Pornography: A Christian Critique*, found a definite connection between the escalation of rape and the availability of pornographic materials. It also concluded that pornography encompasses more than adult videocassettes. Pornography reflects a social condition or state of mind. There are men, women, and even cities that are pornographic by sheer lack of values. Recently, Gay Pride Week was celebrated across the nation. In major cities throughout America, hundreds of thousands of homosexuals rallied to boast their gay lifestyles and, in at least some of the celebrations, illustrated how we have become a pornographic society.

An article in the *Oklahoma City Times* described one such parade:

> Gay pride week fetes marred by violence—Hundreds of thousands of homosexuals...rallied around the nation to cap Gay Pride Week.... Spectators often joined the festive procession, which included men dressed in evening gowns or garter belts, or wearing black leather vests and skimpy shorts.... The paraders, many scantily dressed in the hot sun, marched and danced toward West Hollywood Park.[56]

The ultimate form of idolatry, and a cardinal indication that a society has come under siege to demonism, is socially accepted hypersexualization. In every historical survey of past great civilizations, openly practiced hypersexualization preceded the demise of that society. This was true of Noah's day, Sodom, Gibeah, Corinth, Rome, Germany, and many others.

Regarding homosexuality, in the beginning it appears to have been

EVIDENCE OF INVASION AND FIRST RESISTANCE

an attempt of Satan to disrupt the lineage of the Messiah. In Genesis 3:15, we find the protoevangelium—the promise that the seed of the woman would someday come forth, being born of a virgin, and would destroy the serpent's power. Soon after the promise was given, fallen angels had intercourse with the antediluvian women in an attempt to intercept, pollute, and destroy the righteous seed. God responded by judging the giants (nepheli, the offspring of this union), and by commanding Israel not to intermarry with the heathen populations. This was so there might be pure seed in Israel.

When Satan saw that his plan had failed, he began to fill the hearts of men with passion for each other. If men preferred men and women preferred women, no children would be born. Satan's strategy was to cut off the bloodline of the Messiah. The Bible records Paul's warning against sexuality outside the bonds of marriage: "Neither fornicators, nor idolaters, nor adulterers, nor effeminate, nor abusers of themselves with mankind...shall inherit the kingdom of God" (1 Cor. 6:9–10).

America's acceptance of hypersexualization, as well as other forms of aberrant behavior, illustrates contemporary demonism. Hypersexualization is demonic, and when openly practiced it is *pornographic*.

A spirit of pornography is ravaging America. The physical toys or objects of pornography (videocassettes, magazines, etc.) are not the core problem, but the symptoms or fuel of a deeper problem. Just as loss or change of appetite accompanies physical illness, so pornography's conquest of America is symptomatic of a deeper spiritual condition—a sickness of the soul of our nation.

Every form of media in the United States today is racing to keep up with the baser appetites of young and old. Television, radio, fashions, education, cyberspace, Hollywood, and advertising are all drifting daily into greater depths of pornography. Like ancient Corinth, we stand blinded by our own intellectual achievements, while morally we die. We're sliding into a cesspool of sensuality where physical pleasures are exalted above the law of God. Meanwhile, AIDS is a national crisis, children are abused by pedophiles and pornographers, women are demeaned and exploited, and teenagers are abducted by sick minds feeding on perverted fantasies.

Clarence M. Kelly, former director of the FBI, reported that 77 percent of child molesters of boys and 87 percent of molesters of girls admitted imitating behavior seen in pornography.[57] These statistics were overwhelmingly supported in the "Final Report of the Attorney General's Commission on Pornography" released in 1986. Government studies reveal 85 percent of pornography is linked to organized crime.[58]

"As it was in the days of Lot.... Even thus shall it be in the day when the Son of man is revealed" (Luke 17:28, 30). America's infatuation with political correctness concerning hypersexualization and pornography is prophetically reminiscent of the moral condition of Sodom and Gomorrah at the time of their destruction. This serves as a warning for us today.

2. Idolatry

In Acts 7:41–42 we read, "And they made a calf in those days, and offered sacrifice unto the idol.... Then God turned, and gave them up to worship the host of heaven." The Jerusalem Bible says that they worshiped the army of heaven, referring to fallen angels. The Apostle Paul continued this thought by saying, "The sacrifices of pagans are offered to demons" (1 Cor. 10:20). These and other verses reveal that idolatry and demon worship are synonymous. Anything can be idolized, but behind the physical thing worshiped exists the true object of adoration-demons. Thus, a cardinal indication of demonism is the growing cultural sanction and practice of idolatry.

Modern idolatry can be manifested in one of three ways: 1) classical idolatry—honoring images or created objects as divinity; 2) human idolatry—excessive admiration for another person or thing; and 3) occult idolatry—worshiping a spirit other than God, such as one's self or Satan.

Idolatry, in any form, is socially destructive. This has been historically true. Beyond that, it is also condemned by God. The Lord issued a solemn warning to Israel in Deuteronomy 18:9–14, regarding idolatry:

> When thou art come into the land which the Lord thy God giveth thee, thou shalt not learn to do after the abominations of those nations. There shall not be found among you any one that maketh his son or his daughter to pass through the fire, or that useth divination, or an observer of times, or an enchanter, or a witch, or a charmer, or a consulter with familiar spirits, or a wizard, or a necromancer. For all that do these things are an abomination unto the Lord: and because of these abominations the Lord thy God doth drive them out from before thee. Thou shalt be perfect with the Lord thy God. For these nations, which thou shalt possess hearkened unto observers of times, and unto diviners: but as for thee, the Lord thy God hath not suffered thee so to do.

In the 1990s, America is experiencing what would have seemed impossible just fifty years ago: an explosion of idolatry. In the United States alone, there are now more than two hundred thousand registered witches, and that number is expanding at an exponential rate.[59] On college campuses and across the nation, witchcraft, spiritism, New Age practices, and Satanism are gaining ground on American youth. Paganism is exploding as the women's spirituality movement now claims more than five hundred thousand participants in earth-centered goddess cults and the worship of female deities.[60] Thousands of children from daycare centers and preschools have recounted strikingly consistent stories of human and animal sacrifices in connection with strange satanic rituals.

The symbols and evidence are abundant. The upside-down pentagram or "baphomet," seen in graffiti and turning up in ritual sites everywhere, represents the goat's head and is considered the most powerful symbol in Satanism. The worship of Satan in the image of a goat is certainly nothing new. The Levitical Law (Lev. 17:1–7) forbade the Hebrews from offering "sacrifices unto devils" (Sayir or sair, "the he-goat"). One of the oldest and purest forms of Satanism is the worship of Satan in the image of a "shaggy he-goat."[61] Under Jeroboam Satan was worshiped in this way (2 Chron. 11:15). In the Book of Isaiah we find that Satan's cohorts are sometimes depicted in a similar manner. We read of a time when "satyrs," demonic he-goat creatures, would dance in the ruins of Babylon (Isa. 13:1–21, 34:14). Josiah in religious zeal tore down the high places of the he-goats: *shearim, seirim* (2 Kings 23:8).

This and similar forms of Satan worship have persisted throughout time, cropping up whenever nations forgot Jehovah and submitted to demonic control. Today, the he-goat, is being idolized in various ways across America. Since the 1960s there has been a steady increase in idolatrous activity and an acceptance of it on the part of America's citizens. Beginning with Edgar Casey and Jean Dixon, many have moved to embrace such persons as Anton Levay and the First Church of Satan. The grand opening of Levay's church was filled with high-ranking political figures and the Hollywood elite. Indirectly, television programs (like "Bewitched") glamorized the notion of occult activity.

Cartoons and children's programs have suckered our children into the occult, and today our kids are playing with Ouija boards and experimenting with parapsychology more than ever. All of this dramatically points to a growth in the acceptance and practice of idolatry, and attests to the presence of invading evil powers within the United States today.

3. Christian Persecution

According to Christian Solidarity International, more Christians have been martyred for their faith in the twentieth century than at any other time in history. Missionary evangelist Mike Evans was forced to flee Cambodia after government intelligence officials there learned of a plan to assassinate him. It appears that those who wanted him dead

EVIDENCE OF INVASION AND FIRST RESISTANCE

despised his Christian testimony. According to *Charisma & Christian Life* (February 1995), *National and International Religion Report* was advised that persecution of Christians is also growing in Iran, where they claim that the Iranian government was responsible for the recent slayings of three Christian leaders. Additional reports of religious persecution are coming in from countries around the world where it is believed that more than 150,000 Christians are murdered each year.

When we hear of the sufferings of our brothers and sisters in lesser developed countries, we are troubled. We should be. As citizens of the United States, we have not had to suffer great resistance to the message of the Gospel in the past. That's changing now as persecution of Christians is on the increase in the United States.

Recently, a woman in Houston, Texas, was ordered by local police to stop handing out Gospel tracts to children who knocked on her door during Halloween. She was informed by the officers that such activity is illegal (not true) and that she would be arrested if she continued. On another front, the Ohio Education Association has been busy trying to eliminate conservative religious activity from the state's public schools. The Freedom from Religion Foundation was allowed to distribute pamphlets to public school children in Madison, Wisconsin, called "We Can Be Good Without God."

Religious persecution in America and the growing assault on traditional values are evidence that, as a nation, we have forgotten our Christian heritage. Persecution increases because a growing number of young people mature without biblical instruction—a generation who do not know where they are going or from whence they came. Persecution of Christians in the United States proves that, given enough time, the gradual invasion of anti-God powers will undermine any people, no matter how powerful or religious their ancestors.

Today, Satan's political puppets want our youth to reflect a hostile indifference to Christianity. Public school children are being taught that America was not founded on the Christian faith, and that our forefathers actually wanted a secular society. The proponents of the

SPIRITUAL WARFARE: THE INVISIBLE INVASION

big lie work overtime to stereotype Christians as the "bad guys" and to expurgate any and all contradictory historical religious evidence from our textbooks. The first (and perhaps the greatest) president of the United States, George Washington, said of such men, "Of all the dispositions and habits which lead to political prosperity, religion and morality are indispensable supports. In vain would that man claim tribute of patriotism, who should labour to subvert these great pillars of human happiness."

Nonetheless, it is in the name of patriotism that Satan is motivating the ACLU and their friends to erase the positive role of Christianity from American history. Dr. Paul Vitz, professor of psychology at New York University, worked with a committee that examined sixty social studies and history textbooks used in public schools across the United States. The committee was amazed to find that almost every reference to the Christian history of this nation had been intentionally removed. Their conclusion: the writers of the commonly used textbooks exhibited a paranoia of the Christian religion.

Satan's invading forces target public school curriculum because this is the best place, outside of the churches and families, to indoctrinate children and thus control the future political and cultural landscape. The framers of the Constitution understood this power when they wrote the Northwest Ordinance, which says, "Religion, morality and knowledge, being essential for good government, schools shall be established in the Northwest territories."

It is obvious that the Founding Fathers intended public education to emphasize religion, morality, and knowledge. They considered it essential for good government. The great men who were led of God to write the Constitution understood that every civilization has been based upon either a theistic or anti-theistic foundation. They learned from history that countries whose systems of education embrace national anti-theistic views ultimately come to ruin. Furthermore, they truly believed what George Washington said, when he argued that it would be "impossible to govern without God and the Ten Commandments." For these reasons the Founding Fathers insisted on an America that was one nation under God. John Adams explained that this underlying philosophy was the cornerstone in the framing of the Constitution. He said, "We have no government armed in power capable of contending in human passions unbridled by morality and religion. Our Constitution was made only for a moral and religious people. It is wholly inadequate for the government of any other."

John Adams believed what Satan already knows—that our great American system would only succeed in governing a moral and religious people. He believed that our laws and Constitution would in fact fail if our nation ever abandoned the restraints of God's Word.

When men work to separate Christian principles from American education, they deny people the knowledge of good and keep them from embracing the laws of God. To that extent, they are pawns of evil and subvert and destroy both the message and the messengers of righteousness. John Adams would have been stunned by the tortured logic employed by the Supreme Court when it ordered the Ten Commandments removed from the walls of the schools in Kentucky. They actually said, "Lest the students looking upon these from day to day should be moved to obey them." Can you imagine anything so terrible as schoolchildren laying down their guns and obeying such radical ideas as "honour thy father and mother" or "thou shalt not kill"? The members of the Kentucky Supreme Court obviously did not understand that our Constitution depended on it.

There is a power at work in the United States today that does not want this generation to look upon or obey the laws of God. This power is manifest whenever we hear, "You cannot legislate morality." Or, "Whose morality should we impose, yours or mine?" The fact is, every law is an imposition of someone's morality, either man's or God's. All of us live by one or the other. When society chooses to live by the infallible laws of God, freedom and the good of mankind succeed. But, when we abandon the moral laws of God, we allow an invasion of evil and persecution to corrupt our society. Thus, we endure the spread of the persecution of Christian values in this generation.

Not long ago, the president of Yale argued that we need an intellectual and moral renovation of the students in the colleges of America. He's absolutely right. Growing numbers of Americans believe violence and crimes of intolerance are growing among young people today. But, how do we propose dealing with the problem? Midnight basketball games to get them off the street? Lectures on why kids should not be Nazis? There is only one way to put an end to the moral decay infecting America's youth—reverse the trend that created the problem in the first place. Yes, I'm advocating putting God back in school. I'm advocating putting God back in our courts and institutions—unless we foolishly consider ourselves too wise or advanced for that.

The fact is, while America was guided by the principles of the Bible, we led the world in diversity and cultural acceptance. That was the basis of our greatness. Christianity reached out to all people. Legendary philosopher Alexis de Tocqueville summed it up by saying that America was great because America was good, and that the basis of our goodness was that Christianity had a greater influence over us than over any other people in the world. He also said that America would cease to be great if ever that influence was diminished.

It was the strong religious convictions of the Founding Fathers, combined with their knowledge of history and the Scriptures, that brought about the conception that an invasion of evil can be restrained, not by human laws alone, but only by God's infallible laws of morality. In 1892 this was argued before the Supreme Court of the United States in *The Church of the Holy Trinity vs. United States*. After exhaustive deliberation, this is what the Court said, "Our laws and our institutions must necessarily be based upon and embody the teachings of the Redeemer of mankind.... It is impossible that it should be otherwise; and in this sense and to this extent our civilization and our institutions are emphatically Christian."

Imagine that. A nation whose laws and institutions are based upon

EVIDENCE OF INVASION AND FIRST RESISTANCE

the teachings of the Redeemer of mankind. Why, such a place would surely become the leader in education, invention, and the arts. Such a place would probably become a haven of religious liberty for more types and religions of people than has ever existed anywhere or at any time on earth. Instead of religious persecution and intolerance, such a place would offer hope and opportunity to the huddled masses of the earth.

4. Juvenile Delinquency

The *Chicago Tribune* reports that increasing numbers of teens are not surviving adolescence within the United States. Quoting the national Center for Health Statistics, they state:

- Over 75% of adolescents use birth control.
- Every 31 seconds an adolescent becomes pregnant.
- Every 78 seconds an adolescent attempts suicide.
- Every 90 seconds one succeeds [at suicide].
- Every 80 minutes an adolescent is murdered.[62]

Noted youth speaker Josh McDowell says, "In the 1940's the teacher's main problems were talking, running in halls, and chewing gum in class. Today the problems are different, assault, vandalism, teen pregnancy, and drug and alcohol abuse."[63]

Josh McDowell is correct. The Federal Bureau of Justice reported nearly one-half of a million violent crimes were committed on high school and college campuses in the previous year alone.

In an article entitled "Our Violent Kids," *Time* magazine recently reported "an upsurge in the most violent types of crimes by teens."[64] Through television, "by the age of 16, the typical child has witnessed an estimated 200,000 acts of violence, including 33,000 murders," the article went on to say. A major study by Dr. Brandon Centerwell of the University of Washington's Department of Epidemiology concludes that "exposure to television is related to approximately one-half of the homicides committed in the United States, or approximately 10,000 homicides annually. Exposure to television is also related to a major proportion—perhaps one-half of rapes, assaults, and other forms of interpersonal violence in the United States."[65]

The January 1991 edition of *Charisma & Christian Lift* reported that every day in the United States:

- 105 babies die before their first birthday
- 1,106 teen-age girls have abortions
- 1,849 children are abused or neglected
- 437 children are arrested for drinking or drunk driving
- 211 children are arrested for drug abuse
- 1,629 children are in adult jails
- 30 children are wounded by guns
- 10 children are killed by guns
- 135,000 children bring a gun to school.[66]

Violence of this magnitude reminds one of a time long ago. "The earth also was corrupt before God, and the earth was filled with violence. And God looked upon the earth, and, behold, it was corrupt; for all flesh had corrupted his way upon the earth. And God said unto Noah, The end of all flesh is come before me; for the earth is filled with violence through them; and, behold, I will destroy them with the earth" (Gen. 6:11–13).

In Genesis, chapter 6, we find a precedent that, to this day, continues to mark the collapse of nations—when a people become idolatrous and self-indulgent, they invite the worst kind of influence to invade their culture. They become wickedly perverse, willing to commit acts of violence against the most vulnerable members of their community, if it serves their evil desires. The blood of the innocent cries to God for justice and judgment, and, unless they repent, God delivers the innocent by judging the wicked. This takes us to our next point.

5. Abortion

Nothing is more convincing that Americans are facing a spiritual invasion than the current level of violence occurring in the United States, especially that which targets our unborn children. Sadly, after years of progress by the pro-life movement, President Bill Clinton, on the Saturday following his inauguration, issued four executive orders as follows: 1) he permitted the tiny bodies of aborted babies to be used in medical research; 2) he lifted the restrictions on abortion counseling in federally funded clinics; 3) he lifted the ban on importing the abortifacient RU 486; and 4) he provided federal funding for abortions in military hospitals.

In 1973 abortion on demand became legal with the landmark *Roe vs. Wade* decision. There's no doubt that abortion has become a profitable business for those involved, since abortion clinics have sprung up across the United States, launching a multimillion-dollar industry. One clinic employee admitted recently that she made an average of thirteen thousand dollars per month based on a commission of twenty-five dollars per abortion. She compared her job responsibilities to a phone-in boiler room, where each employee sat at a booth answering calls. When a distraught young lady called in, a sales script was read that had been designed to overcome any obstacle that stood in the way of an abortion. The caller was encouraged to come in for "counseling," and to bring the payment for the abortion with her. Once the abortion was performed, the saleswoman would receive a twenty-five dollar commission. The idea is simple. Used car salesmen and con artists have employed the same system for years.

Abortion on demand is the demonic Baal worship of modern times, and is a leading indicator of invading spiritual forces within the United States today.

King Ahab and Queen Jezebel led the Israelites in Baal worship and the sacrifice of children in the Old Testament. It was believed that Baal held the key to prosperity. People desiring to live in prosperity and ease would bring their firstborn child to the high priest, where scholars say the child would be offered as a burnt offering to the deity. The altar of Baal was in the image of a bull with the head and shoulders of a man. Its arms extended outward and fire belched out from a hole in the chest. The priest of Baal placed the babies on the outstretched arms, where the child would be rolled into the fire. As the child died, the priest and priestess engaged in sexual intercourse, while an orgy occurred among the onlookers.

Recently, archaeologists unearthed a Baal cemetery containing the remains of more than twenty thousand children. The Greek author Kleitarchos described the practice of sacrificing infants three hundred years before Christ:

> Out of reverence for Kronos [Baal], the Phoenicians, and especially the Carthaginians, whenever they seek to obtain some great favor, vow one of their children, burning it as a sacrifice to the deity, if they are especially eager to gain success. There stands in their midst a bronze statue of Kronos, its hands extended over a bronze brazier, the flames of which engulf the child. When the flames fall on the body, the limbs contract and the open mouth seems almost to be laughing, until the contracted body slips quietly into the brazier.

Ancients killed their children for personal convenience and gain, while engaging in promiscuity. Modern Americans have slaughtered more than thirty million for the same reasons. The judgment of God came upon the baby killers of the Old Testament as is revealed in 2 Kings 17. Can we in the United States hope to escape the wrath of God when we have done the same?

"Be not deceived," says Galatians 6:7, "God is not mocked: for whatsoever a man soweth, that shall he also reap." The law of reciprocity is catching up with America. Biblically based tenets of morality that have guided our nation for more than two hundred years have

EVIDENCE OF INVASION AND FIRST RESISTANCE

been put aside in favor of situation ethics and hedonism. Never in the history of the United States have we, as a nation, permitted such an assault on the Almighty. Like Pergamum, Persia, Gadara, and Corinth, we have opened the door for a hostile takeover of demonic proportions within the United States. When a government acts apart from God, in His place, or against Him, it invites an invasion of evil. If this is allowed to continue in the United States another ten years, I believe the entire superstructure of American culture will collapse like a house of cards. The philosophy of situation ethics, the doctrine of open (as long as it's safe) sex, the epidemic of AIDS and other rampant forms of sexually transmitted diseases, the redefining of the family unit, and other abandonments of traditional standards of morality will come to their dangerous and natural conclusion.

Gen. Douglas MacArthur, at the close of World War II, said, "History fails to record a single precedent in which nations subject to moral decay have not passed into political and economic decline. There has been either a spiritual awakening to overcome the moral lapse, or progressive deterioration leading to ultimate national disaster."[67]

In other words, it's time for believers in the United States to overthrow the kingdom of darkness through repentance. We must turn from sin and beseech our heavenly Father for revival. D. M. Paton said that revival is the inrush of the Spirit into the body that threatens to become a corpse. That's what America needs. During the famous Welsh revival of 1904, judges were presented with white gloves; they had no criminal cases to try. No rapes, no murders, no robberies, no embezzlements—nothing. People 100,000 strong were converted to Christianity in 150 days! The District Consuls actually met in emergency meetings to discuss what to do with the police, now that they were unemployed. So great was the social impact of revival.

It's Time for America to Repent and Pray

At a time when environmentalists who protect streams, seals, eagle eggs, snail darters, and spotted owls are supported through tax monies, while "butchers" legally slaughter unborn babies, it's time for America to repent and pray.

At a time when thirteen-year-old girls are forbidden to drive a car, drink alcohol, get married, take aspirin at school, or get their ears pierced without parental consent, but sex clinics are installed on school grounds so these same girls can acquire condoms, birth control pills, and even abortions without the consent of their parents, it's time for America to repent and pray. At a time when Nativity scenes cannot be erected on public grounds, yet "artists" such as Andrea Serrano, protected by the highest court in the land, are allowed to display a crucifix submerged in their own urine at publicly owned museums, it's time for America to repent and pray.

It's time for citizens to join hands across America in holy dissatisfaction and refuse to continue watching the destruction of the United States by gargoyles from Satan's dark kingdom. They delight themselves in our demise. Surely such evil demands a godly response on the part of the righteous.

Can Christians effectively respond to horrid invisible powers intent on destroying America? If we as a nation have willingly exposed ourselves to insidious powers, and now as a result are reaping the mischief of these unseen forces, can we now reverse the process of cause and effect and liberate our cities under siege? Yes. The repentant church of Jesus is still the power against which the gates of hell cannot stand.

The Weapons of Our Warfare

When Solomon stood before God and asked what the people of Israel should do in light of their sins and subsequent social demise, God provided an answer, spelled out in four biblical fundamentals:

1. They were to humble themselves.
2. They were to pray.
3. They were to seek His face.
4. They were to turn from their wickedness (2 Chron. 7:14).

If Israel would do these things, revival would come. God would hear their prayers, forgive their sins, and heal their cities.

These principles are eternal. God is unchanging. Jesus is the same yesterday, today, and forever, and the law of precedence suggests that what He has done for others He will do for us. The dynamic of spiritual weaponry, that was born of repentance and worked for both Old and New Testament believers in reversing social decay, will work in the twentieth century to overcome evil and will revive the United States of America.

But, let's not kid ourselves. The fact that believers have access to spiritual dynamics doesn't mean they will respond properly. God's command to Solomon was to do something. It involved energy and will power. Will the church rise to this occasion? And, based on the answer, where is America headed? Some say the church is asleep and Satan's invasion will succeed. Others prophesy revival.

I believe that the future of this nation could include revival—the kind of spiritual awakening sufficient to overwhelm and overcome the efforts of Satan, and to liberate our cities. In 1905 240 department stores closed from eleven to two each day for prayer in the streets of Portland, Oregon. In Atlantic City, only fifty people, from a population of fifty thousand were unconverted in the same year. This could happen again.

But, if indeed America's future is brightened by the possibility of revival, what causes could set it in motion? What would cause believers to humble themselves, pray, and seek God?

History has concluded that societies, including believers, have the potential to experience revival through the catalyst of two different stimuli: revival through crises and revival through repentance alone.

Revival through Crises

Revival can come through crises. Throughout the course of history, God, at times, has allowed a crisis to grip the soul of a nation, so that through it men might come to the end of their human abilities; and, in desperation, cry to God for forgiveness, healing, and restoration.

SPIRITUAL WARFARE: THE INVISIBLE INVASION

The Old Testament proves repeatedly that tribulation or trials often become God's only means of redemption. The God who chastens whom He loves will allow famine, military aggression, economic woes, or whatever may be necessary to turn the heart of the nation back toward Himself again.

During the American operation against Iraq called Desert Storm, several major magazines pointed out an undeniable historical link between crises and revival. Banners across the United States were seen everywhere: "GOD, GUNS, & GUTS!", "PRAY FOR AMERICAN BOYS!", etc. During times of prosperity in the United States, our cultural tendencies reflect measurable declines in religious interest, while during times of crises our interest in church attendance and faith toward God have increased historically.

For that reason America's future might include calamities or crises. For thousands of years prophets have forecasted calamity for the time just before the year 2000. As we approach the seventh millennia, Americans may face the greatest shaking since the country was formed. Some Bible scholars believe this has prophetic merit and emphasize the need to repent while there is time.

REVIVAL THROUGH REPENTANCE ALONE

Revival can also come through open repentance. While a crisis can bring people to repentance long before God sends trouble upon a land, He first sends people of faith (prophets) to announce the impending divine judgment. This is done so that through a last appeal, He might have mercy in place of tribulation.

If God can bring a nation to repentance without introducing a crisis, this is the choice God obviously prefers. In Ezekiel 18:30, the prophet says, "Repent, and turn from your transgressions; so iniquity shall not be your ruin." Repentance is the key.

When Jonah, the reluctant prophet, spoke to the people of Nineveh concerning the impending judgment of God, that judgment was certain, but open repentance would provide a means of escape. When the

EVIDENCE OF INVASION AND FIRST RESISTANCE

king of Nineveh heard the prophetic preaching of Jonah, he believed the true prophet and repented in sackcloth and ashes. The result was a revival of righteousness without the need for crisis. Thus, the destructive spirits over Nineveh were foiled. Could not God spare modern America in the same way? It's possible that God did something similar to this in 1940 when prayers were made, and Germany's Third Reich disintegrated as its leadership began making mistake after mistake.

During these crucial days, God is looking for church leaders who will preach repentance in love. The Bible says, "Repentance and remission of sins should be preached in his name among all nations, beginning at Jerusalem" (Luke 24:47). Calling a people or a nation to repentance is not an easy task. It's easier to preach things people want to hear and will applaud. The time has come when all true ministries will include altars of repentance.

In 1 Kings 22:15–23, we find a time when God grew weary of Israel's negligence of the truth and allowed a "lying spirit" to fill the mouths of the prophets. They prophesied deception and caused the people to trust in a lie. God tolerated this in order to expedite a crisis against Israel for refusing to repent. I believe something similar to this began happening in the United States in the late sixties, and has continued to the present. While some church leaders continue to speak the truth, others have given in to a lying spirit and preach only the popular doctrines that please their audiences. Instead of righteousness, service, and devotion to God, many are made to feel at ease while they dine on doctrines of self-rights and privileges for believers. Portions of these teachings are true, but they are often without balance, and that is a deadly poison.

Many pastors avoid talking to their congregations about repentance for fear of losing their attendance and support. So, they rob them of their true spiritual life, while seducing them with untrue doctrines and feel-good theology. In 1 Timothy 4:1 we read, "Now the Spirit speaketh expressly, that in the latter times some shall depart from the faith, giving heed to seducing spirits, and doctrines of devils." Later, in 2 Timothy 4:3–4, Paul wrote, "For the time will come when they will not endure sound doctrine; but after their own lusts shall they heap to themselves teachers, having itching ears; And they shall turn away their ears from the truth, and shall he turned unto fables." This verse is very contemporary. It describes a portion of sermonizing today.

If America is to escape a national crisis, we need, as never before, church leaders who will decry the sins of our nation and people, and that will call America to repentance. It may not be too late for the United States, but we must recognize our fallen condition and repent. In Isaiah we read, "In the year that king Uzziah died I saw also the Lord" (Isa. 6:1). Upon seeing the Lord, Isaiah discovered that he was unclean, and that he dwelt with unclean people. He called upon Israel to repent. In the days of 1 Kings, chapter 22, Israel would not listen to the true prophets who preached repentance, but preferred the easy messages of the false teachers. Judgment came upon them.

In one year we have had the flood, blizzard, and hurricane of the century. AIDS and other forms of disease are ravaging our citizens. The underpinnings of our society are collapsing. God is talking, but are we listening? The kind of true revival that America needs must begin with the obedience of the Body of Christ. The point of origination is defined: "If my people, which are called by my name..." (2 Chron. 7:14). It may take the catalyst of major crises to stir us toward repentance and prayer, or perhaps we shall simply obey the Spirit's pleading. But, through whatever combined source of prompting, church leaders and their congregations must now turn from the addictions of religious entertainment and humble ourselves in this hour of darkness, pray, seek His face, and turn from every shadow of wickedness.

In so doing, believers will triumph over evil forces and open the door for God's restorative power and the recovery of American society. If we, as the Body of Christ, do anything less, America has no future.

In Acts 3:19 we read this promise: "Repent ye therefore, and be converted, that your sins may be blotted out, [and] the times of refreshing shall come from the presence of the Lord." Thank God; we, like Nineveh, have a choice.

— *Chapter Four* —

THE VICTORS' MASTER WEAPONS

One of the most engaging verses in the Old Testament is Psalm 78:41, where we read, "Yea, they turned back and tempted God, and limited the Holy One of Israel." This verse represents an interesting notion—that men can limit God. How so? Can we enter heaven and tie God's arms so that He cannot arise from His throne? There is only one way to limit God—in our minds; in our concept of Him. In Proverbs 23:7 we read of the enormous ability of the mind, "As he thinketh in his heart, so is he."

When the spies returned from Canaan, they said, "The land, through which we have gone to search it, is a land that eateth up the inhabitants thereof... And there we saw the giants, the sons of Anak, which come of the giants, and we were in our own sight as grasshoppers, and so we were in their sight" (Num. 13:32–33). When the skeptical report of the spies was delivered, "All the congregation lifted up their voice, and cried; and the people wept that night" (Num. 14:1). Their concept of God's power to bring them into the promise land had been diminished. God had not changed, nor was He unprepared at that moment to bring Israel's opponents to their knees. But, Israel limited God conceptually. God had become so small in the mind of Israel, that He became the God of the grasshopper people.

The quality of believers' relationship with God is determined by their concept of Him. If people have a limited concept of the power and nature of God, they will thereby limit God's activity in their lives. When I was a pastor, I would leave the hospital and one of the nurses would say, "Good bye, chaplain." That was their concept of me. But, when I went home, my wife referred to me as "honey," and received me as her husband. My staff just called me "boss." Although I never changed, I became separate things to different people. Consequently, my relationship with each individual was determined by his or her concept of me.

In matters of spiritual warfare, we need a concept of God based on Exodus 15:3, where we read, "The Lord is a man of war: the Lord is his name." Truly, God is militant, and we need to perceive Him as such. Upon the extermination of Amalek, God revealed Himself to Moses as Jehovah-Nissi, the Lord our Banner (Exod. 17:15). He is our banner—the One who goes before us into battle.

For a believer to have an effective, militant prayer life, we must perceive God as a "man of war." If the United States will see her cities delivered from spiritual bondage, we must understand and join the battle-ready side of God. Our nation cannot afford modern believers who, like ancient Israel, "turned back...and limited the Holy One" (Ps. 78:41).

Erwin Lutzer in *The Rebirth of America*, notes, "Only the people of God can arrest our slide into the cesspool of sensuality. But the question is whether we have the moral fiber to put our own house in order so that we can speak to the world."[68]

Thankfully, God is a ready captain. As He provided weapons by which Solomon might see deliverance and restoration for the nation of Israel, so today, American Christians need not stand idly by observing the decline of Western civilization. We, too, can be sufficiently equipped as vessels of power and authority, fully capable of turning back Satan's invading forces.

What are the liberating weapons available to the Body of Christ, through which the Church may induce spiritual awakening and secure a climate aimed at social renewal?

Weapon #1: Humility

God said in the verse cited in 2 Chronicles 7:14, "If my people will humble themselves." Although the primary focus in this chapter is to consider militant prayer, and much has already been said about the need for humility, it must be noted finally that humility plays a positive role in creating effective prayer warriors. Humility keeps us focused on the need for prayer. Humility brings us to repentance and keeps us keenly aware that without God's ongoing help, we will never prevail. Humility forbids false pride and persuades man of his need for preserving and redeeming grace.

Today, many Bible expositors theorize that we are living in the antithesis of humility—the Laodicean age of the church. It's a time when the organized church appears wealthy, popular, and entertaining—modern juntas run by affluent preachers who enjoy all the "perks" of successful, upscale Wall Street businessmen. Sadly, below the surface, many of these leaders and their devotees are inwardly cold, beggarly, and spiritually bankrupt.

In Revelation, chapter 3, Jesus said,

> And unto the angel of the church of the Laodiceans write:... Because thou sayest, I am rich, and increased with goods, and have need of nothing; and knowest not that thou art wretched, and miserable, and poor, and blind, and naked: I counsel thee to buy of me gold tried in the fire, that thou mayest be rich; and white raiment, that thou mayest be clothed, and that the shame of thy nakedness do not appear; and anoint thine eyes with eyesalve, that thou mayest see. As many as I love, I rebuke and chasten: be zealous therefore, and repent. (Rev. 3:14–19)

Like some congregations today, the Laodicean church exalted itself. This exciting, dynamic fellowship enjoyed numerical growth and political power. Yet despite its fine achievements, many of which were undoubtedly godly, these believers were either ignorant or indifferent to the words of the Apostle Paul, as he witnessed to the church in Galatia, "God forbid that I should glory, save in the cross of our Lord Jesus Christ" (Gal. 6:14a). Instead, they declared, "We are rich and increased with goods, and have need of nothing!" The Lord evidently viewed Christian success differently than did the believers in Laodicea. He explained that while they were outwardly rich, the Laodiceans were, in His eyes, "wretched, and miserable, and poor, and blind, and naked." Because of the material progress enjoyed by Americans over the past forty years, the subtle possibility of an infection of Laodiceanism is a real and present danger for any congregation.

Compared to other nations we are rich. If we want something, we buy it. If we need ministry, we hire it. If we don't like the way it looks, we pay to have it changed. And, if it convicts our hidden sins, we take our money elsewhere. We tend to get the window dressing just right so that when we enter the sanctuary on the Lord's Day, we are comfortable and entertained.

While there is nothing inherently wrong with prosperity or success, Christians must understand that God is looking for servants. He resists the proud but gives grace to the humble. He uses finances, but He wants people whose first devotion is to rely upon Him and His power. The heathens trusted in Mammon—the Aramaic god of wealth and earthly power. God wants children who are dissatisfied with anything less than the manifestation of His holy presence.

The strength of America is sometimes the biggest problem in the church. Like Laodicea, we are proud, wealthy, and powerful. There's nothing wrong with that as long as we are not deceived by our strength and arrogantly forget God.

On 30 April 1863, Abraham Lincoln wisely said,

We have been the recipients of the choicest bounties of heaven. We have been preserved, these many years, in peace and prosperity. We have grown in numbers, wealth and power, as no other nation has ever grown. But we have forgotten God. We have forgotten the gracious hand which preserved us in peace, and multiplied and enriched and strengthened us; and we have vainly imagined, in the deceitfulness of our hearts, that all these blessings were produced by some superior wisdom or virtue of our own. Intoxicated with unbroken success, we have become too self-sufficient to feel the necessity of redeeming and preserving grace, too proud to pray to the God that made us! It behooves us then, to humble ourselves before the offended Power, to confess our national sins, and to pray for clemency and forgiveness.[69]

Abraham Lincoln would tremble if he could see America today. If we as the church in the United States are to win in the battle against principalities and powers, we must begin on our knees in humility confessing the inadequacy of our ceremonies and programs, and our absolute need of God the Father, the gifts of His Holy Spirit, and the power of His Son, Jesus Christ. With the proper repentant attitude we are more than conquerors through Jesus Christ. Anything less is an unholy mixture, a strange fire in the presence of God. It may draw crowds and make churchgoers cheer, but when the civic auditoriums close up for the night, we still live in a nation under demonic siege unless, "My people will humble themselves."

Angelic Help for the Humble Christian Soldier

For the purpose of a successful military crusade, God provides the humble Christian with heavenly helpers—angels and spiritual armor. First, let's discuss angels for the humble.

Although they have existed since the dawn of time, angels are again a hot topic in both the secular and Christian worlds. Bookstores of every kind offer a wide variety of angel publications that continue to appear on the best-sellers list month after month. As the only true source for accuracy, we look to the Bible for an authoritative view on angels and their role in spiritual warfare.

From the Old and New Testament accounts, we find the activity of angels as it relates to spiritual warfare defined in the following way: In relation to God, angels serve His person and military program. In relation to the world, angels assist God's action in guiding the nations. In relation to the church, they help in an assortment of critical areas whenever and wherever it's deemed necessary by God for a successful military campaign. Angels are not under the church's command, but they protect the believers and the message of God while they are on the battlefield.

The New Testament word *angelos,* like the Old Testament word *malak,* simply means "messenger." The idea is that angels serve the Lord on earth and in the heavenlies. While the ministry of angels is vast, let's consider four categories that come under spiritual warfare:

1. Angels Participate in Guiding the Nations

Angels, both good and evil, take part in the spiritual battle for nations. Throughout biblical history, we find clear evidence that angels have regularly participated in influencing world governments and in shaping human history. While angels are actively involved around the world, they are particularly interested in nations that relate to Israel and prophetic fulfillment. In Exodus 23:20 we read, "Behold, I send an Angel before thee, to keep thee in the way, and to bring thee into the place which I have prepared." When God brought Israel out of Egypt, He made a promise that His angel would go before them and would assist them in the development of their nation. In recent years, we have witnessed an ongoing involvement of angels with regard to Israel. Following the Six Day War, eyewitness testimonies came in from across Israel of "fiery chariots" that had appeared in the skies above the Jewish soldiers, and that had apparently assisted in their military victory. Some of the best confirmation of these angelic chariots came from the prisoners who swore that they had been frightened into surrender by a heavenly host.

THE VICTORS' MASTER WEAPONS

In Daniel 12:1, we discover that the Archangel Michael will play a role in guiding the nation of Israel during the tribulation period. We read, "And at that time shall Michael stand up, the great prince which standeth for the children of thy people: and there shall be a time of trouble, such as never was since there was a nation even to that same time." Throughout the seven years of tribulation, we read of angels helping God in shaping the future of the nations by dispensing His will and judgment upon the kingdoms of the world. The angels in the Book of Revelation assist in wars and affect "natural" phenomena—such as earthquakes and storms—in ways that will serve the plans of God in directing the world's future.

America's forefathers believed that heavenly providence played a role in the formation and establishment of the North American continent. Over the past few years, we in America have experienced the most destructive weather in hundreds of years, and in some cases the most devastating storms on record. When we understand that angels strive with the nations by controlling natural phenomena (such as weather), we realize that God may be trying to say something to the United States today. In 2 Chronicles 7:14 we read, "If my people...will humble themselves, and pray, and seek my face, and turn from their wicked ways; then will I hear from heaven...and will heal their land." If we participate in militant prayer and repentance, God will send forth His "heavenly host" to assist in guiding our nation back into moral and spiritual recovery!

2. Angels Are Battlefield Messengers

Messagebearing is the first and most recurrent function of angels. Thus the title *angelos-messenger*. Angelic message-bearing is most common during decisive events of a celestial order, such as the birth of Christ or national spiritual warfare. It was an angel that brought God's prophetic message to Mary concerning the immaculate birth of her Son, Jesus (Luke 1:26–38). Earlier, a similar message had been delivered by an angel to Zechariah about the conception of his son, John the

Baptist (Luke 1:5–25). After Jesus was born, the angels moved into a battlefield-messenger role, delivering a warning message to Joseph and instructing him to flee with Mary and Jesus into Egypt. The angel said, "Flee into Egypt, and be thou there until I bring thee word: for Herod will seek the young child to destroy him" (Matt. 2:13).

In the Book of Acts, we find an example of how angels can serve the Church as God's messengers during spiritual warfare. Satan had filled Herod's heart with hatred for the Church. James was killed and Peter had been imprisoned for preaching the Gospel. When the believers understood that Herod was also planning to kill Peter, "prayer was made without ceasing of the church unto God for him" (Acts 12:5).

Peter was in a strict prison confinement, sleeping between two Roman soldiers in chains. During the night, an angel entered the prison and hit Peter on the side. "Arise up quickly," the angel said, "Gird thyself, and bind on thy sandals...and follow me" (Acts 12:7–8). Peter thought that he was dreaming as he followed the angel out of the prison and past the guards. It was not until he was outside and standing on the street that Peter realized that the *angelos,* the messenger of God, had spoken God's message and delivered him from the Roman prison.

Other accounts of angels serving the military purposes of message-bearing reveal that angels are sometimes perceived as heavenly beings only after they have departed. Such was the case with the angel that appeared to Gideon in Judges 6:11–24. Hebrews 13:2 says, "Be not forgetful to entertain strangers: for thereby some have entertained angels unawares." When angels appear they can be brilliant and even frightening, but usually they appear in simple human form. It would be interesting to know how many times we have encountered these mysterious "strangers," and how often they have offered us words of counsel. Because one never knows for sure, we should always be listening for the "message behind the speaker's voice." This is especially true during times of important decision making and of spiritual warfare.

3. Angels Provide Battlefield Protection

In an earlier chapter I related the story of a young possessed boy and his attempts to harm me. It has always been my private belief that the "something" that came between me and the young man was a guardian angel.

In the Scriptures we read how angels were assigned to protect Jesus. "For he shall give his angels charge over thee, to keep thee in all thy ways. They shall bear thee up in their hands, lest thou dash thy foot against a stone" (Ps. 91:11–12). Such verses reflect the ancient (and I believe accurate) Jewish belief that God assigns protective angels to those who belong to him.

The writers of the early church, including Origen and Eusebius, believed that each person is accompanied by a personal guardian angel. The followers of Christ evidently held this view, for when Peter stood outside knocking on the door at Mary's house, they said, "It is his angel" (Acts 12:15). This is certainly true of children according to Matthew 18:10, but whether or not the continual presence of guardian angels applies to adults in every situation is difficult to prove. In any case, I believe the duty of protective angels in escorting us through the battlefield is a certain biblical reality.

In Hebrews 1:14 we read, "Are they (angels) not all ministering spirits, sent forth to minister for them who shall be heirs of salvation?" Protecting the saints is a vital part of angelic ministry. In Daniel 6:1–23 this was illustrated in the familiar story of Daniel in the Lions' den. After a sleepless night of fasting, King Darius ran to the lions' den and cried, "O Daniel, servant of the living God, is thy God, whom thou servest continually, able to deliver thee from the lions?" Daniel answered, "O king, live for ever. My God hath sent his angel, and hath shut the lions' mouths" (Dan. 6:20–22).

Another illustration of angels protecting the servant of God is found in 2 Kings 6:13–17. The king of Aram hated Elisha and sent spies out to track him down. When they found Elisha in the city of Dothan, they surrounded him with a great army. "And when the servant of the man of God was risen early, and gone forth, behold, an host compassed the city both with horses and chariots" (2 Kings 6:15). The servant of Elisha said, "Alas, my master! how shall we do? And he answered, Fear not: for they that be with us are more than they that be with them" (2 Kings 6:15–16). Elisha prayed that God would open his servant's eyes and allow him to see the angelic realm. "And the Lord opened the eyes of the young man; and he saw; and, behold, the mountain was full of horses and chariots of fire round about Elisha" (2 Kings 6:17).

During spiritual warfare, people often pray for God to surround their homes and to provide their children with angelic shelter. Volumes of reputable testimonies have been given to confirm the verity of such angelic protection. Obviously, this is a great source of comfort for Christians who are on the battlefield. Sometimes angels deliver messages. Sometimes they deliver themselves as guardians!

4. Angels Bring Comfort and Strength to the Battle-Weary

The Prophet Daniel had been in militant prayer and fasting for three weeks. He was interceding to God and conducting war in the heavenlies for the future of the nation of Israel. While he stood on the bank of the Tigris River, the Angel Gabriel suddenly appeared before him. Daniel fell on his face saying, "How can the servant of this my lord talk with this my lord? for as for me, straightway there remained no strength in me, neither is there breath left in me" (Dan. 10:17). Daniel fell down trembling—overcome by the extent of his fast and by the glorious presence of the angel. Then the angel touched him, saying, "O man greatly beloved, fear not: peace be unto thee, be strong, yea, be strong" (Dan. 10:19). When the angel touched Daniel, he delivered strength to the prophet. Daniel was afterward energized and continued in spiritual warfare.

Psalm 34:7 is a beautiful verse that was written from the soldier's battlefield perspective. It says, "The angel of the Lord encampeth round about them that fear him, and delivereth them." It was an angel that ministered strength and deliverance to Elijah in 1 Kings, chapter

19, when the prophet was running for his life and trying to escape from the wicked queen Jezebel. In the New Testament, we find angels ministering strength to Jesus after His fast and temptation in the wilderness (Mark 1:13). Thankfully, the ministry of angels is not limited to great prophets or to Christ alone, but as the Apostle Paul taught, they are ministering spirits, sent forth to deliver battlefield strength to all of God's children (Heb. 1:14).

Armor for the Humble

In Ephesians 6:13–17 we read about the second heavenly helper—spiritual armor. It's interesting that before we are commanded to pray (verse 18), we are told to put on the whole armor of God. To the world it may sound foolish to speak of armor for the humble. The world's view is that the humble will ultimately get squashed, that might is right, and that only the strong will survive. That's what the mighty Roman Empire believed, and they laughed at Jesus for preaching a message that said, "the meek shall inherit the earth." But today there's nothing left of the old Roman Empire, and Christianity has encircled the globe.

To the Greeks knowledge was all powerful. People from around Asia migrated to the Parthenon to venerate Athena, the Greek goddess of wisdom, and to listen to the greatest known human intellects argue that the mind was the mightiest force of all. But, today the majestic temple of Athena is in ruins, and the once great Parthenon is the habitation of goats.

The point is, you cannot judge the church's power by human measurements. As we humble ourselves before the Almighty, we are directed by the Holy Spirit to put on the Christian's coat of mail. This is supernatural equipment designed by a supernatural God for supernatural warfare.

1. The Girdle of Truth

First of all, we are commanded to gird our loins with truth. In New Testament times, the soldier's girdle was the broad leather belt that was buckled around the waist. It protected the loins and harnessed the sword.

A great deal has been written about the girdle of truth with the focus usually on speaking the truth or quoting the Word of God. But, this verse is actually talking about Christian character. In ancient times, it was believed that the essence of a man's character issued forth from his loins. It's clear from this analogy that Paul wanted the Ephesians to see how important, and how powerful, truth is to our Christian experience. What we do and say in truth is very important in spiritual warfare.

But, having our loins girt about with truth addresses more than human endeavor. It speaks of an internal reaction to the consistent presence of God, in which we are made partakers of God's divine nature. God is truth. As we walk in the Spirit, we experience God in devotion and service until we are overtaken by a nature that loves and embraces the righteousness of God, and despises everything that makes a lie. "This then is the message which ye have heard of him… that God is light, and in him is no darkness at all" (1 John 1:5).

It's easy to see why the girdle of truth is a powerful guard in protecting us from the enemy. Satan is the antithesis of truth; he is the father of lies and cannot approach the presence of God's light and truth.

2. The Breastplate of Righteousness

Secondly, we are to put on the breastplate of righteousness. The breastplate was actually two plates, one on the front and the other on the back, hung over the neck and tied together on the sides. It protected several vital organs, but primarily the heart.

Today, we think of our minds as the seat of volition. But in ancient times the heart was considered the area from which our free will and resolve flowed. The sixth chapter of Ephesians reveals that the soldier's resolve is to be based, not on our good deeds, but on God's perfect righteousness. It's very important for the believer to understand that while our good works are important, they will never sustain us when we are confronted by the enemy. Sometimes Christians approach the

THE VICTORS' MASTER WEAPONS

battlefield on the basis of their good deeds, only to experience discouragement and defeat. Satan attacks their righteous acts with accusations and condemnation, deriding and questioning their motives until they often lose faith in themselves and their accomplishments. But, Satan cannot question the righteousness of God, and when His righteousness is the believer's breastplate, we can march into battle having full confidence in the imputed righteousness of Christ.

3. Shoes of the Gospel

Thirdly, we are to shod our feet with the preparation of the Gospel of peace. Here we find one of the central functions of spiritual warfare—advancing the Gospel. Our feet are to be carried into battle on the same material that can liberate Satan's captives. The preaching of the Gospel is to be the dynamic that provides our authority, our footing, and our military stability.

Today, Christians in the United States face an unfriendly Supreme Court, a hostile public education system, and a liberal federal government. While these entities are good at opposing the church, they offer no answers for the social decay troubling our nation. They vainly study and introduce social programs only to watch them miserably fail. But, the simple preaching of the Gospel breaks the bands of wickedness. It makes junkies come clean, criminals repent, and fathers come home to their children. It can repair marriages, convict corporate cheats, and even rebuild society if we will give it a chance. It was Paul who confirmed to the Romans that the Gospel of Christ was "the power [*dunamis*, dynamo] of God unto salvation" (Rom. 1:16). As warriors of God's kingdom, we can enter into battle with a full assurance of victory, when our feet are born along by the power of the Gospel.

4. The Shield of Faith

The fourth part of our armor is the shield of faith and speaks of our confidence in God. Trust in God is the Christian's first line of defense, and is the protective gear used during spiritual warfare to quench the fiery darts of the wicked one. The Roman soldier used his shield to hide behind in the heat of the battle, but we find that the battle shield was useful for even more. The shield was about four feet high and over two feet wide and made of a thick leather hide. Because it was common in ancient times to douse the end of the arrows in an oily mixture, and then ignite them before shooting or throwing them at the enemy, the experienced Roman soldier would soak his leather shield in water for several hours before going off to war. Once on the battlefield, his shield would provide him with an effective defense against the enemies' fiery darts and arrows.

The Apostle Paul likened our faith in God to a shield that will not burn. When our confidence is in God, rather than in human skill, we win battles day by day as we learn to put our faith and trust in Him.

5. The Helmet of Salvation

The fifth part of the Christian's armor is the helmet of salvation. A soldier can receive wounds to most parts of his body and live to fight again, but a serious wound to the head is usually fatal. The helmet of salvation is needed to protect the believer's thought life. First, it's important that we understand with our head, as well as with our hearts, that we are saved by faith in the redemptive work of Christ. Secondly, we need an ongoing source of protection for our thought life each and every day. In the field of spiritual warfare, none dare enter without a divine helmet of salvation. Those who do, often fall on the battleground, injured by arrows of lust and deception.

The helmet of salvation is the Christian's best defense against demonization. While I do not believe that a born-again Christian can ever be demon possessed, I do believe that some Christians are troubled by demons (oppressed). There are different ways that a Christian can wind up demonically afflicted, but usually it begins in the mind. Satan hammers at our thought life continually. He knows that all of us are tempted and enticed to sin, and so he preys on our individual weaknesses. If he can once get us to fall into and persist in an ongoing debauched thought process, his battle is nearly won. Thankfully, we have a "thought shield" if we will put on the helmet of salvation.

6. The Sword of the Spirit

The sword of the spirit is the Word of God and is the last of the soldier's hardware. Unlike the other articles of armor, the sword is both defensive and offensive. Paul undoubtedly drew this analogy from the example of Jesus, who exemplified for every believer the power of the Word. For Jesus, there was no greater sword than the written Word of God. He overcame every obstacle, from the scoffing of the Pharisees to Satan's tempting in the wilderness, by the power of the Word. As the Word incarnate and the head of the church, Jesus now leads His people into battle. We must follow our captain's lead, take up the sword of the Spirit, and let God's Word quicken and direct us from victory to victory. In the Old Testament, we read of Eleazar (2 Sam. 23:10) who fought with the Philistines so long and hard that his hand melded to the handle of his sword. This is the victor's goal: to have the Word of God so engrafted in our hearts, that it fuses to our hands in the day of battle.

Weapon #2: Prayer Power

After we put on the armor of God, we are then commanded to "pray always with all prayer and supplication" (Eph. 6:18).

Robert E. Lee (famed southern preacher) once wrote, "Knowing that intercessory prayer is our mightiest weapon and the supreme call for all Christians today, I pleadingly urge our people everywhere to pray. Believing that prayer is the greatest contribution that our people can make in this critical hour, I humbly urge that we take time to pray—to really pray."[70]

In 2 Chronicles 7:14, God continues saying, "If my people will… pray." In the eleventh chapter of Luke, the disciples came to Jesus and said, "Lord, teach us to pray." This is the desire of every true believer—to know how to pray as we ought.

Clearly there are different ideas about prayer. Some teach that what we say, confess, and claim is the point and power of our prayer life. But, if we give in to that kind of pop theology, we hold in contempt God's sovereignty. We arrogantly claim our will as more important than God's will and wisdom. Instead of name it and claim it, Jesus taught His disciples to pray, "Your will be done on earth as it is in heaven" (Matt. 6:10).

As we submit to His will in prayer, we grow and mature in three basic areas of prayer.

First, there is devotional prayer. Daily appointments with God where people offer prayer and praise to God and open their hearts and receive spiritual sustenance. This is very important.

Then there is intercessory prayer. This type of prayer often accompanies militant prayer but is equally distinct in that its primary purpose is to intercede or act on behalf of another. During times of war, the U.S. Air Force will fly flights of interdiction. This means that when the enemy sends their aircraft into strategic areas to fight American soldiers, the U.S. Air Force responds by sending out aircraft to cut them off at the pass, heading them off or intercepting their planes. This is the basic objective of intercessory prayer. It is one believer interdicting the enemy on behalf of another.

Finally, there is militant prayer, which concerns itself not only with interdiction, but actually initiates the aggression. Let us consider militant prayer.

All Christians need devotional prayer. Some practice intercessory prayer. The time has come for mature Christians throughout America to operate in militant prayer. John Knox was so well known as a prayer warrior that the queen of Scotland, "Bloody Mary," confessed that she feared the prayers of John Knox more than an army of soldiers. Born of a repentant heart, this is the kind of exercise in spiritual authority that will turn back archons and liberate communities held captive by spiritual powers.

The Need for Militant Prayer

Currently, many developing countries are experiencing the greatest revival in their respective histories. In each of these nations, we find that the liberating factor includes militant prayer.

THE VICTORS' MASTER WEAPONS

Ed Silvoso, a native of Argentina, founder of Harvest Evangelism, and an integral part of the present Argentinian revival, writes, "All kinds of prayers are offered in Argentina, but the most unique prayer is in the context of spiritual warfare. Christians seem to have two focuses in their prayers: God, to whom they address all honor and praise; and Satan, whom they boldly and aggressively rebuke."[71]

Ed Silvoso goes on to describe how believers in Argentina believe that militant prayer plays a vital, active role in God's plan of redemption, and that, without the Church's prayers, God will not reclaim territories invaded by Satan.

Omar Cabrera, considered by some to be the dean of power evangelism in Argentina, has made a habit of secluding himself in a hotel room for days of militant prayer before ministering in a new city. He prays, binding the demon who controls the air or heaven above the city. Afterward, he goes public announcing to the people that they are now free to come to Christ. Like slaves freed from their shackles, thousands run to give their lives to Jesus.

Every verse in the Bible dealing with spiritual warfare indicates that the action must begin on earth. Jesus commissioned Paul to preach to the Gentiles and to "open their eyes, and to turn them from darkness to light, and from the power of Satan unto God" (Acts 26:18a). It is the believer's responsibility to ask before God will respond. We must bind and release on earth for heaven to do the same. Part and parcel to the great commission is the Church's responsibility to cast out demons, and to tread over the power of the enemy.

Invading Satan's Headquarters through Militant Prayer

In Nehemiah 9:6 the prophet spoke of more than one heaven: he saw the heavens and the "heaven of heavens." These were not peripheral heavens as taught in Mormonism, but heavenly divisions as Paul referred to in 2 Corinthians 12:2, saying, "I knew a man in Christ above fourteen years ago, (whether in the body, I cannot tell; or whether out of the body, I cannot tell: God knoweth;) such an one [was] caught up to the third heaven."

Satan was called Beelzeboul, "lord of the height," by the Jews. Some Bible expositors believe when Paul referred to a third heaven, he was speaking from his scholarly upbringing as a Pharisee concerning three heavens which included a domain of air (the kosmos), or height, controlled by Satan. In pharisaical thought, the first heaven was simply the place where the birds fly, anything removed from and not attached to the surface of the earth. On the other end of the spectrum and of a different substance was the third heaven—the dwelling place of God. This was the place from which angelic spheres spread outward. Between the first heaven where the birds fly and the third heaven "where dwells the throne room of God" was a war zone called the second heaven. This was the kosmos—the Hebrew equivalent of the Persian Arhiman-abad—the place where Satan abides as the prince of the power of the "air" (*aer*, the lower air, circumambient), a sort of gasket heaven, the domain of Satan encompassing the surface of the earth. From here kosmokrators could overshadow cities, intrude upon, and attempt to influence the affairs and governments of men.

It was also believed that the kosmos not only influenced earth's governments and puppeted human counterparts, but that Satan's minions sought to close the heavens above the city so that God's blessings could not flow into it. Later, it was believed that when saints bent their knees in prayer, they had to pray through walls of opposition contained within this gasket heaven. The level of spiritual opposition to the saints' prayers depended on how far the city had fallen under Satan's control.

This continues today. When our prayers leave our lips they go upward through the devil's domain to the throne of God. If Satan considers the prayers significant, he rises up to oppose them, both going to and coming from the throne of God. Therefore, the second heaven is considered a war zone for our prayer life and the residence of the power of the air.

From the air above our cities, evil powers seek to influence church direction, social philosophy, and legislation. The effectual, fervent prayers of the righteous are the battering rams that can push through all demonic opposition enroute to and from the throne of God. This was illustrated in the tenth chapter of Daniel, where the prophet prayed for twenty-one days until the angel broke through and delivered God's answer. The persistence of our prayers, when they are prayed "according to His will," creates activity within the second and third heavens. In turn, the heavenly responses affect every level of spiritual and physical society. In cities where prayer is active, the heavens can be opened so that the healing power of God flows in freely. Daniel prayed until he pushed a hole through the walls of demonic opposition and the heavens opened with spiritual revelations. Elijah continued in prayer until the heavens opened and the rains fell. The disciples continued until their prayers penetrated the heavens and the glory of Pentecost came rushing down from the throne of God. Jacob prayed and the heavens opened. Angels ascended and descended. Elisha prayed and his servant beheld the heavens opened and the host of heaven standing upon the mountains to help them.

Repentant Christians in Portland, Chicago, New York, and other places in America, regardless of size, must pray until the heavens open and archons are set to flight as the skies are cleansed of demonic rule. Thus the blessings and restorative power of God will flow freely into our cities.

The Yalu River

As one considers the idea of militant prayer, there is what I call the Yalu River Dilemma. From 1950–53 America fought one of her most bloody and forgotten battles—the Korean War. My father served in this conflict in which the dictator of North Korea, Kim Il Sung, obtained military help from the U.S.S.R. dictator, Joseph Stalin. During this time the Chinese army, on 26 November 1950, surprised Gen. Douglas MacArthur by crossing the Yalu River in great force. Hitting the exposed flanks of MacArthur's forces, the Chinese stunned the allies and forced them back. By Christmas of the same

SPIRITUAL WARFARE: THE INVISIBLE INVASION

year, the United Nations forces were once again fighting below the 38th Parallel.

It was this point that would set President Truman and General MacArthur at opposing positions. Truman—thoroughly frightened by China's action and fearing the possibilities of a world war—moved to limit the confrontation, while MacArthur pressed to bomb the bridges at the Yalu River and expand the war into China proper. Truman refused and decided to allow only the Korean halves of the Yalu bridges to be bombed. By March 1951, Truman announced his limited war policy. This compromise infuriated MacArthur, who in turn released his Military Appraisal—a document that amounted to an ultimatum to the Chinese and to President Truman. This resulted in Truman's decision to dismiss MacArthur. "By this act," the president said, "MacArthur left me no choice—I could no longer tolerate his insubordination." MacArthur was ordered to return home—relieved of duty. Afterward, MacArthur addressed the Congress where he made his famous statement: "There is no substitute for victory!"

Douglas MacArthur wanted to end the war by a total military victory in Asia. Truman chose to continue a limited engagement. In the spirit realm we face this same type of dilemma. As a local church or as individuals, we war in prayer. When apparent victory comes, we slack off in our prayer assault, only to discover later the same problems resurfacing. In cities under demonic siege, it's critical for Christian soldiers to remember this key point. A limited war policy or passive approach to prayer will result in the enemy's retreat behind his own Yalu River (stronghold)—there to regroup, strategize, and attack again when prayer has ceased.

Whether your prayer concerns are corporate or individual, recognize that God gives you what the U.S. government refused to give MacArthur during the Korean War—the power to move beyond the protective bridges of your enemy's stronghold. God allows the contrite saint to invade the opponent's headquarters through the power of fervent prayer, to identify and bind the ruling prince through the power of Jesus' name, and to persistently fast and pray until heaven's anointing annihilates the gates of hell, destroying the fortress walls of nefarious warlords until there is no place within their gates to counsel among themselves. Instead, these servants of Satan are offered no quarters as they are set to flight before the power of persistent and prevailing militant prayers.

It is this kind of fervent military response, commanded by repentant hearts, that the kosmos cannot withstand. While prayers of compromise are mocked among the kosmos, the saint whose steadfast heart is controlled by God's Spirit will gain victory over the enemy and over geographic demonization.

Attributes of Effective Militant Prayer

During times of emergency, God has special people whose primary concern is the moral health of the nation. These have been known as revivalists and radicals. We refer to them here as prophets of prayer. Such men were Elijah, Jeremiah, and John the Baptist. At critical times in history they appear on the scene to reprove, rebuke, and exhort the Church toward righteousness, and to battle with principalities and powers. Their home is the watch tower. They are often labeled as extreme, negative, fanatical. In some ways they are. This is because their single-minded calling does not allow for politics. They trouble many and offend others. Liberals are repulsed by them. But, they are called by God to exhort the church to do battle with Satan, and to live holy in wicked times. The church cannot repay the debt these prophets of prayer are owed.

There are several key things we can learn from their effective prayer style. First, there is sincerity. Those who are not sincere should avoid militant prayer. When one engages with principalities in battle there is demonic confrontation. If the believer is sincere, God goes before them into the battle and makes the difference. Sincere Christians need not fear the enemy, for we, and our house, belong to the Lord. But, if people are not sincere, they might bring trouble upon themselves.

This was illustrated in the Book of Acts when the sons of Sceva tried to cast out a demon. We read, "And the man in whom the evil spirit was leaped on them, and overcame them...so that they fled out of that house naked and wounded" (Acts 19:16).

Another part of effective militant prayer is praise. All prayer should begin with praise. This is especially true during militant prayer because Satan cannot endure praise toward God. The Bible tells us that God inhabits the praise of His people. This is our goal, to create a habitation for God and His people, and where demons cannot dwell. When Saul was troubled by an evil spirit in 1 Samuel 16:14–23, David played a harp and sang praises to the Lord. This drove the evil spirit away. Individual or corporate attempts to organize prayer for our cities must begin with times of praise and thanksgiving to the Lord.

The third key to effective militant prayer is urgency. When my wife was rushed into emergency surgery with complications, my prayer life went from casual to urgent. When my youngest daughter lay unconscious after accidently ingesting an adult prescription drug, my prayers became urgent. Sometimes circumstances make urgent prayer necessary. A ruler came to Jesus saying, "My little daughter lieth at the point of death: I pray thee, come and lay thy hands on her, that she may be healed; and she shall live" (Mark 5:23). His prayer was urgent.

Today, one can read the paper or watch the evening news and find cause to pray for America with urgency. When the king of Nineveh understood that his city was under sentence of judgment, he commanded all of Nineveh, saying, "Let everyone call urgently on God. Let them give up their evil ways and their violence. Who knows? God may yet relent and with compassion turn from his fierce anger so that we will not perish" (Jon. 3:8–9 NIV). Serious prayer warriors feel a sense of urgency as they pray.

They are in tune with the times and recognize cultural disintegration. In fact, the renewed emphasis on militant prayer within the United States today is in response to what many see happening within our society.

Another key ingredient to militant prayer is fasting. Jesus made it clear that fasting is an integral part of effective spiritual warfare. He prepared Himself with fasting before being tempted of Satan in the wilderness. When His disciples were unable to exorcise a demon, He said, "This kind can come forth by nothing, but by prayer and fasting" (Mark 9:29). Through fasting Daniel brought down the demon prince of Persia.

Later we shall discuss how fasting works, and why it is vital for the church today.

Militant prayer is also specific. Because each community is different, militant prayer must be specific. We must discern the strongholds within our particular city and target them with militant prayer. This includes understanding the political as well as the spiritual climate of our community. For example, cities like San Francisco and Portland are dominated by spirits that leave people complacent, over-sexualized, and depressed, while areas such as Las Vegas suffer from spirits of greed and lust. Jesus gave spiritual discernment to the church so that we can pinpoint Satan's strongholds within our community and respond with militant prayer.

The sixth key to effective militant prayer is confessing authority. "You will receive power when the Holy Spirit comes on you" (Acts 1:8, NIV). This verse identifies the authority granted to humble believers. Peter said to the cripple: "Silver and gold have I none; but such as I have give I thee: In the name of Jesus Christ of Nazareth rise up and walk" (Acts 3:6). This was authority in action.

God gives authority to the humble. Because of this we have boldness to enter into prayer warfare, and to speak authority for our city. Both fear and authority can speak. Fear spoke when Job said, "For the thing which I have greatly feared is come upon me" (Job 3:25). Fear spoke again when the spies who entered Canaan said, "We be not able to go up against the people; for they are stronger than we" (Num. 13:31). But, authority spoke when Caleb replied, "Let us go up at once, and possess it; for we are well able to overcome it"

(Num. 13:30). Like Caleb, we have God's authority to claim our cities through militant prayer.

Several years ago in our church, we responded to this realism by starting the Care Ministry, which follows the basic format of most cell-group ministries, with some important additions. Each of our Care groups ends its weekly meetings by prioritizing authority in prayer. First, people pray for each other. Just as Daniel first chastened himself in prayer, so there must be an ongoing self-discipline in prayer before we engage in spiritual combat for our cities. Prayer is offered during this time for the specific needs of the group members.

Each Care group then turns its attention outward and prays toward the north, south, east, and west of that particular Care group location. Spiritual authority is released as each group does the following:

1. Binds spiritual powers from advancing any further against the people in that neighborhood. The name of Jesus is hallowed above every spiritual influence, and specifically against the kosmokrators over Portland. This is done in anticipation of the day when invisible walls crumble and the Lord visits Portland with revival.
2. Releases spiritual captives by interceding in prayer. They pray for the Holy Spirit to open the eyes and ears of those who are spiritually bound, so they might see and understand their need of Jesus.
3. Prays that the kingdom of God will be enlarged through their ministry efforts, and that God will use all group members to evangelize their neighborhood with the Gospel. They pray for boldness and sensitivity so they will recognize daily opportunities to witness.
4. Prays that those liberated from demonic power will find a Bible-believing church that can best minister to them on the basis of their individual needs.

5. Prays for our nation, and that the moral laws of God will be established within our society. During this time specific laws and legislation are targeted. They pray for a national revival.

Through this weekly exercise in spiritual authority, our people have come to see, even expect, a weekly harvest of souls liberated through militant prayer. Equally important, many have come to realize that every child of God is given this opportunity, and that when it comes to engaging principalities and powers, failure can only come by default. As David said in Psalm 149:8–9, "To bind their kings with chains, and their nobles with fetters of iron; To execute upon them the judgment written: this honour have all his saints. Praise ye the LORD."

Another part of militant prayer is proper focus. Effective militant prayer focuses on God, not on Satan or his demons. Mature believers do not seek to confront Satan personally. Instead, they seek the Father and allow Him to fight the battle through them by providing insight and guidance concerning spiritual warfare.

When Michael the archangel was disputing with the devil about the body of Moses, he did not confront him on a personal level, but said, "The Lord rebuke thee" (Jude 9). Usually, a Christian should not pray, saying, "I command you Satan" to do this or that. This tends to make the battle their own. We are to focus on the Lord and allow Him to direct the battle.

Jesus said, "If ye abide in me, and my words abide in you, ye shall ask what ye will, and it shall be done unto you" (John 15:7). When we are in communion with Him, it is the nature and authority of Christ speaking through us that penetrates the kosmos and brings down Satan's stronghold.

Number eight in effective militant prayer is defense. While the believer's normal duty in spiritual battle is offense, the very nature of encountering evil forces often requires Christians to pray for a fence of protection around themselves, their children, and their nation.

SPIRITUAL WARFARE: THE INVISIBLE INVASION

In the Scriptures, we find that Satan could not touch Job while the protective fence of God was up and around him. It was only when God lowered the fence and allowed Satan to test Job, that Satan could enter the scene. Today the fence is down around America, and spiritual darkness is invading the United States from the four corners of the earth. As never before, Christians need to know how to protect themselves and their children from Satan's insidious presence.

For the purpose of spiritual warfare I have developed a simple but effective prayer outline that can be used for building a protective fence. When necessary, this outline can be used by believers to protect their children and family members, or as an intercession for America. As we enter covenant prayer with God, we erect a supernatural picket fence, beyond which Satan cannot enter. Each plank of the fence is divided into six five-minute segments, and each is "nailed up" during the following specific half-hour of prayer:

Praise. The first five-minute segment of prayer is in praise toward God and produces a three-fold spiritual benefit. First, we fulfill the commandment to enter God's presence with praise, humbling ourselves and recognizing the supremacy of God. Second, God joins us by inhabiting our praise. Third, since Satan cannot endure praise toward God, we thus fulfill the first primary goal of warfare—to create a habitation for God and His children where Satan cannot dwell. Praise is the first plank in building a protective fence.

Confession. The second plank is raised through confessing our sins and receiving forgiveness. This is very important in spiritual warfare because Satan can otherwise use our unconfessed sins against us and try to bog us down in a quagmire of condemnation and ineffectiveness. When we follow our praise time with confession, we neutralize Satan's power and condition our hearts for spiritual combat. If we are trying to pray a protective fence around a loved one or location, we should also ask that God will make them aware of the need for confession. Empowered by the forgiveness of sins, we can then move forward in confidence.

Praying Scripture. Jesus used the Scriptures like a soldier uses a sword in combat. In Jeremiah 23:29 we read, "Is not my word like as a fire? saith the Lord; and like a hammer that breaketh the rock in pieces?" The wise Christian soldier learns to quote Scriptures that correspond to his specific needs. Satan may be able to resist our own personal thoughts or commands, but he cannot defy the Word of God. This is key in building a supernatural fence of protection. Some try to build a fence out of philosophy. Others try psychology. But five minutes of praying the Word, and we can securely fasten the next supernatural plank.

Intercession. During this five-minute segment, we focus on the persons or things at the center of our concern. We hold them up in the presence of God and intercede for their protection. We may need to pray for a hedge of protection around their minds, or their homes. Satan's attack might include one or more members of the same household. Or, as in the case of our country, it could even include whole segments of society. In 1 Timothy 2:1–2, we are commanded to intercede for all who are in authority. Following that directive, we can pray a fence of protection around the local mayor, the city council, or our state representatives. In each of these scenarios we are walking in obedience to the Word of God, and are directly intervening for our leaders in the heavenlies.

Waiting and Listening. The next plank erected during the half-hour of power comes from waiting on the Lord. This five-minute segment helps us to discern our marching orders. It is also during this time that we receive insights concerning the battle, and we learn to recognize the Shepherd's voice. In Ecclesiastes 5:2 we read, "Be not rash with thy mouth, and let not thine heart be hasty to utter *any* thing before God: for God is in heaven, and thou upon earth: therefore let thy words be few" (emphasis added). In other words, there is a time to speak, and there is a time to be silent and listen to the voice of the Lord.

Praise Again. We install the final plank by devoting the last five minutes to praise. We offer praise and thanksgiving to the Lord of protection. We praise Him for who He is, and we thank Him for hearing us. Through this simple but effective half-hour, we can close ourselves in with God and build a defensive hedge, beyond which Satan cannot enter. This is the defense of militant prayer.

The ninth and last major ingredient of effective militant prayer is expectancy. In James 4:7, the apostle says, "Be submissive to God. Stand up to the devil and he will turn and run" (NEB). We also read, "Therefore I say unto you, what things soever ye desire, when ye pray, believe that ye receive them, and ye shall have them" (Mark 11:24). This means that individual prayer warriors can expect things to happen when they pray. Sometimes in looking at the awesome scope of a national crisis brought on by submission to evil, we as individuals feel powerless, as though our individual prayer lives will be of little effect. But, this is not true. A nation is simply a multitude of individual persons. Each time an individual decides to live for God, we move one person closer to revival.

Historically, every notable revival began with the individual. The Reformation began by the convictions of Martin Luther. Paul stood alone in Ephesus, a city ruled by an unsurpassed religious and political machine, yet he was used of God to establish a church there, which helped release the minds of men and women from the deceptions of Diana worship. When Charles Finney launched into evangelism, he took onto his team a man named Nash, who made prayer his only role. When Finney preached, Nash stayed behind and prayed. As many as fifty thousand accepted the Lord in one week. Jonathan Edwards, George Whitefield, Gilbert Tenant, Shubal Stearns, Daniel Marshall, Billy Sunday, and numerous others proved one cannot underestimate the power of a single Christian in prayer.

The Canaan Illustration

The story of Joshua and Caleb, and their entry into Canaan, illustrates the ability of individual believers to overcome the efforts of archons and change the trends of cultural development. In Numbers, chapter 13, we find the children of Israel upon the mountains above Paran overlooking the land of Canaan. For forty years, Israel wandered in the wilderness until they found themselves at the entrance to the blessed Promised Land. It was here that God instructed Moses to send twelve spies, leaders from the tribes of Israel, to enter secretly into and spy out the land of Canaan. But, they were soon confused. Upon entering Canaan, the spies found not only fertile fields, an abundance of beasts, and unlimited milk and honey, but giants—the nepheli, the dreaded sons of Anak. Demonic people had moved into the Israelite's inheritance and laid siege upon the *haraboam,* the land promised to Abraham. The cities had thick, towering walls and strongholds with towers, and fortifications were strategically positioned throughout the land.

This is a picture of the children of God overlooking the land God had given them, aware that it was theirs, but also aware that it was infiltrated by evil. Canaan was under siege to Satan. How do we conclude that the ancient occupants of Canaan were demonically inspired and pawns of the kosmokrators ruling that area? There are three contributing factors.

First, Canaanites had moved into the land that God had given to Abraham and his seed (Gen. 17:8). The Bible emphasizes that Satan tries to steal, kill, and destroy all that belongs to the children of God. It is probable that when God told Moses to go up to Egypt (Exod. 3:1–10) and make a public declaration that Israel was headed for a promised land, Satan heard and realized that Canaan was the land to which God referred. At this point, he summoned his dark forces to precede the Israelites (while God was dealing with them in the wilderness) to lay siege to the area, in order to challenge later the will of God for His people.

Second, the name *Anak* comes from the Hebrew word meaning "to strangle," or "to compass about" as with a chain. When used in a military sense it means "to encompass or garrison about." Since these sons of Anak were by birth the progeny of the cursed nepheli, this action should be seen as demonic originally.

Third, we conclude that Canaan and its inhabitants were an area besieged by demons because nepheli are thought by many Bible scholars to be half-human and half-demon creatures. Their origins may be found in an ancient intercourse between fallen angels and antediluvian women. In the apocryphal Book of Enoch, we read, "It happened after the sons of men had multiplied in those days, that daughters were born to them elegant, beautiful. And when the angels, the sons of heaven beheld them, they became enamored of them, saying to each other: Come, let us select for ourselves wives from the progeny of men, and let us beget children" (7:1–2).

Correspondingly, we read in Genesis 6:4, "When mankind had spread all over the world, and girls were being born, some of the supernatural beings saw that these girls were beautiful, so they took the ones they liked.... In those days, and even later, there were giants [nepheli] on the earth who were descendants of human women and the supernatural beings" (TEV).

The offspring of this unholy union were a race of now-extinct mutant beings called *nepheli, gibborim,* and *rephaim*.[72] While the gibborim were noted for their impiety (Num. 13:33; Deut. 25:18–19), the rephaim were associated with ghosts and the spirit forces of Sheol. "Hell from beneath is moved for thee to meet thee at thy coming: it stirreth up the dead [rephaim] for thee, even all the chief ones of the earth...they shall speak and say unto thee, Art thou also become weak as we? Art thou become like unto us?" (Isa. 14:9–10).

Whatever their origin or estate, when the people of Israel arrived at the Promised Land, they found that demonic people had taken hold of God's desired possessions for Israel. Like the prince of the kingdom of Persia, these wicked ones had hearts governed by the stratagems of evil spiritual forces whose primary purpose was to seize both the property and wealth God had planned for Israel and bring it to destruction.

The Pattern Continues

Believers in the nineties need to understand that this pattern continues to the present. Israel had an incredible inheritance, but in the midst of it sat enemy forces—settled and hostile.

This picture portrays the current status of many American cities and the challenge faced by many local congregations. Church bodies are confronted with increasing economic needs, yet for most American congregations the problem is not a lack of local money. The problem is not a lack of local people needing to be saved, nor is it a lack of real estate upon which a house of God might be built. Rather, the problem is that the nepheli have entered the area. While the children of God have consumed their energy longing for the pleasures of Egypt, the true blessings of Canaan have come under siege to dominant demonic powers who intend for those lands, provisions, and peoples to be brought to destruction.

Look around your city. Is there an abundance of money vested in other interests? Is there still real estate available? Are there enough people to fill your auditorium many times? In the Greater Portland area, there are an estimated one million unchurched souls controlling 98 percent of the local wealth and resources. The problem in our city is not a need for more money or land, but rather that those provisions already provided by Jehovah-jireh be brought in and surrendered for service to the Lord.

Is the situation similar in your city? As important as it was for Israel to claim their "city" by confronting and destroying spiritual strongholds in 1490 B.C., so today God's elect must understand that to please God we must "cast out devils" (Matt. 10:8). With this, many verses agree.

> "And these signs shall follow them that believe; In my name shall they cast out devils" (Mark 16:17).

> "The kingdom of heaven suffereth violence, and the violent take it by force" (Matt. 11:12). "The people that do know their God shall be strong, and [cause to dissemble, to drive away archons] do *exploits*" (Dan. 11:32).

Only two Israelite men from Numbers, chapter 13, eventually entered into Canaan—Joshua and Caleb. The name *Joshua* means "Jehovahsaved," while *Caleb* means "forcible," or "forceful." The message is: the Jehovah-saved must always be forceful in their reaction to nephelim or archons. As David boldly stood up to Goliath (a nepheli), we must stand and embrace the authority of the biblical reality, "Whatsoever thou shalt bind on earth shall be bound in heaven: and whatsoever thou shalt loose on earth shall be loosed in heaven" (Matt. 18:18), and let the church of the firstborn understand that in the exercise of militant prayer, humble saints are more than able to overcome Satan's invading forces. We must "go up at once and possess it; for we are well able to overcome [them]" (Num. 13:30). We can do it—if we will pray.

Weapon #3: God Himself—
The Source of Prayer Power

Peter Marshall once wrote,

> The choice before us is plain, Christ or chaos, conviction or compromise, discipline or disintegration. I am rather tired of hearing about our rights and privileges as American citizens. The time is come, it now is, when we ought to hear about the duties and responsibilities of our citizenship. America's future depends upon her accepting and demonstrating God's government.[73]

Almost as though the emphasis to pray does not alone quite focus the soul, God continues saying, "If my people will...seek my face." Isn't prayer seeking the face of God? Not necessarily. Prayer often includes the pursuit of godly direction, material help, divine healing, supernatural intervention, binding, loosing, and other necessities important both to God and man. However, all these are at best the by-product of our Christian experience—part of the inheritance, but never the central objective. In prayer, God is to be the object of our desire. God gave the gift of fasting and prayer so that we could commune with Him. "That I may know Him and the power of His resurrection" (Phil. 3:10) is our goal. "This is eternal life that they may know you, the only true God, and Jesus Christ, whom you have sent" (John 17:3). The psalmist said in 42:1, "As the hart panteth after the water brooks, so panteth my soul after thee, O God." The pursuit of God, for no greater reason than to know Him and be known of Him, is our objective.

One can pray religiously, devotionally, or even as an intercessor, and not seek after Him. All sincere forms of prayer should mature to this level. Discipline is the chief mandate for developing such a prayer life, and is observed by heaven as the memorial of one who loves God. Such an example is found in the life of Cornelius. In Acts, chapter 10, the angel of the Lord visited Cornelius saying, "Thy prayers and thine alms are come up for a memorial before God." What a testimony: to have pursued the Father with such loving fervor that heaven itself memorializes the discourses of your life! What love. What power. What quintessence of the Christian faith.

Seeking the Father through Fasting

Fasting *(nesteuo* meaning "not eat"), combined with prayer, is the biblical method for seeking the Father. David, Isaiah, Jeremiah, Samuel, Nehemiah, Ezekiel, Daniel, Moses, Abraham, Paul, Jesus, and almost every important biblical figure practiced fasting as an approved method for seeking God. Furthermore, seeking the Lord through fasting is biblically defined as reaping greater spiritual rewards than prayer alone. There are levels of spiritual power, insight, and deliverance that come only to the soul who is committed to a fervent pursuit of God through fasting.

Jesus taught that power in prayer is increased through fasting. He said, "This kind can come forth by nothing, but by prayer and fasting" (Mark 9:29). This indicates that there are levels of spiritual opposition within the demonic realm, and the greater powers and the locations of their rule will only be defeated as militant Christian soldiers descend from the mount of fasting. "This kind" requires more than religious ceremony. "This kind" is not intimidated by clever three-point sermons. Prayer alone will not bring down "this kind." Triumph over these is found only by those who are in pursuit of God through fasting.

Satan understands the power of fasting. His most deliberate moments in tempting Jesus came not while He was performing miracles, but earlier, when He was fasting. The miracles Jesus would later perform in delivering those who were oppressed by the devil, would simply be the release of an inner power earlier received. If Satan were going to keep Jesus from being powerful in the Spirit, he would first have to cut Him off from the source of that power. Therefore, before Jesus began His public miracle ministry, Satan came to tempt Him in an effort to break His fast. Satan said, "If you are the Son of God, command these stones to be made bread (Luke 4:3)." Satan wanted Jesus to think about eating in order to stop His fast, thereby attempting to cut Him off from the source of spiritual power. Satan's focus has not changed these past two thousand years. He continues to tempt the believer with substances pleasing to the flesh, in order to lead the Christian away from God's sources of power. His efforts are succeeding in some areas. While "this kind" invade cities across America and around the world, believers have often been led away from altars of fasting and prayer to pursue the bread of indulgence. Fat on delectable doctrines, they inquire like the disciples of old, "Lord, why could we not cast out this spirit?" The conquest of powerful spirits still requires fasting and prayer.

It's easy to follow the pathway of power revealed in the life of Jesus Christ. In Luke, chapter 4, He was led of the Spirit into the wilderness to fast. Afterward He came down in the power of the Spirit and immediately began to perform miracles. As our supreme model, Jesus exemplified the life of one who seeks the Father. In so doing, He illustrated the powerful results of fervent prayers, intercessions, and fasting.

How Does Fasting Work?

One might wonder how fasting, as practiced by ancient Jews, was so successful in increasing divine energies. What was there about fasting, as a method for seeking God, that the Father so honored? Some say it's simple obedience. Others say God honors fasting because of its sacrifice and self-denial. But, the primary directive of original Jewish fasting was to refocus the human spirit upon the Father. It provided a time of reflective meditation and communion with God, uninterrupted by earthly cares. When the Father communes with us, we are visited by an increase in the manifestation of His presence, and thus of His power. That is the key. Fasting serves a twofold purpose—it facilitates the plea "If my people will…seek my face" and provides an important addition to the arsenal of the child of God.

The most important thing in the believer's life isn't the observance of the mechanics of religion, but rather knowing upon whom to focus. Fasting empowers us because it reminds us of where to glory, and upon whom our adoration is to be fixed. This is not to suggest disengagement from organization or religious structure, but these are at best the outgrowth of our adoration of our God. When this is clouded or reversed, and the focus of our glory is buildings, gowns, and service structure, the church is, at best, impotent and incapable of fruitful spiritual warfare. Evil never prevails so greatly within society as it does when the righteous are merely religious, having forgotten where to glory.

To glory in anything other than God produces spiritual anemia. Why? Because when we give glory to something, we give it attention, devotion, and sometimes allegiance. Reciprocally, it becomes our inspiration and power. Whatever we glory in receives our adoration, and in return gives us inspiration and motivational strength. For example, if you fanatically collect antique cars, these cars are what you glory in; they are the object of your attention and devotion. In return antique cars inspire you, motivating and empowering you to press for the advancement and preservation of the world of antique cars.

SPIRITUAL WARFARE: THE INVISIBLE INVASION

There is nothing wrong in collecting antique cars, but if the one dedicating his life to this pursuit suddenly faces problems such as emotional attack, marital discord, terminal illness, or demonic attack, can he call upon his antique cars to save him? No. Automobiles have no spiritual propensity whatsoever. One rightly concludes that what you glory in is of the utmost spiritual importance.

If people glory in church functions or personalities, rather than glorying in the Lord, they will be incapable of opposing principalities and powers. Material objects and human charisma will not be able to deliver them when they are confronted by the enemy. But, if their dedication to the functions of the local church merely facilitates their adoration of Him, not only is He the object of their adoration, but the source of edification, inspiration, and deliverance in the time of need.

Jeremiah speaks of this principle as he rebukes Israel:

> A conspiracy is found among the men of Judah, and among the inhabitants of Jerusalem. They are turned back to the iniquities of their forefathers, which refused to hear my words; and they went after other gods to serve [glory in] them.... Therefore thus saith the Lord, Behold, I will bring evil upon them, which they shall not be able to escape.... Then shall the cities of Judah and Jerusalem go, and cry unto the gods unto whom they offer incense: but they shall not save them at all in the time of their trouble. (Jer. 11:9–12)

Jeremiah points out the failure in glorying in the wrong thing. Today, especially in the evangelical movement, people tend to think that, as modern believers, they are incapable of losing sight of where to glory. High-tech Christians often proudly say, "We are the people of power and glory," considering themselves distinct from older mainline denominations which have sometimes gone the way of cold, rigid formalism.

Is it possible in these enlightened days that a part of the American church has forgotten where to glory, and is lacking in authority? The

THE VICTORS' MASTER WEAPONS

Old Testament Jews did exactly that, and, like the claims of evangelicalism today, the Old Testament Jew had a God who revealed Himself in power and glory. The children of Israel were visited with His manifested glory in the pillar of fire, beside the Red Sea, and throughout the wilderness journey. In every way He was revealed to them in glory. But, they were not satisfied simply having the glory of God. They yearned for something more. They wanted a building. So God allowed them to build a temple, and when it was finished, the program was on!

The people immediately learned proper ceremonial conduct. Everyone knew when to stand, when to sit, and when to sing. Everyone read the liturgy. One can almost see the priests as they marched in four and twenty square, ready for the big religious service. Then God chose to show His glory. Solomon had completed his great prayer when suddenly the glory of the Lord flooded the temple of God, and the radiance of His presence was so powerful that the priests could not enter the house of the Lord in order to carry out their ceremony. Did God upset the proper order? No. God's glory was greater than the ceremony. His presence was more important than the service coming off without a hitch. But, over time Israel got their eyes on the temple rather than on the Lord. They began to glory in everything but their Creator. Finally, as God's people found the mechanics of religion more worthy of attention than the presence of God, the lamp of God went out in the temple of the Lord. "Ichabod" was written upon the temple, and the glory of God departed from Israel.

When Jesus Christ came into the world hundreds of years later, the mechanics of religion were still in operation. The temple was there. The priests were there. The holy days were there. The only thing missing was the glory of God. The Scribes and Pharisees stood on the street corners praying their prayers and receiving their own psychological answers. But, when Jesus—the long-awaited Messiah—finally arrived, they called Him a liar, a rebel, and a deceiver. They crucified their own Redeemer. Having forgotten where to glory, they were pawns of the unseen princes of this world (1 Cor. 2:8).

Soon afterward, their enemies swept upon them and their temple was destroyed.

If the eyewitnesses of God's majestic power forgot where to glory, then we must not be so foolish as to consider ourselves incapable of repeating the same mistakes. This is the goal of a regular diet of fasting: to refocus the mind and spirit upon the God who will not share His glory. When He's the object of our adoration, we are at one with Him. His lordship and nature can then be manifested through us. The gates of hell cannot stand before that power. Such men were the Apostles who refused to leave altars of fasting and prayer, and about whom it was said by evildoers "they have turned the world upside down."

Encouragement and Discernment through Fasting

There are three basic kinds of fasting described in the Bible: the normal fast, which involved abstaining from food but not from water; the absolute fast, which denied the body both food and water; and the partial or "pleasant bread" fast that was basically a restriction on the diet. Each of these is seen as providing spiritual benefits for the believer.

Jesus overcame Satan in the wilderness by His power during a normal fast, while 0lieen Esther outwitted Haman and escaped the hangmen's gallows through conducting an absolute fast. She instructed Mordecai to "hold a fast on my behalf, and neither eat nor drink for three days" (Esther 4:16). Then, we find that Daniel received supernatural revelations through holding a partial fast. We read, "In those days I, Daniel, was mourning for three weeks. I ate no delicacies, no meat nor wine entered my mouth" (Dan. 10:2).

In each of these examples, supernatural benefits were provided to individuals who participated in fasting. The Bible contains many examples of people receiving everything from physical deliverance to visions of the future, through the potency of fasting. It is in the context of spiritual warfare that fasting provides two of the most essential items needed for the church to conduct a successful military campaign: battlefield encouragement and spiritual discernment.

Battlefield Encouragement through Fasting

A few years ago while pastoring in Portland, Oregon, I had the opportunity of recommending one of the young girls in our church as a state finalist in the Missionettes (an Assemblies of God discipleship program based in the local church) youth competition. Her name was Brenda, and she went on to become *Miss Missionette* for the state of Oregon that year. A while back, at the age of twenty, Brenda Wright died of a rare blood disease. At the time of her death, Brenda was engaged to be married.

After twelve years of pastoring, Brenda's memorial service was as beautiful as I can remember. Even so, her young age caused some to question, "Why?" Everyone agreed that Brenda was now in a better place, and they were glad that her suffering was over. But, looking at her young memorial pictures nestled among the flowers, a few people couldn't help but wonder why.

Some teach that to grow discouraged or question why is to be lacking in faith. But, I believe that to ask "Why?" is a natural response to the difficulties of life. A person's attitude should be right. We must not question or challenge the sovereignty of God, but from Gideon to Jesus Christ, the finest examples of Christian faith have had those moments when, from the midst of their greatest discouragements, they looked heavenward and asked, "Why?"

Gideon's response to the angel of the Lord was "If the Lord be with us, why then is all this befallen us?" (Judg. 6:13). Gideon was discouraged and questioned why, and Gideon was called a mighty man of valor. From the depths of his trials, Job asked why he had been born—yet, Job was considered a perfect man. Even our Lord cried from the cross and said, "Why has thou forsaken me?" It does not trouble God for His children to wonder why and seek to find meaning to their discouraging circumstances when they ask from a sincere and humble heart.

If you're struggling with discouragement and growing weary in the battle, you need to discover the refreshing power of fasting. Fasting has a way of putting things into perspective, and of holding up the battle-weary soldier and helping him focus on the war's projected end. As a reassurance, let us consider a few of the encouraging military benefits of fasting.

1. Fasting Reminds Us that Bad Things Happen in Every Earthly War

The Book of Corinthians states that physical suffering and death are a part of this earthly battle, and are an ongoing enemy of the believer. Satan has been overthrown; separation from God has been overcome; but, the human body is still dying, and the final victory for the church is to overcome death. Although provision for premature suffering and divine healing have been provided for in the atonement, the dying mechanism will eventually overtake us all. Our bodies are running down and getting old, and it is the process of aging and dying that provides many of the trials suffered by Christian soldiers.

Unlike the unsaved, the believer has hope when facing death. While we naturally fear what we've never experienced, our fear of death is not the same as it is for the lost. We have a home beyond the grave. The physical death of a believer can even provide profound spiritual good. This is true, not only because we are joined to God and our earthly chores are over, but multitudes have found Christ when faced by the certainty of death while attending a Christian's funeral.

2. Fasting Reveals the Purpose For Our Battle Scars

One of the great mysteries of the New Testament is that God became flesh so that (among other reasons) in Christ Jesus the incarnate God might experience what it was like to be human.

Jesus suffered as a man so that we would have a mediator in heaven who understands our pains and suffering. He knows how we feel because He has experienced it. Similarly, God often allows believers to acquire battle scars so that we can learn to identify with the sufferings of those around us. Our great struggles sharpen our military readiness and open doors of ministry to the hurting, and of witnessing to the lost, that cannot be opened in any other way.

3. Fasting Helps Us to Make the Proper Battlefield Choices

During war our choices can help or hurt ourselves or those around us. I knew a young man in California whose mother was in spiritual warfare for his salvation. During that time, he suffered brain damage from a motorcycle accident. Because his mother was a Christian, some in the area asked, "Why did God do that to him?" The truth is that he had been out drinking and was so intoxicated that he hit a tree at sixty miles per hour. God did not injure the young man; he did it to himself Battlefield injuries can also be the result of a soldier's poor choices. Sometimes choices that we've made will return to trouble us years later. For this reason, we should go to the Lord in prayer and fasting before making battlefield decisions that could affect our lives and family. If you have made choices that have come back to trouble you, take it to the Lord in repentance. If we humble ourselves and repent of the wrongdoing, God will help us through the circumstances and turn things to our benefit no matter how impossible the problem may seem to be.

4. Fasting takes our enemies in their own snare

The Book of Esther tells the story of Haman's gallows and reveals that fasting can turn the tables on those who intend to do us harm. Fasting generates circumstances that will take our enemies in their own trap. It looked bad for Mordecai, but Haman swung on his own gallows. It looked bad for Daniel, but it was his enemies that died in the lions' den. It looked bad for Joseph, but it was his scheming brothers that returned to serve him. If it appears that evildoers are prevailing against you, remain sweet and continue in your fast. God will be your vindication.

5. Fasting Keeps Us On the Military Course

Paul said that some in the church at Corinth were suffering military defeat because they were living in error concerning the Lord's body.

Other Scriptures reveal that sin and rebellion open the door for defeat on the field. Much of the Old Testament is dedicated to stories about Israel forgetting God, and afterward how God turned the heart of Israel back to Himself by allowing them to experience battlefield defeat. The God who chastens whom He loves will allow us to face trials if that is the only way to turn us from our destructive course and guide us back to Himself But, fasting keeps our insights keen and saves us from falling in battle by warning us of our impending error.

6. Fasting Helps to Perfect Our Military Disciplines

The Bible reveals that fasting was an integral part of the early Christians' disciplines. In the Gospels we learn that fasting was a regular part of our Lord's earthly experience. God uses fasting to develop our military readiness in the same way that a parent teaches a child restraint. No child wants to learn discipline, and no loving parent delights in administering correction, but anyone who has ever raised a child understands the need for correction. Are you experiencing discouragement? Perhaps your loving Commander is calling you to the disciplines of fasting.

7. Fasting Reminds Us that it Rains On Every Soldier

We are not of this world, but we are temporarily in it. We are therefore subject to most earthly trials. Jesus said, "In the world ye shall have tribulation" (John 16:33). The difference for the believer is that God has promised to make all things work together for our good. God is at work in our battles perfecting His will through circumstances that appear to be negative and beyond our control. The life of Joseph illustrates how God establishes His kingdom through circumstances that seem to be without purpose. Joseph was betrayed by his brothers and sold into slavery. But, Joseph maintained his character and revered the Lord in spite of the unjustified suffering this caused him. Because he kept his dignity and submitted to God's will, Jehovah controlled the circumstances and exalted Joseph. When hungry stomachs led the older brothers into Egypt a few years later, they found the same boy who had been sold into slavery sitting in authority at the right hand of Pharaoh.

Are you discouraged and growing weary in the battle? You will find wisdom and strength in the practice of fasting.

Spiritual Discernment through Fasting

Fasting produces three kinds of discernment needed to conduct a victorious military crusade: 1) discernment for witnessing, 2) discerning of spirits, and 3) discernment for church activity.

Discernment for Witnessing

Preaching the Gospel and personal witnessing are central to spiritual warfare, and are vital for the purpose of reclaiming the streets of America. Because the unsaved are each different in personality and philosophy, the experienced Christian soldier understands the need for discernment. Fasting helps to clear our minds and sharpens our spiritual judgment. Fasting teaches us when to speak, when to listen, and when to stop and go. I learned about the value of this years ago when I was a youth pastor in a small church. One day we decided to use the public school gymnasium and to show the film, *The Cross and the Switchblade,* based on the book by David Wilkerson. The public was invited and I was supposed to give an altar call at the end of the film. I remember fasting and praying that the Holy Spirit would use the film to reach the local youth. To our surprise, so many people came that it filled the available seating and people had to be turned away. I was so nervous looking at the crowd that all I could do was pray and ask God to give me the right words to say. He did, and hands went up all over the auditorium for salvation.

When the altar call was over, I began to feel an urge to go outside and look around, so I excused myself and walked towards the front door of the gymnasium. As I went, I heard a voice in my mind saying, "Go left here…now follow the trail out to the road." Although it was

SPIRITUAL WARFARE: THE INVISIBLE INVASION

dark outside, I felt as if an invisible companion was leading me each step of the way. When I arrived at the street in front of the school, I turned around and looked down the road. I noticed a woman walking on the sidewalk towards me. She was crying. "Tell her about Jesus," the voice said. I was afraid and didn't know what to say, but I took a deep breath, walked up to her and said, "Are you O.K.?" She told me about her problems, and I assured her that Jesus cared about her and would help. Right there on the sidewalk she repented of her sins and accepted Jesus as her Savior. When I left, she was still standing on the street corner with her hands in the air praising the Lord.

This was possible because fasting produces a special kind of discernment for witnessing. There's nothing else like it. It draws us close to God, and impresses upon us His compassion for the lost and His plan for witnessing. In this way fasting empowers us with dynamic abilities. We are equipped to listen, speak, and to stop and go as the Lord directs.

Discerning of Spirits

For the sake of spiritual warfare, we sometimes need to know what kind of a spirit is at work in a person or community. At other times, we need to understand the nature of a spirit's position in the person or community. Both of these circumstances can be understood when spiritual discernment has been enhanced through fasting.

A woman in a church that I once pastored approached me one day and said, "One of my family members is in a mental institution. She's coming home on a weekend pass and I'd like to bring her to church. I believe that her mental condition is due to a spiritual possession. Would you pray for her?" I agreed, but requested that the information be shared with only a few other selected members.

We fasted and prayed during the week, and on Sunday the young woman was brought to the front of the auditorium for prayer. The elders anointed her with oil and began to intercede. A moment later I joined them, placing my hand on her shoulder and intending to pray. Suddenly I felt strange, as if a dull electrical charge was moving through my arm. Somehow, I was being repulsed, so I pulled my hand back and to my surprise I felt better. I stepped over to the side of the auditorium and said, "Lord, what's going on?" The answer came swift and it astonished me. "Don't pray for her" was my immediate impression. I could hardly believe it. Yet, I felt very strongly that the Lord was saying to me, "Leave her alone. She's possessed because she wants to be. The demons are her friends. If you make them leave, she'll just ask them to come back. It's her choice."

Never before had such a thought entered my mind. Was this spiritual discernment? I opened my eyes and saw the young woman standing across the auditorium; her eyes were fixed on me, and she was laughing with maniacal laughter.

Years later my wife and I revisited that same church. When we met with the new leadership I noticed that the senior pastor looked tired. I asked him if it had been a busy week, and he proceeded to tell me about an exorcism that they had participated in a few days earlier. As he talked about a certain possessed lady and how the church had prayed for seventeen hours commanding various demons to come out of her, I realized that he was talking about the girl from the mental institution. I kept quiet while he repeated the exhausting story, telling of their struggle and how they worked all night in fasting and prayer and spiritual confrontation. He related how the last spirit finally came out, and how "it moved like a cloud through the room and went and stood by the front door." The young girl sat up, and for the first time she had a cognitive look on her face. They asked her if she wanted to accept Jesus as her Savior, and she emphatically said, "No!" Instead, she started calling out to mysterious individuals by name (the demons), and she became irate with those around her for making her "friends" go away. She began crying and asking the spirits to come back. As she did, the cloud by the front door moved through the room and entered her again. Her facial expression changed and she lost control of her mental faculties. The exorcism ended.

While that was the only time I have felt that God did not want me to pray for a person, fasting provided me with the ability to discern the accurate spiritual condition of a fallen soul and of the spirits that controlled her. Fasting protected the body of Christ from powerful spiritual forces, and kept the spirits from toying with the time and energy of the church.

Discernment for Church Activity

Unlike other religions, the Gospel of Jesus Christ is alive and contemporary. Each generation experiences new and exciting things as the church is regularly visited by an eternal and living God. While one era may be renewed in the gifts of the Spirit, another is refreshed through an outpouring of miracles. At certain points in history, the moving of the Spirit has been accompanied by revelation knowledge, while at other times it has exhibited more of a physical phenomenon. While all of this produces an appreciated excitement, it creates a need for discernment within the activities of the church.

Satan understands that supernatural occurrences have a way of generating excitement and of motivating the church toward godly activity, including spiritual warfare. It is therefore his intention to infect and corrupt every church activity that is breathed by the Holy Spirit, in order to frustrate the equipping of the saints.

In Mark 1:23 we read, "And there was in their synagogue a man with an unclean spirit." Satan attempts to infiltrate the church and to distort her doctrines and endeavors. His goal is to draw believers away from kingdom—enlarging activities, and into a carnal and divisive human ambience. But, a regular diet of fasting is the sure-fire antidote for Satan's insidious scheme. Fasting sharpens our insights and improves our ability to make judgment calls, and when necessary, to discern the difference between an authentic move of God and evil orchestration. Fasting helps us to "prove all things; hold fast that which is good" (1 Thess. 5:21).

Fasting derails Satan's military ploy by regularly helping believers to remember and discern the following:

1. *All church activity must be based upon the Word.* All Scripture is the inspired Word of God and is the final authority in all church activity. If a situation within the church contradicts the clear teachings of the Scripture, then the activity must be disregarded. We look to the model of the church in the Book of Acts and ask: Is this activity something we see happening in the first church? Is there a biblical precedent for it? These were the guidelines used by the participants of Azusa Street when they found justification for speaking in tongues.
2. *All church activity must be decent and orderly.* There's no doubt that unusual things happen when people experience the reality of God. The manifest presence of God often brings a spontaneous and emotional reaction from those who experience it. People often behave in otherwise uncharacteristic ways in the liberating presence of the Holy Spirit. But, Paul cautioned the church at Corinth not to allow their newfound liberty in Christ to become a stumbling block to the unsaved or to confuse those who were weak in the faith. He commanded, "Let all things be done decently and in order" (1 Cor. 14:40).
3. *All church activity must bring people to repentance.* Repentance is central to the preaching of the Gospel and is vital for the miracle of the new birth to occur. Jesus commanded that "repentance and remission of sins should be preached in his name among all nations, beginning at Jerusalem" (Luke 24:47). It is the twofold pattern of evangelism—preaching the Gospel and bringing people to repentance—that contains "the power of God unto salvation to every one that

believeth" (Rom. 1:16). Satan would abolish this activity, but all true manifestations of God will include opportunities for repentance.

4. *All church activity must exalt Jesus Christ.* In Revelation 19:10 we read, "And I fell at his feet to worship him. And he said unto me, See thou do it not: I am thy fellowservant, and of thy brethren that have the testimony of Jesus: worship God: for the testimony of Jesus is the spirit of prophecy." If you want to know whether a manifestation is from God, ask a simple question: Does it seek to focus glory on Christ or someone else? It is always the function of the Holy Spirit to glorify Jesus.

5. *All church activity must edify the body. Some* people confuse this with "entertain" the body. While there is certainly nothing wrong with laughing and enjoying our church services, there is a very real difference between edification and entertainment. Jesus said that a "tree is known by its fruit" (Matt. 12:33). The end result of all church activity should serve to build us up in our most holy faith and unify us in singleness of purpose and service toward God. Also, Paul taught in 1 Corinthians, chapter 13, that every manifestation of the Holy Spirit should produce a love among the believers. If an activity within the church causes us to love and accept one another with a godly love, then that activity should be encouraged.

6. *All church activity must nurture evangelism.* This brings us back to the incentive for spiritual warfare. Our Lord's greatest command is, "Go ye into all the world, and preach the gospel to every creature" (Mark 16:15). When an activity within the church is breathed of God, it will ultimately result in evangelism and spiritual warfare. It is impossible to separate the two. Jesus commissioned His followers to go into all the world and preach the Gospel. He followed

that by saying, "These signs shall follow them that believe; In my name shall they cast out devils" (Mark 16:17). Part and parcel to the preaching of the Gospel is the believers' responsibility to take authority over Satan's kingdom. Through the discerning of spirits, battlefield encouragement, and keeping our focus on Christ, fasting empowers us to join ourselves to God's activities, and to march forward in reclaiming our communities for Jesus.

Weapon #4:
If My People Will Turn
from Their Wicked Ways

"P.T.L. SCANDAL!" "WELL KNOWN PASTOR RESIGNS UNDER ALLEGATIONS!" "EVANGELIST CAUGHT WITH SEXY SUSIE IN A MOTEL TRYST!" Literally thousands of newspaper and magazine headlines have sensationalized the well-publicized sins of the church over the past few years. Tabloid television has thrived on recruiting willing "Christians" ready to sell their salvation and the loyalty of their comrades for the fast big buck and glitter of Hollywood. Christianity's modern heroes have fallen from the pedestals on which they were placed, only to reveal that the vulnerability of the human heart is still alive. What a surprise this must have been to the charismatic followers who exalted them to places of fame, and took up stones at their judgment.

What a revelation it has been, these past few years, to watch the God who chastens whom He loves opening the doors to His sleeping fold wide, letting us see ourselves as we really are. While a remnant have shown faithful the keeping power of Christ in the midst of subtle corruption, others have discovered their true reflection, and do not like what they have found. Christians who know all the right doctrine, who use the proper words, and who strictly adhere to the fashionable things equated to popular Christianity, sometimes live amidst great wickedness.

Among the church's closet skeletons brought to light recently is an increasing justification for indulgence in the baser desires—drugs and alcohol, financial mismanagement, sexual improprieties, and other expressions of worldliness.

But, are these revelations divinely directed so that condemnation can overwhelm and drown us without pity? Not at all. The God who saved us by His grace shall keep us by His power. Should that include disciplined correction and reinforced accountability, so be it. That is our only hope, and that is America's only hope. No secularized sin-saturated "church" will rise to defeat the powers of darkness or change our country for God. A congregation made up of carnal sin-filled believers is a powerless vehicle to stand in authority against the powers of hell.

In Joshua, chapter 7, the armies of Israel could not stand before the men of Ai. Joshua tore his clothes and fell before the Lord inquiring the reason for their failure. And, the Lord said to Joshua,

> Get thee up; wherefore liest thou thus upon thy face? Israel hath sinned, and they have also transgressed my covenant which I commanded them: for they have even taken of the accursed thing, and have also stolen, and dissembled also, and they have put it even among their own stuff. Therefore the children of Israel could not stand before their enemies, but turned their backs before their enemies, because they were accursed: neither will I be with you any more, except ye destroy the accursed from among you. Up, sanctify the people, and say, "Sanctify yourselves against tomorrow: for thus saith the Lord God of Israel, there is an accursed thing in the midst of thee, O Israel: thou canst not stand before thine enemies, until ye take away the accursed thing from among you." (Josh. 7:10–13)

"Get thee up; wherefore liest thou thus upon thy face?" Never has this comment been more appropriate than it is for the church today. Nothing would make Satan happier than for American Christians to retreat apologetically, embarrassed by the turmoil surrounding the upheaval of certain religious empires, merely accepting a broad-brushing identification of Christianity as a whole. The wisdom from heaven says, "Get up! Don't lie there on your face! Repent! Sanctify yourself and remove the unclean things! Handle your internal matters with sternness and with love! Demand of yourself honesty and uprightness before your God, and He will heal your land."

"If my people will...turn from their wicked ways" is the heavenly mandate for right living. Biblical righteousness is best defined as the separation from evil that naturally occurs as one draws near to God. This kind of righteousness demands as much doing that which is right, as it does avoiding that which is wicked or improper.

In James 4:17 we read, "Therefore to him that knoweth to do good and doeth it not, to him it is sin." God's standard of righteousness carries an equally important priority between doing, and not doing, things that are right and wrong.

This includes involvement in politics. While evil powers manipulate human counterparts within the governments of men, there are more than equal numbers of the heavenly host who intercede in the affairs of earth as they are guided by the compulsions of saintly intercessions.

Many worthy legislative causes will succeed against the tide of wickedness in America if the church is awakened by revival. Every citizen has the right to lobby for moral good. The splendid opportunity to stem the tide of evil and set America on track toward social and spiritual recovery is very real as activism and Christian campaigns address the need for participation in legislative issues important to us all. Thank God for ministries that are currently involved in political issues where the unified voice of the Body of Christ can make a social and moral difference.

Having so noted, it is the burden of this book to point out that a different and nonlegislative method is needed to create social change (albeit a companion method), and that is first of all the combating of supernatural forces through spiritual weaponry—the root cause of social change through spiritual awakening. Every effort in the secular arena, no matter how righteous or worthy, must be simply the outgrowth first of a heart in pursuit of God. In *The Rebirth of America*, John Price notes, "Repentant Christians in prayer will be able to do more for America than all the government programs rolled into one. They will find the purpose and power that allows them to take public stands in league with their fellow believers which could radically change the future of America."[74]

Satan's invasion will fail if the church in America returns its faith and attention to the Lord. Faith in human relationships, religious plotting, pious programming, and most human endeavors will fail to endure. But, faith in our heavenly Father will never disappoint us. From deep unto deep comes the still plea from God the Father, "If my people will seek my face." Only in His presence is strength and purpose found to live upright in a wicked world. When one enters into fellowship with Him, all things are brought into the light of perfect reason. Being fashioned in the image of His Son, desires change. When appetites change, things take on new meaning, and we want to live and serve and honor our Lord.

Much of our nation is under demonic siege. Christians must now turn from the secular theology that teaches us to live for community affluence and financial gain. These have their place in life. But, if we are to succeed against Satan, our primary goal must be for God Himself, who cries in the face of material things, saying, "If my people will…humble themselves…pray…seek my face…and turn from their wicked ways, I will heal their land" (2 Chron. 7:14).

I am convinced that God is the author of our country's greatness and the grantor of U.S. dominance on a world level. The Bible is replete with the fact that all power, government, and responsibility for that authority are given by God. God established America as a world leader for the Gospel's propagation. It's no surprise then that, of all nations, Satan should attack the United States with all his fervor.

Never has a nation sacrificed more to preach the Gospel to the ends of the earth or been such an ally to Israel during troubled times.

God has blessed America; yet, it seems—as Abraham Lincoln confessed— "We have forgotten the gracious hand which preserved us." May God grant the church in America insight regarding its failures and space to repent, lest after having preached to the four winds of the planet, this generation of Americans witness the terminal invasion of demonic powers resulting in the decline of Western civilization, and the fall of the greatest nation ever established by the hand of God.

Where Is America Going?

I listened to the pastor of a large church in Texas recently as he preached a blistering sermon on the social decay troubling America. Over and over he drove home the question, "Where is America going?" He made me wonder.

Across the U.S., well-respected minds are offering a disturbing forecast for the future of America. Social academics and cultural scientists are concerned that for the past fifty years we have separated moral principles from social policies, and that consequently we are at the breaking point in the stability of our culture. They point out that even our language has been contaminated by a new political correctness, and that we are no longer capable of speaking with a public moral certainty. What our citizens once called promiscuity has become known as "sexually active," and cold-blooded murderers are now called "victims of rage."

These facts coupled with the latest statistics on crime, drug abuse, and juvenile delinquency, reveal what should be obvious to everyone by now—without a moral and spiritual awakening, America is headed for calamity.

History students have looked with interest at the French Revolution, which was followed by the horror of death and torture under Robespierre. They have compared it to the Revolutionary War in America that resulted in an unprecedented cultural and monetary success. While citizens were rejoicing in America over their newfound freedoms, in Paris more than twenty thousand people died in the guillotine. The years to follow in France would see a reign of terror leading up to totalitarianism and Napoleon. Why were the American and French Revolutions followed by such contrasting conclusions? The difference was that the American Revolution was fought on Christian principles, while the French Revolution was anti-God. The forces behind the French Revolution were out to eliminate God as the enemy of France. They placed a statue of a nude woman upon the altar in the church at Notre Dame and proclaimed the God of Christianity as dead. Soon afterward, the French government collapsed.

America's Founding Fathers believed that all human governments have the potential to guide societies toward good or decay depending on whether their social policies respond to the moral supremacy of God. Men like George Washington and John Adams studied the historical triumphs and tragedies of this realism, from the great Flood to the fall of the Roman Empire, and they wisely chose to rely upon the Bible and the leading of the Holy Spirit as their moral handbook in formulating the politics of early America.

When we understand our nation's Christian roots, we are forced to conclude that America has lost sight of her guide. Like a ship adrift at sea and needing direction to find land, modern America stands "lost at sea," blinded by our intellectual achievements while facing certain moral drowning. For the past five decades, we've allowed the liberal Left to defend the use of public funds for pornography, explicit sex education, and anti-Christian curricula. The Hollywood elite have denigrated Judeo-Christian belief and have mocked the virtues of purity. The highest courts in the land have ruled with contemptuous decrees against God, against prayer, and against the free expression of religion. The net result has been that the United States has quickly become the most profane and violent society in the industrialized world. The question is, what can we do about it now? Is there any way to reverse the destructive trend and set America on track toward moral and spiritual recovery? Yes. If America will do the right things, there is still time for a spiritual awakening and deliverance for her cities under demonic siege.

There are ten things the church must do:

1. We must be willing to see and accept the truth about where we are as a nation. We must humble ourselves and restore the message of repentance, integrity, and accountability to the pulpits of America.
2. We must be willing for revival to begin in the church. Righteousness must begin in the house of the Lord through repentant saints refreshed with a new anointing.
3. We must pray. Not just hold seminars on the mechanics of intercession, but implement its sacred activity within our closets as well as sanctuaries. S. D. Gordon has accurately said, "The greatest thing anyone can do for God and man is pray. It is not the only thing, but it is the chief thing. The great people of the earth are the people who pray. I do not mean those who talk about prayer; nor those who say they believe in prayer; nor yet those who can explain about prayer; but I mean those people who take time to pray."[75]
4. In addition to prayer, we must seek the Father through fasting. We must refocus ourselves upon the supreme object of the believers' adoration—the Godhead. In this we will find ultimate power.
5. We must commit ourselves to spiritual warfare. "Pray without ceasing" was the message Paul sent to the troubled saints in Thessalonica (1 Thess. 5:17). In 1 Corinthians 15:32 he recalls his struggle with "the beasts of Ephesus." To the Romans he wrote, "And the God of peace shall bruise Satan under your feet shortly" (Rom. 16:20). To the Thessalonians he said that he would have come to them, "but Satan hindered us" (1 Thess. 2:18). And to young

Timothy he admonished, "Endure hardness, as a good soldier of Jesus Christ. No man that warreth entangleth himself with the affairs of this life: that he may please him who hath chosen him to be a soldier" (2 Tim. 2:3–4).
6. The church must wholly commit itself to the vocal community declaration of the Gospel of Jesus Christ. It is the preaching of the Gospel of Christ that embodies "the power of God unto salvation, both to the Jews and the Gentiles."
7. We must intercede specifically for our political leaders. 1 Timothy 2:1–2 says, "I exhort therefore, that, first of all, supplications, prayers, intercessions, and giving of thanks, be made for all men; For kings, and for all that are in authority; that we may lead a quiet and peaceable life in all godliness and honesty."

Praying for our leaders is the most effective tool we have in restoring God to the center of social policy. Believe it or not, prayer can change people dramatically. I've experienced it. I was a mean little boy. According to my mother, I would greet new friends by asking if they wanted "to play or fight?" She says I was always ready for either. I don't remember that, but I do remember a lot of other mean things I did while growing up as a child.

I had an Alaskan Huskey, which is a very hairy dog, and I lived in the hot Arizona desert. As best I can remember, he was solid black with a white circle on his back. We called him Eightball. The only thing that poor dog ever wanted was a place in the shade. I still remember how he would lie under a tree with his tongue hanging out, trying to cool off while he slept. That's when I would creep up and grab that big tongue.

The object was to see how long I could hang on before he got away. It's a miracle he didn't eat me.

I wish that tormenting Eight-ball had been the worst thing I had ever done. It wasn't. My meanness as a boy in the small Arizona town

THE VICTORS' MASTER WEAPONS

of El Mirage was legendary. Most of our neighbors considered me a menace and prayed for the day when I'd be gone. Thank God for a few saints who understood the life-changing power of prayer. I recall an old Christian lady who lived across the road and was nice to me in spite of myself. There were Sunday school teachers who took time to tell me Bible stories and lead me in the sinners' prayer almost every week. Lord knows I needed it. There was Brother Kay. He was the pastor of our small church and the closest thing to a fire-breathing dragon I had ever seen. When he preached the rafters shook. But, when he prayed the heavens shook. Of course, there were my parents and grandparents. I'm sure they have great treasures in heaven for putting up with me. Many of these people went to their graves wondering if this menace of a kid would ever straighten out. I did, but not without the compulsions of their prayers.

I'm older now. I've been a business, ministry, and community leader for more than eighteen years, and I've learned about the importance of praying for our leaders.

8. Our representatives in Congress need to hear from us immediately. A single call or letter to your congressman is considered by most legislators to reflect the opinion of many thousands of other Americans. Remember, the only thing necessary for evil to prevail is for good people to do nothing. Congress needs to hear from us now!

9. We must participate in the political healing process. To do nothing would be a sin. We can talk to the public school teacher and explain why our children will not be allowed to attend explicit sex education classes. We can call the local public broadcasting channel and explain why we will no longer support PBS if they continue to air programs that vilify our religious faith. We can attend local campaign rallies and town hall meetings and express our feelings on issues regarding religious liberty. We can form

a citizens' group of four or five people, educate ourselves on the issues, and meet privately with our representatives and senators when they are in town. Many congressmen report that this is the best way to get legislation through Congress.

10. At the forefront of each of our activities, let's remember the biblical admonition: "If my people...will humble themselves, and pray, and seek my face, and turn from their wicked ways; then will I hear from heaven, and will forgive their sin, and will heal their land" (2 Chron. 7:14). Revival is the primary key to overcoming America's moral decay.

Where is America going? It depends on who our guide is. If we continue following the social architects who have guided the United States for the past thirty years, then we are in trouble. But, if we look for guidance from the God who originally multiplied and enriched and strengthened us, then there is reason for great hope concerning our nation's future. May God grant believers a holy resolve not to allow this moment in time to slip away. Instead, may this become known in the near future as the time of the Great Spiritual Awakening in American history. Repentance, righteousness, prayer, fasting, a commitment to spiritual warfare, and evangelism are the weapons of our warfare that are mighty through God to pull down strongholds and to liberate cities under demonic invasion.

I Believe

In conclusion, I believe there can be a great revival in the United States in this generation. If our Lord should tarry, a sovereign outpouring could sweep across America until the glory of God flows from sea to shining sea.

That's the way it could be. I also believe America's cities are coming under siege to demonic power at this present time. Satan's forces have no original claim to the earth or its inhabitants. Everything they

THE VICTORS' MASTER WEAPONS

hold, they do so with adverse possession. But, a time could come when the children of God grow tired of the propagation of deception, of perversion, of degradation—a time when dissatisfaction with material pursuit gives way to a revival of spiritual hunger. With holy resolve, God's children could respond with weapons against which our enemy has no recourse—no Yalu bridges, no option to regroup or reseize their captives. Rather, with total victory, the Jehovah-saved could resound, "Let us go up and possess the land, for we are well able to overcome them."

I hope that time is now. I pray that time is come.

THE GODS
WHO WALK AMONG US

By Thomas R. Horn
& Donald C. Jones, Ph. D.

THE GODS

*To the memory of William Cornish (W.C.) Jones,
Charles K. (C.K.) Barnes, and Orville R. (O.R.) Cross,
faithful ministers of the Gospel of Jesus Christ.*

FOREWORD

The Gods Who Walk Among Us is a most enlightening and insightful book on a subject about which we need to know more. It graphically describes the gods of this world and their wide-ranging influence upon individuals and upon peoples. This book is most unusual and timely. For the most part, today's generation is unaware of, even blind to, the dangers of ideas and teachings regarding the spirit-world that have become so commonplace. Demons, worship of demons, occult activities, and the like, have been topics somewhat apart from evangelical believer's concerns. Most of us have given little thought or study to such things. We have felt almost untouched or untainted by them. How dangerously mistaken we have been. Authors Thomas Horn and Donald Jones have researched the subject remarkably well. Not only have they done a superb job of identifying the gods of antiquity and their functions, but they have, in scholarly fashion, shown that these same gods command the attention and allegiance of multitudes of modern men and women. While Horn and Jones suggest that the names of some of the gods may have been altered to a degree, they demonstrate quite conclusively that their nefarious activities have remained constant. After reading this book, we are suddenly aware of the "ever-present darkness" and find that we can no longer afford to be blind to what we have previously ignored. It is evident that pagan worship and rituals are going on today. Of particular interest is the revelation that all of Egypt's plagues were direct affronts to her recognized and revered deities. In every instance, we see how Jehovah effectively demonstrated his vast and unequaled superiority.

Horn and Jones recognize that the gods of this world are, in every instance, and in every manifestation, representations of the evil supernatural; in fact, they are representations of Satan himself. They believe, and with good reason, that the New Age Movement is, at its core, a cleverly devised scheme whereby Satan is seeking to acquire the allegiance of all of mankind; they provide adequate illustration to support this thesis. The suggestion that possibly some things that occur during worship times in our churches today are similar to things that happened in pagan worship is, to say the least, frightening. Horn and Jones ascribe a measure of credibility to UFO sightings, and are persuaded that the evil supernatural is making alarming and ever-increasing inroads into modern culture. They believe this sets the stage for the Antichrist. This book is an eye-opener for some of us who grew up in a day when most people believed in the God of the Bible, even if they did not strive to obey Him. No doubt we were simplistic, even naive about the spirit world, especially the evil spirit world. No longer! It is time to pay attention to what Horn and Jones say, for to be well-informed is to have the possibility of being well-prepared. We are at the end of the age. The coming of our Lord is near. Let us sound the trumpet in Zion!

—R. L. Brandt

ACKNOWLEDGMENTS

I wish to acknowledge the following people without whose help and inspiration this book would not have been possible: Dr. Donald C. and Joyce Jones for their willingness to work with me on this project. Pastor Rance and Jaynie Kinser for their unconditional love and support. Judy Vorfeld for her tireless technical and research assistance. R.L. Brandt for providing a thoughtful forward. Superintendents William O. Vickery and William I. Gallaher for their steadfast leadership example over the years. My mother Virginia (Sally) for a lifetime of love and support. My sister Vida for sharing deeply personal information on the possible spiritual aspects of the UFO abduction phenomenon. My big brother Clarence (Amil) for illustrating what it means to be a pastor. And to my wife Juanita, and our children Althia, Joe, and Donna, for being the greatest family on earth.

— *Chapter One* —

THE ORIGIN OF THE GODS

> "Were (the Sumerian deities) the 'mythologizing' of certain ancient heroes, or…the result of an extraterrestrial 'alien' visitation, which gave birth to the legends and mythological gods?"
>
> —Tom Horn (later in this chapter)

Birds skipped among groves of date palms along the marshy banks of the Euphrates in the year 3500 B.C. As the sun arose above Sumer, the alluvial desert of the Middle East came alive with agricultural activity. In a valley forged between the twin rivers of the Tigris and the Euphrates, magnificent walled cities awoke to the chatter of busy streets and marketplaces. In what the Greeks would later call "Mesopotamia" (between the rivers), the world's first great trade center and civilization developed. The opulent Sumerian cities of Ur—the home of Abram—Uruk, and Lagash, had become the economic machines of the ancient Middle East, and industries from as far away as Jericho, near the Mediterranean Sea, and Catal Huyuk, in Asia Minor, competed for the trade opportunities they provided. Laborers from the biblical city of Jericho exported salt to Sumer, and miners from Catal Huyuk prepared obsidian, used in making mirrors, for shipment to the ancient metropolis. But while the prehistoric people of the East looked to the Sumerians for their supply of daily bread, the Sumerians themselves gazed heavenward to the early rising of Utu (Shamash), the all-providing sun god, as he prepared once again to ride across the sky

THE GODS WHO WALK AMONG US

in his mule-drawn chariot. In 3500 B.C., Utu was not alone among the gods.

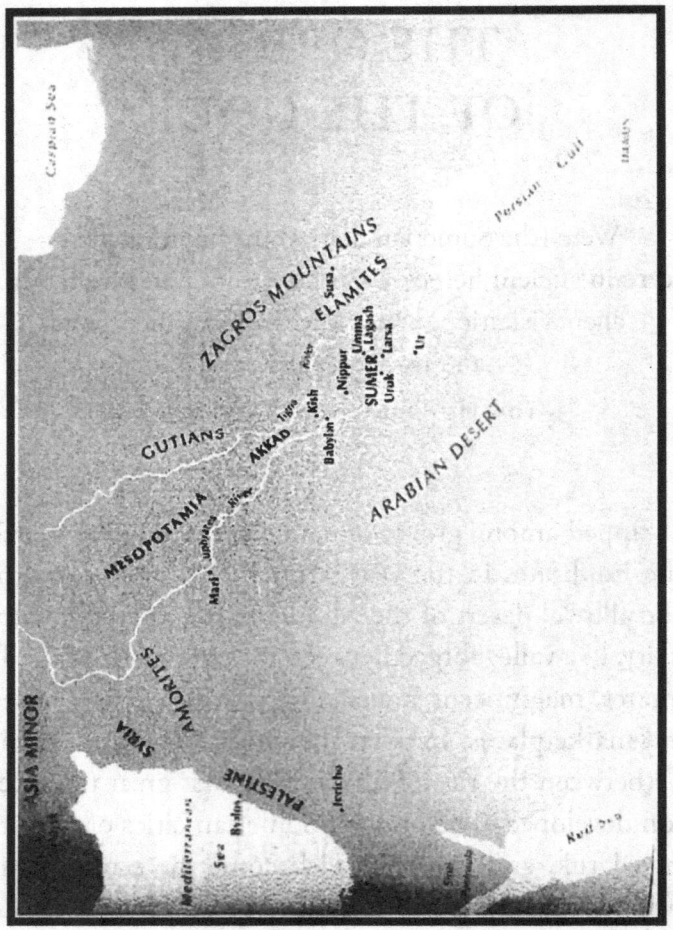

Ancient Sumeria/Mesopotamia

By now, the Sumerian pantheon provided the earliest known description of organized mythology, consisting of a complex system of more than 3,000 deities and covering nearly every detail of nature and human enterprise. There were gods of sunshine and rain. There were vegetation gods, fertility gods, river gods, animal gods, and gods of the afterlife. There were the great gods, Enlil (prince of the air), Anu (ruler

THE ORIGIN OF THE GODS

of the heavens), Enki, (the god of water), and so on. Under these, existed a second level of deities, including Nannar, the moon god, Utu, the sun god, and Inanna, the "Queen of Heaven." But, where did the gods of Sumeria come from?

Since the religion of Sumeria was the first known organized mythology, and would greatly influence the foundational beliefs of the forthcoming nations of Assyria, Egypt, Greece, Rome, and others, this question has interested scholars and historians for more than a millennium. Specifically, where does one find the historical beginning of the ancient gods of Sumeria? Were the Sumerian deities the product of human imagination, or the distortion of some earlier prehistoric revelation? Were they the "mythologizing" of certain ancient heroes, or, as some New Age followers suggest, the result of an extraterrestrial "alien" visitation, which gave birth to the legends and mythological gods? More importantly, did the gods of Sumeria reflect the emergence of a real and spiritual power operating through pagan dynamics, or were the gods purely the creation of primitive imagination?

These questions are both fascinating and difficult since the gods and goddesses of ancient Sumeria/Mesopotamia continue to be shrouded in a history of unknown origins. As though, out of "nowhere," the Sumerians sprang onto the scene over 5,500 years ago, bringing with them the first written language, a corpus of progressive knowledge from complicated religious concepts, and an advanced understanding of astrology, chemistry, and mathematics. The questionable origin of the Sumerian culture has caused some theorists to conclude that the gods of Sumeria, and the subsequent mythologies that grew out of them (Assyrian, Egyptian, etc.), were the diabolical scheme of a regressive and evil "supernatural presence." If this is true, does the ancient power continue to work within our world? Do primordial and living entities, once worshipped as "gods," coexist with modern man? There are three competing theories regarding the origin of the early mythological gods: 1) the Euhemerus view; 2) the New Age view; and 3) the Biblical view.

The Euhemerus view was based on the historical theories of the Greek scholar Euhemerus, who claimed that the pagan gods originated with certain ancient and famous kings who were later deified. The more widely accepted theories, the New Age view and the Biblical view, have succeeded in becoming the popular authorities regarding original paganism, and are, therefore, the focus of our attention. What can we learn from these two views?

THE NEW AGE VIEW CONCERNING THE ORIGIN OF THE GODS

A growing doctrine within the New Age Movement claims that the origin of the gods, and the human race, as we know it today, is the direct result of extraterrestrial (UFO) activity. In the introduction to his bestselling book, *Chariots of the Gods?*, Erich von Daniken, who, it might be argued, is one of the fathers of the New Age Movement related to UFOs, said, "I claim that our forefathers received visits from the universe in the remote past, even though I do not yet know who these extraterrestrial intelligences were or from which planet they came. I nevertheless proclaim that these 'strangers' annihilated part of mankind existing at the time and produced a new, perhaps the first, *homo sapiens*."[1]

As depicted in the Hollywood films *Contact* and *Close Encounters of the Third Kind*, Erich von Daniken's hypothesis took America by storm in the 1960s with the proposition that mankind was possibly the offspring of an ancient, perhaps ongoing, extraterrestrial experiment. New Age UFO experts like Daniken assert that the gods of mythology may have been themselves evidence of, and a reaction to, an encounter with other-worldly beings. They claim that ancient men would have considered space travelers as gods and would have recorded their arrival, their experiments, and their departure, in hieroglyphs, megaliths, and stone tablets, as supernatural encounters between gods and men. Von Daniken wrote,

While [the] spaceship disappears again into the mists of the universe our friends will talk about the miracle, 'The gods were here!'...they will make a record of what happened: uncanny, weird, miraculous. Then their texts will relate, and drawings will show, that gods in golden clothes were there in a flying boat that landed with a tremendous din. They will write about chariots which the gods drove over land and sea, and of terrifying weapons that were like lightning, and they will recount that the gods promised to return. They will hammer and chisel in the rock pictures of what they had seen, shapeless giants with helmets and rods on their heads, carrying boxes in front of their chests; balls on which indefinable beings sit and ride through the air; staves from which rays are shot out as if from a sun.[2]

Von Daniken also claimed that the odd appearance of some of the gods, as depicted in various hieroglyphs, (human-like creatures with falcon heads; lions with heads of bulls, etc.) could be viewed as evidence that "aliens" conducted experiments of cloning and cross-mutated ancient people and animals.

Some people accept this part of Von Daniken's hypothesis as a humanistic alternative to the Biblical account of creation. It's uncertain how many people believe such a theory, but a full eighty percent of Americans claim they believe in the possibility of extraterrestrial life. Some, like the 39 members of the Heaven's Gate cult who committed suicide in Rancho Santa Fe, California because they believed they were being summoned by a UFO trailing the Hale-Bopp Comet, subscribe to an eerie amalgam of mysticism and conventional religion. Not surprisingly, the growing interest in UFOs and the paranormal has given birth to a host of popular television specials and weekly programs depicting such otherworldly creatures and those who claim to have encountered them. One of the more disturbing aspects of such UFO phenomena are the reports, which continue to come in from around the world, of nighttime abductions by small, wide-eyed creatures who supposedly pilot UFOs, and conduct various medical experiments on their victims. The New Age Movement argues that such activity would be proof of an ongoing experiment between humans and aliens, and they note that the radical aspects of such experiments have included impregnating victims and later removing the hybrid embryos.

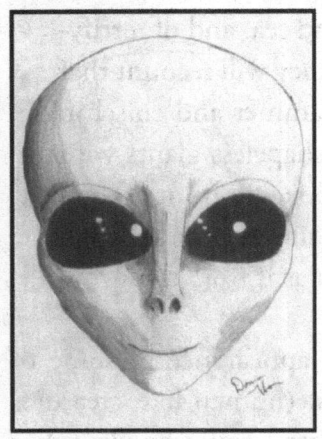
Intergalactic New Age Scientist?

Ancient Chinese folklore includes stories of a distant land of "flying carts." A Sanskrit text, *The Drona Parva*, documented "dogfights" by gods in flying machines.³ But men like Von Daniken claim that the Bible is their best advocate and is the "greatest UFO book of all time!" The "wheel" in Ezekiel 1:15; the "pillar of cloud" in Exodus 13:21–22; and Elijah's "chariot of fire" (2 Kings 2:11), are all viewed as examples of UFO sightings by New Agers. It's true that we do find a biblical record of mysterious celestial creatures invading the earth and conducting procreative experiments. In Genesis 6:4 we read, "When mankind had spread all over the world, and girls were being born, some of the supernatural beings saw that these girls were beautiful, so they took the ones they liked. In those days, and even later, there were giants *[nepheli]* on the earth who were descendants of human women and the supernatural beings" *(TEV)*. But is Genesis 6 a description of reproductive experiments conducted by advanced extraterrestrial creatures? Or is it a record of something even more sinister?

A Christian Analysis vs. the New Age View

Regardless of one's interpretation of these and other ancient records, one fact remains: Thousands of years ago, heavenly beings visited the earth. They engaged in sexual experiments resulting in a race of mutant beings called *nepheli*. The final result appears to have been an immediate judgment from God, who ordered Israel to destroy the *nepheli* and its descendants. Thousands of years later, Jesus spoke of the events that occurred during the days of Noah as being comparable to the days leading up to the rapture of the Church (Matthew 24). This prophecy is remarkable when one realizes that after God judged the celestial beings who cohabited with the Noahtic women, all such comparable activity apparently ceased until about 1940. Then, following the infamous Roswell incident which occurred in New Mexico in 1947, people from around the world began encountering strange creatures conducting procreative experiments with increasing regularity. One is forced to wonder, what's going on? Who are these creatures? Are the current UFO visitors the same as those of Noah's day? If so, what is this reproductive experimentation about? Perhaps the answer to this question (the Christian's analysis vs the New Age view on "aliens") is hidden in the first six chapters of Genesis.

Very soon after the fall of man, we find in Genesis 3: 15 the protoevangelium (the promise that the seed of the woman would someday bring forth a child [Jesus] capable of destroying the serpent's [Satan's] power). In response to the promise, supernatural beings (fallen angels?) appeared from the heavens and performed reproductive experiments on human women (Genesis 6). Was Satan attempting to intercept, pollute, and thereby destroy the righteous seed? Was he trying to cut off the birth line of the Messiah? Perhaps. Satan's ancient goal included cutting off the line leading to the Messiah. Satan led Pharaoh to destroy the Hebrew children so the deliverer might not be born. Herod sought the baby Jesus in the *New Testament* in order to have Him killed. In Revelation 12, we see the devil (dragon) waiting to destroy the messianic seed as soon as it is born of the woman. But Dr. I.D.E. Thomas, in his book, *The Omega Conspiracy*, suggests that Satan had even bigger plans at work in Genesis 6. He claims that Satan (as opposed to aliens) was trying to produce a race of mutant warriors by breeding fallen angels with women in an effort to exterminate the children of God.

From a Christian's point of view, this could explain how people like the Sumerians of Mesopotamia, who were enemies of Yahweh, appeared out of nowhere around 3500 B.C., bringing with them a pantheon of deities, the first written language, and a superior knowledge of earthly sciences. This may also explain why many of the religions that followed Sumerian mythology, including Greek mythology, emerged from the original idea that powerful beings, with names like "Zeus" and "Apollo," visited the earth, intermarried with women, and fathered half-human children. Dr. Thomas believes recent UFO abduction activity may point to the birth of a new race of anti-God warriors, as we approach the end of the age and the coming of Armageddon.

Does Genesis 6 support the New Age theory that alien creatures traveled from distant planets in UFOs, performed reproductive experiments on women, and were afterward honored in the images and folklore of the gods of mythology? Or, is Dr. I.D.E. Thomas correct in stating that the story in Genesis is a record of fallen angels acting in accord with Satan? What, if anything, could this tell us about the origin of the gods and the current interstellar phenomena? Are we experiencing an ongoing invasion of earth by intergalactic scientists, or is Satan busy advancing the most sophisticated con game in history? We know that the rapture of the Church will be accompanied by "fearful sights and great signs from heaven" (Luke 21: 11). Perhaps Satan is contriving an "alien invasion" to explain the disappearance of so many people at once! If 80 percent of the population believes in the possibility of extraterrestrial intelligence, wouldn't this be a powerful form of deception? Since New Age theology produces a growing belief among some contemporary church groups that flying saucers will be the method God uses to retrieve the Christian community during the Rapture, couldn't the UFO sightings phenomenon play a part in the great deception that will pervade the earth following the Rapture?

We read in 2 Thessalonians 2:8–12,

> And then shall that Wicked [one] be revealed…whose coming is after the working of Satan with all power and signs and lying wonders…. And for this cause God shall send them strong delusion, that they should believe a lie: That they all might be damned who believed not the truth, but had pleasure in unrighteousness. (brackets added)

The world authorities remaining to make up the governments of the Antichrist will need an explanation for those taken in the Rapture. People from around the world will be missing! Now imagine if the Rapture was followed by hundreds of "space craft" landing on earth piloted by creatures who appeared to be advanced humanoids, couldn't these beings claim to have removed the Christians into some kind of a high-tech "rapture," and simultaneously present their leader (antichrist?) as the messiah? Couldn't they point to ancient mysteries, megaliths, pyramids, and the gods of mythology, as proof of an ancient visitation of planet earth?

The late Pulitzer Prize-winning author and agnostic Carl Sagan was, until his death, working on a screenplay about the ramifications of just such a savior who appears in the coming millennium![4] Humanists like Sagan argue that evidence such as the meteorite,[5] which has been hypothesized as indicating that microscopic life existed on Mars millions of years ago, is proof that prehistoric life forms could have moved throughout the universe for untold millennia. Not long ago, people who supported UFO activity were the object of scorn. Because of accumulating evidence and reputable eyewitness accounts; this is no longer the case. That some kind of unexplained phenomenon, called the UFO experience by some, occurs, is beyond question. UFO reports are coming in at the alarming worldwide rate of about six sightings per hour! Whatever or whomever they are, the reality of this activity can no longer be doubted. One concludes that these beings are either advanced humanoids from outer space, or that this activity signals an ongoing deception of demonic design. If the current UFO activity is demonic and indicates that Satan has for centuries planned an "alien" visitation in order to, among other things, explain the Rapture of the church, wouldn't it be reasonable to believe that his plans have heretofore included indoctrination and advanced intelligence? Military invasions always involve preliminary and clandestine maneuvers, and one should believe Satan's plans to deceive in the past, the present, and the future World Order, would first involve covert strategies of brainwashing, political manipulation, and the positioning of his agents in places of power.

While I believe that the New Age Movement's interpretation of UFO phenomenon and the origin of the gods is erroneous, I do credit New Agers for recognizing the high possibility that the gods of mythology were a result of, and perhaps a first step toward, the developing of the schemes of a super-intelligent force, a power which may energize the UFO phenomenon today. But what New Agers describe as the goals of a "highly advanced alien civilization," I call the plotting of an evil supernatural creature.

The Biblical View of the Origin of the Gods

The biblical (and I believe correct) view of the origin of the pagan gods begins with Original Revelation. This means there was a perfect revelation from God to man at the time of creation. The first man, Adam, was one with God and perceived divine knowledge from the mind of God. Adam was "in tune" with the mental processes of God, and understood, therefore, what God knew about science, astronomy, cosmogony, geology, eschatology, and so on. After the fall, Adam was "detached" from the mind of God, but retained an imperfect memory of divine revelation, including a knowledge of God's plan of redemption. Two things began to occur in the decades after the Fall: 1) information from the original revelation became distant and distorted, as it was dispersed among the nations, and passed from generation to generation; and 2) the realm of Satan seized upon this opportunity to receive worship, and to turn people away from Yahweh, by distorting and counterfeiting the original revelation with pagan ideas and gods. This point of view seems reasonable when one considers that the earliest historical and archeological records, from civilizations around the world, have consistently pointed back to and repeated portions of the original story. In their startling book, *The Discovery of Genesis*, the Rev. C.H. Kang and Dr. Ethel R. Nelson confirm that prehistoric Chinese ideographic pictures (used in very ancient Chinese writing) depict the story of Genesis, including the creation of the Man and Woman, the Garden, the Temptation and Fall, Noah's flood, and the Tower of Babel. In his book, *The Real Meaning of the Zodiac*, Dr. James Kennedy claims that the ancient signs of the Zodiac also indicate a singular and original revelation, a kind of gospel in the stars. And that the message of the stars, although demonized and converted into astrology after the Fall, originally recorded the Gospel of Go. Kennedy writes:

> There exists in the writings of virtually all civilized nations a description of the major stars in the heavens, something which might be called the "Constellations of the Zodiac" or the "Signs of the Zodiac," of which there are twelve. If you go back in time to Rome, or beyond that to Greece, or before that to Egypt, Persia, Assyria, or Babylonia, regardless of how far back you go, there is a remarkable phenomenon; nearly all nations had the same twelve signs, representing the same twelve things, placed in the same order.
>
> The book of Job, thought by many to be the oldest book of the Bible, goes back to approximately 2150 B.C., 650 years before Moses came on the scene to write the Pentateuch; over 1,100 years before Homer wrote the *Odyssey* and the *Illiad*; and 1,500 years before Thales, the first philosopher, was born. In Job 38, God finally speaks to Job and his false comforters. As He is questioning Job, showing him and his companions

their ignorance, God says to them, "Canst thou bind the sweet influences of Pleiades, or loose the bands of Orion? Canst thou bring forth Mazzaroth in his season? Or canst thou guide Arcturus with his sons?" (Job 38:31–32). We see here reference to the constellations of Orion and Pleiades, and the star Arcturus. Also in the book of Job, there is reference to Cetus, the Sea Monster, and to Draco, the Great Dragon. I would call your attention to Job 38:32a: "Canst thou bring forth Mazzaroth in his season?" Mazzaroth is a Hebrew word which means, "The Constellations of the Zodiac." In what may be the oldest book in all of human history, we find that the constellations of the zodiac were already clearly known and understood.

Having made it clear that the Bible expressly, explicitly, and repeatedly condemns what is now known as astrology, the fact remains that there was a God-given Gospel [universally acknowledged original revelation] in the stars which lies beyond and behind that which has now been corrupted.[6]

In his book, Kennedy strongly condemns the practice of astrology, while asserting his view that the constellations of the zodiac were likely given by God to the first man as "record-keepers" of the original revelation of God. If the primary assumption of the Biblical view is correct, that an original revelation was corrupted after the fall of man and subsequently degenerated into the mythologies of the pagan gods, one should be able to find numerous examples of such corruption from the beginning of history, in various civilizations around the world.

Since the myths behind the gods would thus be "borrowed" ideas, the corrupted texts would be similar to the original truth, and, in that sense, evidence of a singular and original revelation. Furthermore, if the distortions of the original revelation were in fact energized by an evil supernaturalism, the goal of the alterations would be to draw people away from the worship of Yahweh. In certain ancient legends, such as the *Enuma Elish*, the *Adapa Epic*, and the *Epic of Gilgamesh*, we discover early traces of the kaleidoscope of the original revelation, plagiarized for the purpose of constructing the mythologies of the pagan gods.

Early Traces of Corruption

Evidence suggests that the earliest legends of mythology were preceded by a belief in "the God" *(Yahweh* to the Hebrews) as the creator of all things and the "ruler of heaven." Later, Satan was described as "the god of this world" (2 Cor. 4:4), and the "prince of the air" (Eph. 2:2). A fascinating struggle between the "ruler of the heavens" versus the "power of the air" occurred in early Sumerian mythology after Enki, the god of wisdom and water, created the human race out of clay. It appears that Anu, who was at first the most powerful of the Sumerian gods and the "ruler of the heavens," was superseded in power and popularity by Enlil, the "god of the air." To the Christian mind this is perceived as nothing less than Satan, the god of the air, continuing his pretense to the throne of God, and his usurpation of Yahweh, "the Lord of the heavens." It also indicates a corruption of the original revelation and perhaps an effort on the part of Satan to trick the pagan Sumerians into perceiving him as the "supreme" god (above the God of Heaven) and, therefore, worthy of adoration.

Correspondingly, in the *Enuma Elish* (a Babylonian epic), Marduk, the great god of the city of Babylon, was exalted above the benevolent gods and extolled as the creator of the world. Marduk was symbolized as a dragon (as is Satan in Revelation 12:9) called the *Muscrussu,* and his legend appears to contain several distortions of the important elements of the biblical account of creation. The *Adapa Epic* tells of another Babylonian legend that is also roughly equivalent to the Genesis account of creation. In it, Adapa, like Adam, underwent a test on food consumption, failed the test, and forfeited his opportunity for immortality. As a result of the failure, suffering and death were passed along to humanity.

Finally, the *Epic of Gilgamesh* is a Sumerian poem, which, like the *Adapa Epic,* is deeply rooted in ancient Assyrian and Babylonian mythology. In 1872, George Smith discovered the Gilgamesh tablets while doing research on the Assyrian library of Ashurbanipal at the British Museum. Because of the strong similarity to the biblical account of Noah and the great flood, Bible scholars have viewed the Gilgamesh epic with interest (and suspicion) since its discovery. As the legend goes, Gilgamesh, the king of the city of Uruk, was told about the flood by his immortal friend, Utnapishtim (the Sumerian equivalent of Noah). Utnapishtim described for Gilgamesh how the great god Enlil decided to destroy all of mankind because of its "noisy" sins. A plague was sent but failed to persuade mankind of better behavior, and, consequently, the gods decided on a complete extermination of the human race. Enki, the lord of the waters, was not happy with the other gods for this decision and warned Utnapishtim of the coming deluge, instructing him to tear down his house and build a great boat. Utnapishtim obeyed Enki, built a great vessel, and sealed it with pitch and bitumen. The family of Utnapishtim loaded onto the boat together with various beasts and fowl. When the rains came, the doors were closed and the vessel rose up above the waters. Like Noah, Utnapishtim sent out a dove, and later a swallow, to search for dry land. They both returned. Later, a raven was released and it never came back. After several more days the boat came to rest on the top of a mountain where Utnapishtim built an altar and offered a sacrifice of thanksgiving to the gods. As the gods smelt the sweet offering, all but Enlil repented for sending the flood. In my first book, *Spiritual Warfare: The Invisible Invasion,* I described an interesting example of the original revelation of God as distorted and plagiarized by Satan in order to draw men away from the worship of Jehovah. Concerning Asclepius, the Greek god of healing, I wrote:

> At the base of Pergamums hill stood the shrine of Asclepius, equipped with its own library, theater, sleeping chambers used in healing rituals, and long underground tunnels joining various other shrines to which pagans journeyed to receive the

healing powers of Apollo's favorite son. The Christian Church considered these mystical powers as demonic, for the worship of Asclepius focused on the image of a serpent, sometimes called Glycon, an enormous serpent figure some historians see as the origin for the modern symbol of healing, a serpent winding about a pole. Asclepius carried the lofty title, the hero god of healing. In Numbers 21, Moses designed the brazen serpent on a pole that was used of God as an oracle of healing. Seven hundred and forty-three years later, in 2 Kings 18:4, we find that Israel had began to worship the brazen serpent with offerings and incense.

From here the image was adopted into Greek mythology where it became the symbol of Asclepius, the Greek god of healing. Asclepius was reported to have cured untold numbers from every conceivable disease, even raising a man from the dead. This caused Apollo, through his Oracle at Delphi, to declare, "Oh Asclepius! Thou who art born a great joy to all mortals, whom lovely Coronis bare to me, the child of love, at rocky Epidaurus." Such a healer was he reported to be, that Pluto, god of Hades, complained to Zeus that hardly anyone was dying anymore, and so Zeus destroyed Asclepius with a thunderbolt. Afterward, Apollo pleaded with Zeus to restore his son and this intercession so moved Zeus that he not only brought Asclepius back to life, but immortalized him as the god of medicine. First at Thessaly, and finally throughout the Greek and Roman world, Asclepius was worshiped as the god of healing.[7]

Thus, we find a glaring example of God's "revelation" plagiarized for demonic purposes. Greek mythology represented Asclepius had the power to heal the sick and bring the dead back to life by drawing blood from the side of the goddess of justice. Asclepius was symbolized by a serpent winding about a pole, and he was called the great "Physician."

The obvious intention of the serpent on a pole in Numbers 21 was to focus mankind on the coming Messiah, the true Great Physician, who would hang upon a pole and would deliver His followers from sickness and death by the blood that ran from His side.

THE ENERGY OF THE GODS

Time does not allow for a full disclosure of the many other examples of corruption that occurred with regard to the Original Revelation. They include distortions or "knock-offs" of the virgin birth, Heaven and Hell, the Resurrection and Final Judgment, water baptism, communion, etc. In addition to the corruptions of the original revelation which pre-dated the gods of mythology, the Biblical view of the origin of the gods makes the following important assumptions: 1) that there exists within our universe real and supernatural powers; 2) that these powers are divided by their nature into two separate camps or "kingdoms," one evil, the other good; 3) that these kingdoms are presided over by rulers, the biblical Satan over the evil and Yahweh over the good; and 4) that the kingdom of Satan provided the historical energy or "life" within and behind the gods of mythology as Satan's kingdom solicited human worship through the elements of idolatry.

Quoting again from *Spiritual Warfare: The Invisible Invasion*, I conclude:

> The worship of Asclepius and other such idolatries were, as Paul would later articulate in 1 Corinthians 10:20, *the worship of demons*. [emphasis added] In Acts 7:41–42, we find that when men serve idols they are worshiping "the army of heaven" (Jerusalem Bible). Psalms 96:5 says, "For all the gods of the nations are idols" *('elilim, LXX daimonia)*. Demons. Many other biblical references indicate evil supernaturalism as the true dynamic of idolatry and reveal that idols of stone, flesh, or other imagery are simply "elilim (empty, nothing, vanity), but that *behind these images exist the true objects of heathen adoration: demons.*"[8]

THE ORIGIN OF THE GODS

John Milton wrote in *Paradise Lost* that millions of spiritual creatures walk the earth unseen. The Biblical view of the origin of the gods affirms the idea that "in the beginning" Yahweh created the heavens (celestial beings, planets, etc.) and the earth. Lucifer, "the light bearer," was a crowning achievement of God's heavenly creation and a chief servant of the creative Yahweh. But Lucifer became jealous of the worship Yahweh was receiving from his many creations, and proudly proclaimed, "I will exalt my throne above the stars of God...I will be like the most high" (Isa.14: 13–14). Somehow Lucifer convinced one-third of the celestial creatures to join him in a great rebellion, with the uprising ultimately resulting in Lucifer and his followers being cast out of Heaven. Lucifer (now Satan), driven by a quest for worship and thirsty for revenge against Yahweh, tempted Eve, and, after the fall with its resulting separation between man and God, moved to corrupt the divine truths contained within the Original Revelation by proclaiming himself (the god of the air) more worthy of worship than the God of Heaven.

If such a summary of the Biblical view is correct, that a real and evil supernatural presence exists and has for centuries drawn men away from worshipping Yahweh through the dynamics of various mythologies, the following questions arise: Were the angels that joined Lucifer in the fall also driven by a lust for worship? Did the images and attributes ascribed to the gods of mythology reflect the real and spiritual characteristics of certain unseen personalities operating behind them? More important, is the kingdom of Satan still at work in this manner? Do the living entities of the ancient gods continue to walk among us? If so, do such spirits embody themselves in trees, earth, and idols of stone, or should we assume that modern idolatry has acquired a more selective sophistication and social manifestation? In the following chapters, we'll search for the answers to these questions through a comparison of the various aspects of the gods of mythology. But, be warned, the forthcoming conclusions may startle you.

— *Chapter Two* —

THE GODS WHO WALKED AMONG THE EGYPTIANS

"Oh Egypt! Egypt! Your knowledge will survive but in legends, which later generations will be unable to believe."
—Lucius Apuleius, Roman Philosopher, Second Century A.D.

As the centuries passed by, the god and goddess worshipping cities of the Sumerians began to fade away. The flourishing fields of agriculture that provided the underpinnings of the great Sumerian economy were depleted of fertility through over-irrigation, and residues of salt buildup appeared to chafe the surface of the land. The city-states of Sumeria, Kish, Ur, Lagash, and Umma, weakened by a millennium of ruthless infighting among the Sumerians, finally succumbed to militant external forces. The barbarian armies of the Elamites (Persians) invaded and destroyed the city of Ur, and Amorites from the west overran the northern province of Sumer and subsequently established the hitherto little-known town of Babylon as their capital.

By 1840 B.C., Hammurabi, the sixth king of Babylon, conquered the remaining cities of Sumeria and forged northern Mesopotamia and Sumeria into a single nation. But the ultimate demise of the Sumerian people did not vanquish their ideas. Sumerian art, language, literature, and, especially, religion, had been forever absorbed into the cultures and social academics of the nations surrounding Mesopotamia, including the Hittite nation, the Babylonians, and the ancient Assyrians. A principal benefactor of Sumeria's ideas, and a people who would ultimately make their own contributions to the ancient mythologies, was an old and flourishing population of agrarians known as the Egyptians.

By the year 1350 B.C., Egyptian dominance had spread from Syria and Palestine into the farthest corners of the Fertile Crescent. From northern Mesopotamia to the Baltic Sea, the pharaohs of Egypt had established themselves as the social and economic leaders of the civilized world, ruling an area more than 2,000 miles in length. The military superiority of the Egyptian army demonstrated its ability to subdue the threat of resistance, maintaining a hegemony that extended from the Nubians to the Hyksos. But, in the final analysis, it was the influence of the gods of Egypt, with their magic, myths, and rituals, that provided the Egyptians with a lasting place in history and led the following generations into an immense, enlightening description of the ancient mythologies, including a wealth of information regarding the dynamics and supernatural possibilities of paganism.

Facts about Atum (Ra), Osiris, and Isis

Prehistoric Egyptians believed in the same fundamental idea that most evolutionists subscribe to today, the premise that the oceans both preceded, and, in some way, contributed to the creation of the living cosmos. From the Fifth Dynasty Pyramid Texts, the Heliopolitan theory of creation stated that Atum (the sun god, Ra) independently created himself from a singular expression of self-will, an act visualized by the Egyptians as a divine egg that appeared upon the primordial waters of the all-filling ocean called Nun, out of which Atum (meaning "He who created himself"), emerged. According to myth, a second act of creation developed around

Thoth, by Brooke Townsend

a divine masturbation when Atum, the great "He-She," orally copulated himself and afterward regurgitated his children, Shu and Tefnut, who assumed the positions of god and goddess of air and moisture.

Later, when Shu and Tefnut became lost in the universal ocean of Nun, Atum exhibited his paternal care by sending out his Eye, which had the curious habit of detaching itself from Atum and thinking independent thoughts, to look for them. The Eye of Atum succeeded in finding the child gods and eventually returned to discover that Atum had grown impatient during the wait and had created a second eye. In order to placate the hostility that soon developed between the two divine eyes, Atum affixed the first eye upon his forehead where it was to oversee and rule the forthcoming world of creation. Thus, the Eye of Atum became the jealous, destructive aspect of the sun god Ra.

To avoid getting lost again in the all-filling waters of Nun, Shu and Tefnut procreated Geb (the earth), and Nut (the sky), and thus provided the more stable elements of earth, nature, and the seasons. Later, Geb was conceptualized as cohabiting with Nut and producing four children of his own: Seth, Osiris, Isis, and Nephthys. Of these, Osiris and Isis grew into such important cult deities that the mythology of the Egyptian religion was modified to support the claim that Osiris, with the help of his sister-wife Isis, had nearly overthrown and replaced Ra as the most powerful of the gods, an action that so enraged his brother Seth that the hateful and jealous sibling killed him.

Seth's murderous act was followed by the jackal-headed god, Anubis, assisting Isis with the embalming of her slain husband-brother Osiris, an act which secured the jackal god's position as "the god of embalming." Then, while still in mourning, Isis summoned the wisdom of Thoth, which she combined with her own proficient magical skills and produced a resurrected Osiris, who, in turn, impregnated her with Horus, the god of daylight. Horus promptly avenged his father's death by killing the evil brother Seth. Another version of the myth claims that Horus was born to Isis only after she impregnated herself with semen, which she took from the corpse of Osiris. Yet another story claims that Seth persuaded his brother Osiris to climb into a box, which he quickly shut and threw into the Nile. Osiris drowned and his body floated down the Nile River where it snagged on the limbs of a tamarisk tree. In Byblos, Isis recovered the body from the riverbank and took it into her care. In her absence, Seth stole the body again and chopped it into fourteen pieces, which he threw into the Nile. Isis searched the riverbank until she recovered every piece, except for the genitals, which had been swallowed by a fish (Plutarch says a crocodile). But Isis simply replaced the missing organ with a facsimile and was somehow able to reconstruct Osiris and impregnate herself with the ithyphallic corpse.

This portion of the Isis/Osiris myth probably developed over time in order to provide the legendary background necessary to sanction the kind of temple prostitution practiced during the rituals of Isis. Temple prostitutes represented the human manifestation of the goddess and were available for ritual sex as a form of imitative magic. Much of the details are no longer available, but it appears these prostitutes usually began their services to the goddess as a child and were deflowered at a very young age by a priest, or, as Isis was, by a carved phallus of the god Osiris. Sometimes prostitutes were chosen, on the basis of their beauty, as the sexual mates of the sacred temple bulls. Such bulls were considered the incarnation of Osiris. In other places, such as at Mendes, temple prostitutes were offered in coitus to divine goats.[9]

Regardless, from this time forward Osiris was considered the chief god of the deceased and the judge of the netherworld, the dark and dreary underworld region of the dead. In human form Osiris was perceived as a mummy and, paradoxically, while he was loved as the guarantor of life after death, he was feared as the demonic presence that decayed the bodies of the dead. Such necromantic worship of Osiris and Isis grew to become an important part of several Mediterranean religions, with the most famous cult center of Osiris at Abydos in Upper Egypt, where an annual festival reenacted his death and resurrection. In Abydos, Osiris was called the god of the setting sun, the mysterious "force" that ruled the region of the dead just beneath the western horizon. He was venerated in this way primarily because death, and specifically the fear of one's estate after death, grew to consume so much of Egyptian consciousness.

In the funerary texts, known as the *Book of the Dead*, the most elaborate magical steps were developed around the Osiris myth to assist the Egyptians with their journey into the afterlife. It was believed that every person had a *Ka*, a spiritual and invisible duplicate, and that such *Ka* accompanied them throughout eternity. Since the *Ka* provided each person with a resurrected body in the kingdom of the dead, but could not exist without the maintenance of the earthly body, every effort was made to preserve the human corpse. The body was, therefore, mummified according to the elaborate magic rituals passed down from Isis, who, according to legend, singularly perfected the rituals of mummification through her work on Osiris. Wooden replicas of the body were also placed in the tomb, as a kind of substitute in case the mummy was accidentally destroyed, and additional protection for the corpse was provided through the construction of ingenious burial tombs specifically designed to hide and preserve the human body for eternity. Finally, curses were placed throughout the tomb, as a warning against intruders.

At the death of the Egyptian, *Ka* departed from the human body and, accompanied by the hymns and prayers of the living, used the formulas memorized from the funerary texts to outsmart the horrible demons seeking to impede the *Ka's* progress into the kingdom (or hall) of Osiris. Arriving at the judgment hall, the heart of the *Ka* was "weighed in the balance" by Osiris and his forty-two demons. If they found the deceased lacking in virtue, he was condemned to an eternity of hunger and thirst. If the *Ka* was determined to have belonged to an outright "sinner," it was cut to pieces and fed to Ammit, the miserable little goddess and "eater of souls." But if the deceased was judged to have lived a virtuous life, the *Ka* was granted admission into the heavenly fields of Yaru, where foods were abundant and pleasures unending. The only toil in this heaven was to serve in the grain fields of Osiris, and even this could be obviated by placing substitutionary statues, called *shawabty,* into the tomb.

There is some evidence that the forty-two demons or 'judges" of Osiris were in some way related to the prehistoric legend of the Watchers, the mysterious angelic beings who first appeared in the early cultures of the Middle East. The Egyptian people originally migrated from the biblical land of Shin'ar, which means the "Land of the Watchers." The Egyptians called it *Ta Neter,* the Land of the Watchers "from which the gods came into Egypt." As mentioned in Chapter One, it's possible that a historical event occurred giving birth to the legend of the Watchers, and references to a race of "watcher/gods" who cohabited with women and sought to control the human race is attested to by numerous ancient texts. The Sumerian scribes referred to the watchers as *Anunnaki,* who, they said, "came from Nibiru" to judge/rule the inhabitants of the earth. Some have interpreted Nibiru as "a distant planet," but the actual translation is, "Those Who from Heaven to Earth Came." In the Bible, references are made to the Anakim and to the Nephilim, which also means "those who came from Heaven to Earth." In the *Book of the Dead,* there are prayers for deliverance from the Watchers (Tchatcha, the princes of Osiris), who came from Ta-Ur, the "Far Away Land," and in the Book of Jubilees, also known as the Apocalypse of Moses, the Watchers are compared to the "supernatural beings" mentioned in Genesis 6 as having come down from heaven to cohabit with women, a union ultimately leading to the birth of the giants. The Apocryphal Book of Enoch also associates the creatures of Genesis 6 with the Watchers.

We read:

And I, Enoch, was blessing the Lord of majesty and the King of the ages, and lo! the Watchers called me, Enoch the scribe, and said to me: Enoch, thou scribe of righteousness, go, declare to the Watchers of the heaven who have left the high heaven, the holy eternal place, and have defiled themselves with women, and have done as the children of earth do, and have taken unto themselves wives: Ye have wrought great destruction on the earth: And ye shall have no peace nor forgiveness of sin: and inasmuch as they delight themselves in their children, The murder of their beloved ones shall they see, and over the destruction of their children shall they lament, and shall make supplication unto eternity, but mercy and peace shall ye not attain. (1 Enoch 10:3–8)

From the *Dead Sea Scrolls*, we learn that only 200 of the larger group of powerful angels called "Watchers" ever departed from the higher Heavens and sinned. Thus, Enoch referred to the Watchers in the High Heavens as separate from the ones on earth. The fallen class of Watchers is considered by some to be the creatures referred to in the Book of Jude as the "angels which kept not their first estate, but left their own habitation…[and are] reserved in everlasting chains under darkness unto the judgment of the great day" (Jude 6, brackets added). In either case, it appears the early Egyptian scribes believed that leaders from among the fallen Watchers had become the underworld demons of

Isis, by Brooke Townsend

Osiris whose "terrible knives" exacted judgment upon the *Ka* of the wicked. The Egyptians were desperately afraid of these netherworld "watchers," and a significant amount of time was spent determining how to placate the judgment of Osiris and his forty-two demons. The worship of Isis, the sister-wife of Osiris, thus became integral.

As one of the most important goddesses of ancient mythology, Isis was venerated by the Egyptians, Greeks, and the Romans, as the "goddess of a thousand names," and as the undisputed queen of magical skills. Her enchantments were so powerful that she even forced the reluctant sun god Ra to reveal his most secret name. She accomplished this by conjuring a magic serpent that bit the sun god, a reptile whose venom was so potent that it brought Ra to the point of death, thus he surrendered his hidden and powerful name to the goddess. In response, Isis uttered secret words that drove the serpent's poison from Ra's body. Afterward, the victorious goddess celebrated by adding Ra's powerful and hidden name to her archive of divine words.

Such magic words (of Isis) were considered by the Egyptians to be of the highest importance for the preparation and navigation of this world and the afterlife. This was because Isis not only possessed secret words, but she instructed her followers how, when, and with what vocal tones they were to be uttered. If the proper words were pronounced perfectly—at the right time of day and with the proper ceremony, they would have the effect of altering reality, manipulating the laws of physics, and forcing the being or object to which they were directed into compliance, including evil spirits.

An example of this form of magic is found in the *Theban Recension* of the *Book of the Dead* and depicts Isis providing a spell for controlling the forty-two demons of Osiris. The formula consisted of an amulet made of carnelian that had been soaked in the water of ankhami flowers. It was supposed to be placed around the neck of the dead person, in combination with the spoken words of magic. If performed properly, it would empower the *Ka* of the individual to enter into the region of the dead under the protection of Isis, where the *Ka* would thereafter move about whenever it wanted without fear of the forty-two demons of Osiris. The only Egyptian who did not benefit from this spell was the Pharaoh, and for a very good reason. Although Pharaoh was considered to be the "son of the sun god" (Ra) and the incarnation of the falcon god Horus during his lifetime, he was considered, at death, to have become the Osiris, the divine judge of the netherworld. On earth, Pharaoh's son and predecessor would take his place as the newly anointed manifestation of Horus, and, thus, each new generation of the pharaohs provided the gods with a divine spokesman for the present world and the afterlife.

JUDGMENT OF THE EGYPTIAN GOD KING

While conducting a recent tour of Egypt and the Holy Land, Donald C. Jones (Ph.D. in Biblical History and contributing author of this book), stood outside the Great Pyramid in Giza and pondered what it must have been like to be an Egyptian Pharaoh. As the divine son of Ra, Pharaoh was the earthly representative of the supreme god of cosmic deities; in short, Pharaoh was god on earth. Dr. Jones wondered what the children of Israel must have thought when Moses challenged the mighty arm of a ruler whose kingdom was so vast and powerful. Who would "take on" the leader of a people capable of building a single structure over thirty times larger than the Empire State Building? The Great Pyramid was built over 4,500 years ago of more than 2,000,000 blocks of stone weighing between 2 and 60 tons each, by builders whose knowledge of the earth and the planetary systems was so advanced that the Great Pyramid faces true North, South, East, and West, while also standing at the exact center of the Earth's land mass and at a height exactly that of the earth's mean sea level. One would understand how the leader of such a people would have easily been considered by the ancients as a god on earth.

Dr. Jones in Egypt

Whereas most scholars believe that the Great Pyramid, the last standing monument of the Seven Wonders of the Ancient World, was built around the year 2560 B.C., by Khufu (Cheops), the Pharaoh of the Fourth Egyptian Dynasty, and that Moses probably challenged the pharaoh, known as Ramses II, many other testaments, temples, and pyramids, have survived to reveal that each of the Pharaohs were, in their respective times (at least in the mind of the average Egyptian), the undisputed god-kings of planet earth. Nevertheless, God instructed Moses to go "unto Pharaoh...[and] bring forth my people the children of Israel out of Egypt" (Exod. 3: 10, brackets added). One of the main reasons for the Exodus narrative was, I believe, the historical opportunity for the Hebrew God to reveal Himself as more powerful than the Egyptian gods. In other words, the great "I AM" not only wanted to deliver His people from the Egyptian bondage, but He wanted to "execute judgment" against "all the gods of Egypt" (Exod. 12:12). Numbers 33:4 says, "For the Egyptians buried all their firstborn, which the Lord had smitten among them: upon their gods also the Lord executed judgments."

Thus Yahweh manifested his superiority over Osiris, Isis, Pharaoh, and the various other gods assigned to protect the famous Egyptians. Dr. Jones says, "It would be a mistake to overlook the fact that, taken individually, each plague of the Exodus stands alone as a specific judgment of a particular Egyptian god; while, viewed collectively, the plagues of the Exodus illustrate God's supremacy over, and his attitude toward, the corporate sphere of the gods of mythology."

The Plagues of Exodus

Let's consider a brief overview of the plagues of the Exodus, and their respective condemnations of the Egyptian gods.

1. The Nile Plague

And the Lord spake unto Moses, Say unto Aaron, Take thy rod, and stretch out thine hand upon the waters of Egypt....

that they may become blood...and Moses and Aaron did so, as the Lord commanded; and he lifted up the rod, and smote the waters that were in the river, in the sight of Pharaoh, and in the sight of his servants; and all the waters that were in the river were turned to blood. (Exod. 7: 19–20)

Why would Yahweh turn the Nile into blood? Because the Nile was worshiped as the single most important element needed for the ongoing success of the culture, economy, and paganism of the Egyptian people. The annual flooding of the Nile brought new life and sustenance to over 1,000 miles of Egyptian-dominated settlements, and the watery event was perceived by the Egyptians as the best evidence that the gods of the Nile were pleased. When the Hebrew God challenged the welfare and divinity of the Nile River, He was striking a blow at the core of the Egyptian's faith and pantheon.

First, the waters of the Nile were considered sacred. Blood, on the other hand, was considered an abhorrence to the Egyptian people. The Nile River was supposedly protected from the contamination of human blood and other such impurities by the fearsome ram-headed god, Khnum, who consorted with Sati, the goddess of Elephantine, as the dispenser and protector of the cool waters. Secondly, the Nile was "possessed" by the spirit of Hapi, the son of Horus, who was often depicted as a corpulent man with the breasts of a female (representing the abundance and succoring of the Nile) and was honored as the god who, through using the silt and waters of the Nile, provided the abundant fertility of the land of Egypt. At other times, Hapi was depicted as a mummified man with the head of a baboon, a portrayal in which he was considered the guardian of the lungs of the deceased and the Nile-servant of Osiris. Keeping Osiris happy was important to the welfare of the Nile, because the origin of the Nile was not known in ancient times (the central African location was not discovered until 1862) and the Nile's origin was considered by the Egyptians to be the spiritual bloodstream, or divine "life flow," of the netherworld, Osiris.

Turning the Nile into blood was thus, in part, a mockery of the Osiris blood myth by the Hebrew God, Yahweh. Thirdly, the fish of the Nile were considered sacred and were supposedly protected by two powerful goddesses Hathor, the goddess of the sky and the queen of heaven (who protected the *chromis* or "small fish"), and Neith, the very ancient goddess of war who protected the *lates* (large fish), which were also considered to be her children. Neith was a powerful Egyptian deity, the sister of Isis, and the protectress of Duamutef, the god who watched over the inner stomach of the dead. More importantly, she was the mother of the Nile-god Sobek, an evil god with the head of a crocodile, to whom Pharaoh may have "offered" the Hebrew male children when he commanded the midwives to throw them into the Nile. (Exod. 1:22)

Another Nile crocodile god, Apepi, was the archrival of the sun god Ra, and may have been one of the "serpents" who appeared before Pharaoh and Moses in Exodus 7:10–12. We read, "And...Aaron cast down his rod before Pharaoh...and it became a serpent [*tanniym*, dragon or crocodile]...the magicians of Egypt, they also did in like manner with their enchantments...and they became serpents [*crocodiles*, Sobek and Apepi?]: but Aaron's rod swallowed up their rods." Since the word *tanniym* is not translated "serpent" anywhere else in Scripture, Dr. Jones believes, as do many other Bible scholars, that *tanniym* should be interpreted as dragons or "crocodiles" in the Book of Exodus, as it was thus translated throughout the Books of Isaiah and Ezekiel. Either way, by turning the Nile River into blood, no less than nine separate deities were judged by the Hebrew God and found to be inferior and under His authority; the Nile River, Khnum, Sati, Hapi, Osiris, Hathor, Neith, Sobek, and Apepi. Through the first plague Yahweh confirmed that He alone is the supplier of every human need, and the true Judge of the afterlife and only Sovereign of destiny.

2. The Frog Plague

> And the Lord spake unto Moses, Go unto Pharaoh, and say unto him, Thus saith the Lord, Let my people go.... And if

thou refuse to let them go, behold, I will smite all thy borders with frogs: And the river shall bring forth frogs abundantly.... And Aaron stretched out his hand over the waters of Egypt; and the frogs came up, and covered the land of Egypt. (Exod. 8: 1–3; 6)

When I was a young Christian I had an interesting experience during a time of intercessory prayer. I was fasting and praying for the salvation of a member of my wife's family when suddenly the image of a frog appeared in my mind's eye. The vision startled me, because it was unexpected and powerful. No matter how I tried, I could not shake the uncanny feeling that a "frog" was resisting my prayer. It had the appearance of a typical river frog, but it stared at me as if to warn me that I had wandered into its territory and that it was fully intending to defend its position within the life of the person for whom I was praying. After a while, it became obvious that whatever or whomever the frog creature was, it was not going away, so I rebuked it "in the name of Jesus," and it immediately vanished! Sometime later, I was amazed to discover that certain demons can appear as images of frogs. In the Book of Revelation, we read: "And I saw three unclean spirits like frogs come out of the mouth of the dragon, and out of the mouth of the beast, and out of the mouth of the false prophet" (Rev. 16:13). My experience had been genuine, and, over time, helped me to understand that the Hebrew depiction of frogs as unclean animals was perhaps based on an ancient and spiritual revelation from Yahweh.

To the ancient Egyptians, however, frogs were sacred animals, and, ultimately, the infants of the frog-goddess Heka. Heka played an important role in the development of infants, including humans, beginning at the embryonic stage and continuing up until childbirth. She was, thus, an important patroness of midwives and a powerful goddess of fertility. As the wife of Khnum, she assisted in the original creation of mankind and was closely associated with Hapi, who held the divine frog in his hands as the waters of nourishment flowed from her mouth.

When the *krur* (frogs) increased along the banks of the river during the annual receding of the Nile, it was perceived by the Egyptians as a good Heka omen. It's easy to see how the Plague of the Frogs was a substantial embarrassment to the Egyptians, to have the frog-goddess babies so multiplied that one could not walk upon the ground or move within the house without squashing the divine creatures beneath their feet. Pharaoh could not order the Hebrew slaves to destroy and haul the frogs away, as it was a capital offense to kill a frog in Egypt! How powerful the Hebrew Creator-God must have appeared, compared to the stupidity and stench of the creator-frog goddess, as her infants lay rotting in massive filthy heaps, covering nearly every square inch of Pharaoh's Egyptian empire. Through the plague of the frogs, the mystical power (in the chapter on Greece we shall discuss how Heka was associated with Hekate, the Greek goddess of mysticism and witchcraft) of Heka was reduced to nothing more than a greasy pavement crushed to death beneath the feet of the sorrowful Egyptians.

3. Plague of Lice

> And the Lord said unto Moses, Say unto Aaron, Stretch out thy rod, and smite the dust of the land, that it may become lice throughout all the land of Egypt. And they did so; for Aaron stretched out his hand with his rod, and smote the dust of the earth, and it became lice in man, and in beast; all the dust of the land became lice throughout all the land of Egypt. (Exod. 8:16–17)

Four distinct facts stand out in the plague of the lice: First, the priests of Egypt were immaculate regarding their purifications. Discovering a single louse would have rendered an Egyptian priest unclean, and, as such, incapable of ministering in the temple. The shutdown of the priestly ministry would have been no small matter, as the priesthood numbered in the thousands of men who maintained a strict regimen of daily ministering, bathing, shaving, and sacred purification. Such priests exercised great influence over the common Egyptians, and were considered the uppermost servants of the gods, the "consecrated ones" who carried out the required daily ceremonies of the hundreds of Egyptian temples deemed necessary for the ongoing functionality of the local community. The religious duties of the priests included two main categories: 1) carrying about the little shrines or oracles (small replica temples containing statues of the gods) which were made available to the common people (those who could not enter beyond the veil); and, 2) performing the mystery rituals in the inner sanctums or "holy of holies" of the temples. The difference between the two priestly categories was that the portable gods were publicly available to nod their heads and speak (it's been suggested that the priests spoke for the idols while moving their mouths with a string) while the mystery functions of the priesthood were highly secretive and included the important creation rituals conducted in the inner sanctums of the main temples, like those of Amun-Ra at Karnak, where a priestess known as the "hand of god" performed ritual masturbations on the priests as a form of imitative magic (referring to the Atum masturbation/creation myth). This practice was considered necessary for the ongoing balance of nature, the annual flooding of the Nile, and regulating the seasons.

Moses was a man "learned in [such] wisdom of the Egyptians" (Acts 7:22). As such, he was aware of, and may have been trained in, the mysteries of the Egyptian priesthood. It's even possible that Moses served as an Egyptian priest. The name Moses means to be "drawn out of" or "born of" and was usually associated with a priestly Egyptian deity, i.e., Thothmoses (born of Thoth), Amenmosis (born of Amen), or Rameses (born of Ra). The slight variations of the spelling of Moses (mosis, meses, etc.) did not change the priestly Egyptian meaning. This has caused some scholars to conclude that the Hebrew Moses may have been named after a Nile deity by the Pharaoh's daughter (Exodus 2:10), and that he served as an Egyptian priest who later dropped his Nile deity-name reference upon encountering the omnipotent Yahweh, the

God of his fathers. Whether or not that's true, Moses was raised in the Pharaoh's court, thus he had a special understanding of the far-reaching ramifications of the plague of the lice. Moses understood that when every micro-particle of dust began to crawl upon the Egyptians, the priesthood was ceremonially unclean, and thus immobilized. The masturbation mysteries of Karnak could not be performed. The portable gods could not walk and talk. The seasons could not bring forth their blessings. While this kind of reasoning may seem simplistic, such imitative magic, as performed by the Egyptian priesthood, was central to the Egyptian way of life and was considered of the highest importance.

The second point of interest concerning the plague of the lice involves the fact that Pharaoh was supposedly the incarnation of Horus and the son of the Sun god Ra. He was, thus, god incarnate. The dust of Egypt was, therefore, holy ground. To say the least, it was a serious slap in Pharaoh's face for the Hebrew God to transform the sacred dust of Ra into lice.

The third notable point concerning the plague of the lice is that the magicians (priests) of Egypt could not duplicate the miracle, as they had duplicated the first two plagues. The Hebrew God was perhaps illustrating that He alone has the ability to create life out of the dust of the earth. Even the magicians testified, "This is the finger of God" (Exodus 8: 19).

Fourth, Geb (earth) was the god who protected the soil, while Seth was, among other things, the angry god of the desert sand. In the Osiris myth, it was Seth who raged against the other gods in his bid to become the greatest among the Egyptian pantheon. In the plague of the lice, Yahweh was perhaps mocking the Egyptian religion by causing the dust god, Seth, to literally struggle against Geb, Ra, and Osiris, while leaving the Egyptians to suffer as collateral casualties.

4. Plague of Flies

And the Lord said unto Moses, Rise up early in the morning, and stand before Pharaoh...and say unto him, Thus saith the

Lord...if thou wilt not let my people go, behold, I will send swarms of flies upon thee, and upon thy servants, and upon thy people, and into thy houses...and the Lord did so; and there came a grievous swarm of flies...and...the land was corrupted [destroyed] by reason of the swarm of flies. (Exodus 8:20–24, brackets added).

The beetle was known in Egypt as a fly. The scarab beetle was the sacred emblem of the sun god Ra and was the symbol of eternal life. But the flies of the forth plague were most likely a bloodsucking breed that spread blindness and disease among the populace that lived along the Nile. Whereas such flies were generally disliked by the Egyptians, they were, nevertheless, revered as the servants (demons?) of Vatchit, the Egyptian "lord of the flies." In this context, it's possible that the Hebrew God was administering a threefold judgment: first, of the Egyptians for their veneration of the fly-deities; second, of the sun god Ra, the Egyptian almighty creator; and third, of Vatchit himself, the Egyptian equivalent of Baalzebub (Beelzebub), the ancient god who, according to various eastern religions, was the evil god and "lord of the flies."

The name Baalzebub originally derived from two different words: *Baal* (lord, master), and *zebub* (of flies). While the original meaning is unclear and may have referred to a certain priestly interpretation of the flight path of flies as an oracular communication between a Baal and his followers, some have pointed out that flies are present at decaying bodies, and thus Baal-zebub may have been a kind of Baal-Osiris; a lord-demon of the human corpse.

According to the *Grimorium Verum* and the *Grand Grimoire* (18th century textbooks on magic), Baalzebub manifested himself in the image of a huge fly whenever he was summoned by the sorcerer.[10] Whether Baalzebub, like Vatchit, commanded the flies to do his bidding, or delivered from their nuisance, is unclear. Additionally, since the title "Baal" referred to any lord, deity, or human master, there were many gods of antiquity known as a Baal; i.e. Baal-berith (lord of the covenant), Baal-Gad (lord of the fortune), Baal-hazor (lord of the village), and so on. That some Baals were worshiped by the Egyptians is known from the titles of certain Egyptian provinces; i.e. Baalze-phon ("Baal-of-the-North" or "Hidden Place") of Exodus 14:2. In times of great distress, it was usually a Baal that was called upon for help, and people who sought material prosperity believed their lives could be improved by offering their firstborn child as a sacrifice to the deity. The Greek author Kleitarchos recorded the dastardly process of sacrificing infants to Baal three hundred years before Christ:

> Out of reverence for Kronos [Baal], the Phoeniciens, and especially the Carthaginians, whenever they sought to obtain some great favor, vowed one of their children, burning it as a sacrifice to the deity, if they were especially eager to gain success. There stands in their midst a bronze statue of Kronos, its hands extended over a bronze brazier, the flames of which engulf the child. When the flames fall on the body, the limbs contract and the open mouth seems almost to be laughing [such areas of child sacrifice were often called "the place of laughing"], until the contracted body slips quietly into the brazier. (brackets added)

The sacrifice of babies to Baal was widespread in antiquity and was practiced by the children of Israel under the reign of King Ahab and Queen Jezebel. A recent archeological find illustrated how far-reaching such offerings were. It unearthed the remains of over 20,000 infants who had been sacrificed to a single Baal. Ahaziah, King of Israel, may have authorized such a child sacrifice when he sent messengers to the Philistine city of Ekron to inquire of the fly-god whether he (the king) would recover from his illness. Yahweh intervened and instructed Elijah to prophesy to the King:

> Thus saith the Lord, Forasmuch as thou hast sent messengers to inquire of Baalzebub the god of Ekron, is it not because there is no God in Israel to inquire of his word? Therefore thou shalt not come down off that bed on which thou art gone up, but shall surely die. (2 Kings 1:16)

The Hebrews acknowledged Baalzebub as Satan's highest power and often referred to him as Beelzeboul, "lord of the height," a classification in which he was depicted as the dark atmospheric god who controlled the cosmos, or circumambient "air." Baalzebub eventually developed into a demon-god of such evil reputation that he became known as "the prince of devils" (Matt. 12:24). Milton referred to Baalzebub in *Paradise Lost* as Satan's chief lieutenant, and, in the litanies of the witches' Sabbath, Baalzebub is ranked, together with Lucifer and Leviathan, as an equal member of the supreme trinity of evil. The mocking of Vatchit, as the Egyptian equivalent of Baalzebub, and, thus, as the ultimate manifestation of evil, may have been what the Hebrew God had in mind during the plague of the flies.

5. The Deadly Murrain

> Then the Lord said unto Moses, Go in unto Pharaoh, and tell him, Thus saith the Lord God of the Hebrews, Let my people go, that they may serve me. For if thou refuse to let them go.... Behold, the hand of the Lord is upon thy cattle which is in the field...there shall be a very grievous murrain. (Exodus 9: 1–3)

The first chapter showed how, down through the ages, Satan distorted the various aspects of the Original Revelation of God. The sacred Apis bull of Egypt was a perfect example of such plagiarism in that the Apis bull was a demonization of the life of Jesus, especially of the protoevangelium, the biblical promise of an immaculately born Son of God, who would also be God in flesh. (See Gen. 3:15; Isa. 7:14) Cattle, and especially the Apis bull, were sacred to the Egyptians.

But the Apis bull (also known as Serapis or Osorapis) was special in that it was supposedly born of a miraculous conception when, every twenty-five years, divine moonlight (or lightning) struck a cow and it conceived. The Apis bull was thus considered to be the incarnation of god on earth. During its life span, the Apis was worshipped as both the son, and incarnation, of Ptah, the Universal Architect god. As Ptah incarnate, the Apis embodied the Egyptian logos god who created, according to a later version of the Egyptian creation myth (the Memphite cosmology), all of creation by the authority of his spoken word. In death the Apis supposedly experienced a "resurrection" with Osiris, and thus the Apis bull, identified with Osiris, was a remarkable parallel of the Christian Messiah.

For practical reasons, the Apis bull was, for the most part, kept in seclusion. The Egyptian priests cared for the sacred animal and worked with a team of doctors and nutritionists to maintain the bull's health. At the end of the twenty-five-year cycle, a new bull was chosen with the pomp and ceremony of royalty. A celebration followed the selection and, for a period of forty days thereafter, the Egyptian women raised their dresses and exposed themselves to the bull. Such exposure was thought to capture the fertility energies of the Apis, and to excite the life-giving waters of Osiris. It was also believed that a special generational blessing came upon the exposed women's offspring. At the end of the forty days of "exposure," the new bull was removed to the Apis temple in Memphis where it was kept in a special sanctuary. It was thereafter publicly displayed during special occasions only. We find the Apis sanctuary mentioned in, *The Geography of Strabo* (63 B.C., A.D. 26):

> Memphis itself, the royal residence of the Aegyptians [Egyptians], is also near Babylon; for the distance to it from the Delta is only three schoeni. It contains temples, one of which is that of Apis, who is the same as Osiris; it is here that the bull Apis is kept in a kind of sanctuary, being regarded, as I have said, as god.[11] (brackets added)

Once the new Apis was inaugurated, the old bull was drowned, mummified, mourned, and placed into a huge sarcophagus. The burial rites of the passing bull were so revered and costly that they were paralleled in Egypt only by those of the Pharaoh. The comprehensive nature of such Apis burial rituals was illustrated in 1851, when 60 Apis sarcophagi of red and black granite weighing more than 60 tons each were discovered in Saqqara, just west of Memphis, where the Apis temple stood.

I once took notes on, and photographed, the mummified head of one such bull. It was obvious from the detail and craftsmanship, that great reverence was given to the animal during the mummification process. Especially impressive were the elaborate glass eyes that had been placed into the eye sockets, and the golden sun-disk of Ra that rested between the horns. Such golden discs were similar to the moon-discs worn by other members of the divine bovine family, including those donned by Hathor, the cow-goddess-mother of the sun god, Ra. While other religions have practiced similar veneration of cattle, most notably Hinduism in India where the humped Zebu cow continues to be worshipped as the representative of Aditi, the "sinless cow," nowhere was the deification of such animals more noteworthy than in Egypt.

The ancient Egyptians considered all cattle to be sacred sources of generative power, and the cults of Apis and Hathor thus set the standards of eastern myth and ritual. This fact has caused the plague of the deadly murrain to be considered an especially effective grievance, as, in a single move, it repudiated the six most important aspects of the Apis cult: 1)

Sekhmet, by Brooke Townsend

it devastated the protected livestock of the Egyptians including the vast herds of Pharaoh; 2) it illustrated God's unlimited power when, miraculously, none of the Hebrew cattle died; 3) it humiliated the Universal Architect god, Ptah, and exposed him as a helpless demon; 4) it destroyed the dominion of the sacred Apis and Mnevis bulls of Heliopolis; 5) it judged the goddess Hathor, and the god Osiris, and found them to be inferior; and 6) it nullified the generational blessings of Apis-Osiris (Serapis). Amazingly, after all of this evidence, the foolish heart of Pharaoh was hardened against the Hebrew God.

6. The Plague of Boils

> And the Lord said unto Moses and unto Aaron, Take to you handfuls of ashes of the furnace, and let Moses sprinkle it toward the heaven in the sight of Pharaoh. And it shall become small dust in all the land of Egypt, and shall be a boil breaking forth with blains upon man, and upon beast, throughout all the land of Egypt. (Exod. 9:8–9)

During the third Egyptian Dynasty, at least 1,000 years before the Exodus, a man named Imhotep served as the vizier of the Pharaoh Zoser. Imhotep was an engineering genius and built the first-known massive stone structures, including the great Step-Pyramid (still standing) at Saqqara. From history, we learn that Imhotep's well-founded distinction as a builder was surpassed only by his talent as a skilled magician and healer. When the Egyptians suffered under a seven-year famine that occurred during the reign of Zoser, the king appealed to Imhotep, who in turn consulted the sacred books.

After several days, Imhotep emerged from isolation and announced to the king "the hidden wonders, the way to which had been shown to no king for unimaginable ages." Zoser, impressed with Imhotep's discernment, obeyed the divinations. Simultaneously, Egypt withdrew from the famine and Imhotep was decreed the chief Kheri-heb priest ("son of Ptah") of Egypt. But the popularity of Imhotep's life eventually

THE GODS WHO WALKED AMONG THE EGYPTIANS

gave way to the fame that followed his death, as, later he was elevated, deified, and transformed into a healing god. By the time of the reign of the Pharaoh Menkaure (2600 B.C.), temples throughout Egypt were dedicated to the god Imhotep. Such temples contained incubation or "sleeping" chambers used in the convalescence of the sick and the mentally diseased, and the same became acknowledged as the most potent healing alchemies of Egypt. The incubation-temple of Imhotep at Memphis, for instance, proved to be so popular that the Greeks identified Imhotep with Asclepius, the Greek god of healing, and affirmed his divine membership within the powerful Egyptian "trinity" composed of Imhotep, Ptah, and Sekhmet the lion-headed goddess.

It's said that Imhotep convinced the Egyptians that premature forms of sickness and disease could be ultimately avoided if the proper aspects of healing-magic were carefully employed. The magicians of Imhotep used the magic crystals and incantations of Isis to call upon Sekhmet, the goddess-sovereign of epidemics and diseases, to work with the positive energies of Serapis in the administration of the healing needs of the Egyptians. Such rituals were often accompanied by burnt offerings (sometimes human), and the ashes of the same were sprinkled into the air as a health-blessing for the Egyptians. At other times, the diagnosis called for an extended stay in the temple of Serapis where the sick or injured person was placed under the mystical spell of the katoche. Such katoche supposedly provided the internal coercion of the god and ultimately led to the proper diagnosis, and divine assimilation, of the transmissible and healing energies of the god. The katoche, affiliated with Imhotep's sleep-wizardry, was linked to the mystical crystals of Isis. These, in turn, were joined with Sekhmet's administration of the overall life-giving energies of Ptah and Osiris. Combined, they provided the Egyptian magicians with the powerful and esoteric tools necessary for the overall health (?) of the people. Such magic was, indeed, powerful, and the fame of such men and magic Oannes and Jambres) continued up until the time of the New Testament (2 Tim. 3:8). When the Hebrew God attacked the divine health of the Egyptians by placing a filthy, eruptive disease of boils upon the population, He accomplished what no other surrounding power had attempted to do: 1) He sent the respected Egyptian magicians fleeing, powerless, before Moses—unclean and unable to perform their priestly duties; 2) He illustrated the inferiority of the Egyptian high gods, Ptah and Osiris, and denounced them as helpless demons; 3) He judged the lion-headed goddess Sekhmet and demonstrated her impotence at regulating diseases; 4) He altered the ritual of "casting ashes" and made the ashes a curse instead of a blessing; and 5) He mocked the temples of Imhotep and Serapis, and, thereby, notified the surrounding nations that neither crystals, nor psychic dreams, nor positive energies, nor coercions of men and their gods, can defy the incontestable will of Yahweh.

Seth, by Brooke Townsend

7. The Plague of Hail

And the Lord said unto Moses...Behold, tomorrow about this time I will cause it to rain a very grievous hail, such as hath not been in Egypt since the foundation thereof even until now.... So there was hail, and fire mingled with the hail, very grievous.... And the hail smote throughout all the land of Egypt all that was in the field, both man and beast; and the hail smote every herb of the field, and brake every tree of the field. (Exodus 9:13; 18; 23–25)

The goddess Nut was the Egyptian protectress of the sky and weather, and was depicted in Egyptian art as a woman arched over the earth, with the stars above her back and the earth (her brother Geb) beneath her belly. She was the consort of Osiris, the "blesser" of crops and fertility, and was cherished as the caring mother "sky-goddess" by the agricultural people of the Fertile Crescent. According to myth, Nut elevated herself each morning upon her fingers and toes and thereby provided an expanse between herself and Geb/earth. The spherical covering generated by Nut's towering action allowed the sun god Amun-Ra to coat the earth with light, and the warmth of the new day was received as a blessing of the goddess. At night, when Nut lay down, the expanse closed anew, and darkness covered the earth. To the Egyptians, this was the natural order of things. But when violent storms erupted and the daytime skies were darkened, the same was perceived as a disturbance in the original cosmic scheme.

Nut was displeased with such nonconforming weather, and, at times, the skies grew red with the blood of her wounds (other myths define the red skies as Nut's menstrual period) as she struggled against the storm to restore the cosmic rhythm. For the sake of her people, the Egyptians, Nut bravely fought to maintain the essential universal cycle. Both men and gods depended on the cycle of Nut. Amun-Ra needed her expanse to visit the earth each day. Seth needed the same to dry the desert sand. Osiris needed Nut's meteorological blessings to sustain the agriculture; and Pharaoh desired the sanctions of Nut for two essential reasons: first, she controlled the atmospheric conditions surrounding the Pharaoh's Egyptian empire, and second, she conquered the fierce storms that could herald the death of a king. For these and other reasons, Nut was particularly important to Egyptian devotions.

When the Hebrew God sent a storm of hail and fire "such as there was none like it in all the land of Egypt since it became a nation" (Exodus 9:24), He was repudiating the combined efforts of Nut, Geb, Amun-Ra, Osiris, and Pharaoh, to control the atmospheric conditions that befell the land of Egypt. A similar storm of fire mingled with hail is predicted to hit the earth again during the Great Tribulation. We read, "The first angel sounded, and there followed hail and fire mingled with blood, and they were cast upon the earth" (Rev. 8:7). Just as Pharaoh rejected Yahweh, embraced pagan idols, and hardened his foolish heart, modern men seem destined to repeat the same mistakes. We find "the rest of the men which were not killed by these plagues yet repented not of the works of their hands, that they should not worship devils, and idols of gold, and silver, and brass, and stone, and of wood" (Rev. 9:20). Such verses indicate a latter-day revival of idolatry, and provide the impetus for the last two chapters of this book, in which we discuss the prophetic and extensive aspects of modern paganism.

8. The Plague of Locusts

> Thus saith the Lord God of the Hebrews...if thou refuse to let my people go, behold, tomorrow will I bring the locusts into thy coast: And they shall cover the face of the earth, that one cannot be able to see the earth: and they shall eat the residue of that which is escaped, which remaineth unto you from the hail, and shall eat every tree which groweth for you out of the field. (Exodus 10:3–5)

The locust plague was an awesome spectacle and was one of the most feared pestilences of the ancient world. Such invasions darken the sky and destroy every green thing. An average locust can consume its weight in food daily, and can quickly amass an army of insects numbering in the hundreds of millions per square mile. In 1927, a few African locusts were spotted near a river in Timbuktu. Within three years, the whole of West Africa was besieged by the creatures. Eventually, locusts covered an area more than 2,000 miles wide-extending from Ethiopia and the Belgian Congo to the luxuriant farmlands of Angola. Finally, 14 years after the plague began, 5,000,000 square miles of Africa (an area twice the size of the United States!) had been destroyed by the locusts. In ancient times, the idea of such a calamity brought instant terror to the hearts of the vegetation-dependent Egyptians. To

THE GODS WHO WALKED AMONG THE EGYPTIANS

avoid defoliation created by Edipoda locusts and other living things, the Egyptians prayed to Sobek—the crocodile-headed god of animals and insects. As the son of Neith, Sobek was the underworld demon of the four elements (fire, earth, water, and air). At his cult center in Arsinoe (Crocodilopolis), where devotees cared for his sacred crocodiles, Sobek was ritually associated with Ra (fire), Geb (earth), Osiris (water), and Shu (air). It was believed that Sobek controlled such elements to the extent that he restrained the activity of certain creatures within specific habitats. Thus, Sobek limited the activity of a crocodile within water, a locust within air, etc. His mastery of such elements was demonstrated in the Isis/Osiris myth, when Isis searched the Nile for the severed body parts of her husband/brother Osiris. Sobek, out of respect for the goddess, limited the appetite of the river animals, and thus spared the floating pieces of Osiris.

Sobek, by Brooke Townsend

As an Egyptian demon, Sobek was associated with the goddess Ammit—the crocodile-headed "eater of souls" that dwelt beneath the Scales of Justice in the judgment hall of Osiris. At other times, Sobek and Ammit were depicted as one and the same. In his book, *Egypt, Gift of the Nile,* Walter A. Fairservis, Jr. paraphrased a section of the *Book of the Dead.* In the following paragraph he describes Sobek in the role of Ammit:

> According to the book Meri would at last reach the place of the greatest test of all the Great Judgment Hall. Here in the presence of Osiris, King of the Dead, Anubis the embalmer, Thoth the ibis-headed scribe, and the forty-two gods of judgment, the

heart of Meri would be placed on the scales to be weighed with the "Feather of Truth." If Meri had been a bad man in life, no words or deeds could save him now. His heart would not balance the Feather of Truth, and Meri would be thrown to Sebek (Sobek), the crocodile-headed eater of souls.[12]

In another Sobek-related chapter of the *Book of the Dead*, "Making the Transformation Into The Crocodile-God," we read:

The Osiris Ani, whose word is truth, saith: I am the crocodile god [Sobek] who dwelleth amid his terrors. I am the Crocodile-god and I seize [my prey] like a ravening beast. I am the great Fish which is in Kamui. I am the lord to whom bowings and prostrations are made in Sekhem.

Such prostrations were made to Sobek along the Nile River and at his centers at Korn Ombo and Thebes. Sobek's oblations often included human sacrifices, and this may have been the Pharaoh's intention when he commanded the midwives to throw the Hebrew children into the Nile. The offerings anticipated Sobek's favor in delivering from bothersome insects, and, if a person wanted to eradicate an annoyance, such as locusts, he or she simply made supplications to Sobek while chanting, "To Sobek with it (the locust)!" The modern-day slang, "to Hell with it!" is a derivative of such a ritual.

It was undoubtedly against the demon-god Sobek, and his pestilence-protection rituals, that the Hebrew God initiated the relentless plague of the locusts. In so doing, Yahweh revealed that Sobek was unable to control the elements, or limit the activity of God's insect army. Sobek's companion, the high god Ra (of fire), could not scorch the creatures. Ra's son Shu, the Egyptian god of sun and wind (air), could not blow the consuming insects away.

It was not until the Hebrew God commanded "a mighty strong west wind, which took the locusts, and cast them into the Red sea"

(Exod. 10:19), that the grievous plague was ended. Even so, the heart of Pharaoh was hardened against the God of Israel.

9. The Plague of Darkness

> And the Lord said unto Moses, Stretch out thine hand toward heaven, that there may be darkness over the land of Egypt, even darkness which may be felt. And Moses stretched forth his hand toward heaven; and there was thick darkness in all the land of Egypt three days: They saw not one another, neither rose any from his place for three days: but all the children of Israel had light in their dwellings. (Exodus 10:21–23)

My research companion, Dr. Jones (I call him "Indy" after Indiana Jones), spoke recently of his trek through Hezekiah's Tunnel in Jerusalem. He described the interior of the cave as dominated by a darkness "that could be felt, compounded by feelings of claustrophobia, obscurity, and utter dejection." One can imagine the terrors that the Egyptians must have experienced when the Hebrew God devised a darkness that spread throughout "all the land of Egypt" and lasted for three days! Such an occurrence must have caused an unparalleled despondency, and most certainly would have devastated the Egyptian's religious idea that Amu n-Ra ("The Hidden One") was the incarnation of the midday sun, and the most powerful god in the Cosmos.

The Egyptians referred to Amun-Ra as "the king of the gods." They believed that no deity was superior to him, and that the whole of the pantheon would perish without his symmetry. The sun itself was considered "the Eye of Amun-Ra," and the light and warmth of the midday sun was perceived as the bath of his blessing. Amun-Ra was also called Khepri (the rising sun), and Atum (the setting sun), so that each position of the sun, rising, midday, and setting, was perceived as a posture of Amun-Ra. According to myth, Amun-Ra, like the Sumerian god "Utu" (Shamash), traversed the sky each day. At night, he journeyed through the underworld where the evil god Apepi attempted to prevent him from rising again. With the assistance of the magical masturbation rituals conducted by the Egyptian priests, Amun-Ra was empowered each night to conquer Apepi and become the Ra-Harachte, the bright and morning sun. His cult center at Thebes was the primary location of such rituals, and the same site boasted the largest religious structure ever built, the temple of Amun-Ra at Karnak. Interestingly, the great Temple of Amun-Ra (with its 100 miles of walls and gardens) was the primary object of fascination and worship by the nemesis of Moses, the Pharaoh of the Exodus, Ramses II. It was believed that each pharaoh, including Ramses II (who completed Amun-Ra's temple), reconciled his divinity in the company of Amun-Ra during the festival of Opet. The festival was held at the Temple of Luxor and included a procession of gods carried on barges up the Nile River from Karnak to the Temple. The royal family accompanied the gods on boats while the Egyptian laity walked along the shore, calling aloud and making requests of the gods. Once at Luxor, the Pharaoh and his entourage entered the holy of holies where the king joined his *Ka* (the mysterious ritual is unknown) and transmogrified into a living deity. Outside, large groups of dancers and musicians waited anxiously. When the king emerged "transformed" (supposedly), the crowd erupted in gaiety. From that day forward Egypt was "guarded" by their king and the Pharaoh was considered the son of the sun god—the earthly representative of the creator deity, Amun-Ra.

Subsequently, it was believed that the midday sun arose above Egypt because the Pharaoh had been honored and inaugurated in the Temple of Amun-Ra. If the sun was ever darkened or eclipsed, it was an evil omen for the king. Egypt's priests carefully interpreted such "signs," and even offered life-saving maneuvers to the Pharaoh. But, when three days of utter darkness paralyzed the Egyptians (Exodus 10:21–23), the number three being understood by the Hebrews and the Egyptians as representing divine providence, the king's magicians were uncharacteristically silent. Like the three hours of darkness that accompanied the death of Christ (Luke 23:44), the sovereignty of the Highest was believed to be at work. It would do no good to call upon the goddess Nut. She had been proven to be powerless before Yahweh. If the God of the Hebrews was at work, Nut could do nothing to elevate herself nor could she force the light of Amun-Ra to come forth. The sky-cow-goddess Hathor had been equally humiliated by Israel's Lord during the deadly murrain, and the evil god Sobek had been found impotent at controlling the element of sky. The mystical spells of Isis were useless against Yahweh. The priestly magic, paralyzed, and now, Amun-Ra, the Creator "king of the gods" and champion of the Egyptian pantheon, was confirmed helpless before the God of Hebrew slaves. "And Pharaoh called unto Moses, and said... Get thee from me, take heed to thyself, see my face no more; for in that day thou seest my face thou shalt die. And Moses said, Thou has spoken well, I will see thy face again no more" (Exodus 10:24; 28–29). With this final act, Pharaoh sealed the destiny of his kingdom, and, sadly, his firstborn son.

10. Death of the Firstborn

> And Moses said, Thus saith the Lord, About midnight will I go out into the midst of Egypt: And all the firstborn in the land of Egypt shall die, from the firstborn of Pharaoh that sitteth upon his throne, even unto the firstborn of the maidservant that is behind the mill; and all the firstborn of beasts. (Exodus 11:4–5)

At least six deities were committed to the protection of Egypt's children. They included Heka, the mystical frog-goddess, who oversaw the development of animals and children beginning at the embryonic stage; Isis, the advocate-mother of the children who kept her word; Min, the god of virility who conferred reproductive vigor upon men and who was ritually called upon to produce an heir to the pharaoh; Horus, the son of Isis and Osiris, who protected the Pharaoh's son; Bes, the patron protector of mothers and their children; and the Pharaoh himself—Egypt's protector incarnation of Amun-Ra and Horus. The female deities, Heka and Isis, oversaw different aspects of the children's physical development, while Min and Horus were the powerful male deities responsible for the spiritual progress and overall health of the child.

Min's full name was Menu-ka-mut-f ("Min, Bull of his Mother"), and he was often worshiped in the image of a white bull. At other times, Min was depicted is a bearded man with an oversized phallus. Such iconography of Min served to verify his position as the eminent Egyptian god of male sexuality, while also accounting for his mythological marriage to Qetesh the equivalent Egyptian deity of female sexuality. Egyptian boys supposedly acquired their sexual strength from Min, and subsequently made offerings of lettuce (considered an aphrodisiac by the Egyptians) to this god. The Greeks confused Min with Pan, the Dionystic god of unbridled sexual desire, and thus participated in the orgiastic festivals held in his honor. But the most important area of Min's dominion, insofar as the Pharaoh was concerned, was the mystical relationship between the god and the royal family, including Min's association with the princely heir of Egypt, the pharaoh's son. The pharaoh was so concerned with the blessings of Min that he ceremoniously hoed the lettuce fields during the festival of this god. The idea was to humble himself in the presence of Min and thereby procure divine favor and reproductive synergy. Sexual energy, such as was abundantly produced by Min, was believed to be synonymous with health and longevity. Thus, if the pharaoh and his son were to live long and prosperous lives, they required the favor of Min, the preeminent god of sexual power. Such power of Min would have likely been sought during the death of Egypt's firstborn.

Legend has it that the god Horus was also involved in guarding the pharaoh's son, due, in part, to the mythology that the child Horus had been subjected to rape by the evil god Seth. The adult Horus was, thus, protective of children in general. Equally important, Horus was believed to incarnate himself within the living pharaoh, and to fill the heart of the pharaoh with respect for the father. The virtue of such parental respect was an important part of ancestor ritual and referred to the story of Horus and his war with evil Seth over the murder of his father. Such myths supposedly contributed to the survival of the pharaoh and his son in two important ways: 1) Horus was the protector of the father and child, and perched above and behind the pharaoh, spreading his wings around and guarding the pharaoh's head (another plagiarism reminiscent of the Old Testament passage "in the shadow of Thy wings"); and 2) Horus reminded the royal son of his responsibilities toward the father, especially of the offerings to be made daily at the deceased father's tomb. Such offerings were deemed necessary for maintenance in the afterlife, and amulets (the eye of Horus) placed beside the offerings protected the stomach of the dead. In this way, the living pharaoh (Horus) served the needs of the deceased father, while the predecessor pharaoh conducted himself as the Osiris in the underworld.

In the classic film by Cecil B. DeMille, *The Ten Commandments*, Yul Brynner, in the role of the pharaoh, placed his firstborn son in the arms of the falcon-headed god, Seker (who protected the dead as they passed through the underworld), and said, "Seker, great lord of the lower world, I…bow before you now. Show that you have power above the God of Moses. Restore the life he has taken from my son. Guide back his soul across the lake of death to the place of living men." Ramses II undoubtedly prayed in such fashion for the life of his son. Nevertheless, "at midnight the Lord smote all the firstborn in the land of Egypt, from the firstborn of Pharaoh who sat on his throne unto the firstborn of the captive who was in the dungeon" (Exodus 12:29).

By initiating the death of the firstborn, Yahweh executed His final judgment "against all the gods of Egypt" (Exodus 12:12). Heka was proven powerless. Isis was defunct. Min was unable to energize the pharaoh's son. Horus was equally inept. The pharaoh was without a successor to watch over his tomb. Amun-Ra was without earthly representation. Egypt was without an heir, and the whole of the Egyptian pantheon, with its magic, myths, and rituals, crumbled at once beneath the feet of the Hebrew God. "And Pharaoh rose up in the night, he, and all his servants...for there was not a house where there was not one dead. And he called for Moses and Aaron by night, and said, Rise up, and get you forth from among my people, both ye and the children of Israel; and go, serve the Lord, as ye have said" (Exod. 12:30–31).

Important Notes Regarding the Gods of Egypt

The following notes on the Egyptian deities are important and relate to the last two chapters of the book.

From the example of Amun-Ra we learn: 1) prehistoric Egyptians believed in the same idea that evolutionists subscribe to today—the premise that the oceans preceded and in some way contributed to life on earth; 2) Amun-Ra was a self-existing primordial earth spirit; 3) Amun-Ra was associated with moisture spirits (Shu and Tefnut); 4) sacred prostitution was practiced at the Temple of Amun-Ra as a form of imitative magic; 5) the Eye of Amun-Ra (the sun) was considered a living part of "god"; and 6) the Egyptians treated nature "properly" in order to maintain the blessings of the nature spirits.

From the example of Geb we learn: l) Geb was the original Egyptian "Father Earth"; 2) his sister/wife Nu t was the original Egyptian "Mother Sky"; 3) the earth and sky spirits are the "parents" of humanity; and 4) it is important to care for the earth and sky if we want their ongoing blessings.

From the examples of Osiris and Isis we learn: 1) Osiris was the original Egyptian lord of the dead; 2) the Egyptians believed in a netherworld judgement; 3) the Egyptians believed in the *Ka,* an invisible duplicate body throughout life and provided the person with a new body in the underworld; 4) the goddess Isis was the undisputed Queen of magic; 5) her spells were necessary for the navigation of this world and the afterlife; 6) the magic of Isis, if performed properly (at the right time of the day, with the proper crystals and words) would have the effect of altering reality, manipulating the laws of physics, and forcing the being or object to which they were directed into compliance; 7) sacred prostitution (magic sex) was practiced at the temples of Isis and Osiris as a form of imitative magic; 8) imitative magic extended into the spirit world (i.e., placing a wooden crocodile at the grave of an enemy would produce a real crocodile in the underworld); 9) the Egyptians had numerous oracles, and practiced divining through amulets and crystals; 10) the Egyptians practiced self-healing through psychic dreaming, crystals, and positive energies which were assimilated at the temples of Imhotep; and 11) the Egyptian religion may have started following an encounter with the 'Watchers," a powerful group of fallen angels who visited the earth during antiquity.

From the example of the Plagues of the Exodus we learn: 1) the plagues of the Exodus illustrate God's supremacy over, and His attitude toward, idolatry and paganism; 2) similar plagues are forecast for the Great Tribulation (boils, hail, darkness, locusts, etc.), and, like the plagues of the Exodus, they will be directed at paganism (see Rev. 9:20); 3) Egyptians, like modern pagans, worshiped natural phenomena such as rivers, trees, etc., and attributed divine characteristics to such; 4) the Egyptians treated the earth with respect and believed that, if they did so, she (the earth) would continue the cycle of seasons; 5) the magicians of Egypt were powerful and could mimic many of the miracles of God; 6) the creatures of the Nile (fish, hippos, etc.) were sacred, and, like the environmental movement today, were often placed above the needs of the community; 7) Egyptians, like modern abortionists, often protected sacred animals while sacrificing children; 8) gods (demons) could manifest themselves through animal forms; and 9) the following deities were among those directly impacted by the Plagues of the Exodus: Ammit, Amun-Ra, Apepi, Apis, Geb, Hapi, Hathor, Heka, Horus, Imhotep, Isis, Khnum, Min, Neith, Nile River, Nut, Osiris, Pharaoh, Ptah, Sati, Seker, Sekhmet, Seth, Serapis, Shu, Sobek, Tefnut, and Vatchit.

— *Chapter Three* —

THE GODS WHO WALKED AMONG THE GREEKS

"Mother, what the gods send us,
we mortals bear perforce, although we suffer;
for they are much stronger than we."
—The Homeric Hymns

The Dorians came from out of the north by the tens of thousands. They were nearly invincible Indo-European invaders riding in horse-drawn chariots of war. Between 2800 and 2000 B.C., they conquered most of the indigenous inhabitants of the Middle East, from the inland people of Asia Minor to the Macedonians and beyond, and they did it in the name of their sky god, the thunderous and fearsome Zeus. They came, they conquered, and finally, they forged a new and curious fusion of pagan theologies, of the Dorians, Myceneans, and Minoans, into a new and influential society of gods known as the Olympians. Later, known as the famous (and sometimes infamous) gods of Greece, these powerful deities dwelt together above the towering Mount of Olympus in the north, where they "spent their delightful days." Under Zeus, the greatest of the Olympian gods, were Hera, Poseidon, Hades, Demeter, Apollo, Artemis, Ares, Aphrodite, Hermes, Athene, Hephaestus, and Hestia (later replaced by Dionysus). Simultaneously, a complex system of lesser Greek deities developed beneath the principle Olympian gods including Adonis, Selene, Hypnos, Asclepius, Eros, and, of course, Hercules.

THE MAJOR ORACLE GODS—ZEUS AND APOLLO

In Hesiod's *Theogony* we are told of a time when twelve pre-Olympian gods, known as the Titans, ruled the Universe. These were the children of Mother Earth (Gaia), who gave birth to the "elder" gods by cohabiting with Uranus (Heaven), who also sired the mountains, the sea, the hundred-handed monsters, and the Cyclops. The important Titans included Oceanus, Tethys, Mnemosyne, Themis, Hyperion, Lapetus, and Atlas. But when Uranus attempted to imprison the Titans within the body of his wife (the earth), Cronus, "the youngest and most terrible of her children," conspired with his mother and castrated Uranus with a sickle. The mutilation of Uranus separated Heaven from Earth and succeeded in freeing the Titans. When the powerful Cronus later cast the severed genitals of his father into the sea, a white foam enveloped them, from which Aphrodite was born; thus, the name Aphros, or "foam-born."

As the newly crowned king of the gods, Cronus took note of the beauty of his sister Rhea, and married her. Six famous god-children were born of their union: Hestia, Demeter, Hera, Hades, Poseidon, and Zeus. Since Mother Earth and Father Uranus warned Cronus that his offspring would someday try to overthrow and replace him as the king of the gods, Cronus attempted to circumvent the possibility by swallowing each child whole as it was born. But Rhea, "cunning as the night air," replaced the baby Zeus with a cloth-wrapped stone which Cronus unwittingly swallowed instead. Afterward, Rhea hid the young Zeus at Crete, where he was fed on the milk of the goat Amalthaea and where he remained until adulthood, protected by the nymphs. Years later, Zeus somehow forced Cronus to regurgitate his brothers and sisters. A fierce ten-year war ensued, and the younger and powerful Olympian gods overthrew the older Titans, casting them down into Tartarus (Hell) where they (except for Hecate) were to remain fettered forever.

Eventually, Zeus reconciled with the Titans and proclaimed Cronus the ruler of the Golden Age. But, for the time being, Zeus, fresh from the triumphant victory, summoned his brothers, Hades and Poseidon, and decreed that the universe should thereafter be divided among them. They cast lots, and the sky became the dominion of Zeus; Poseidon was chosen to rule over the sea, and the inner-earth or underworld was declared the haunt of Hades. Notwithstanding, the surface of the earth was determined to be neutral territory, a place where sky, sea, and the underworld joined together, and thus a place where any of the gods could rest, chiefly upon Mount Olympus. Hephaestus was commissioned, and immediately adorned the heavenly stronghold of Olympus with intimate dwelling-places for the victorious gods, each surrounding the beautiful palace of Zeus.

Then, according to a former vow, Zeus bestowed additional privileges upon the Olympians. It seems that Zeus had vowed to his supporters that victory over Cronus and the Titans would result in "spheres of influence" for each of the faithful gods. Consequently, Hephaestus was made the "lord of the fire." Demeter was given the dominion of agriculture. Artemis was placed over the wild animals. Hera, the wife of Zeus, was made the overseer of the various phases of female life. Hermes became the messenger of Zeus and the protector of travelers. Apollo was placed over music, prophecy, healing, and so on. Even so, Zeus remained the preferred god of the early Greeks.

Zeus, by Brooke Townsend

There was scarcely any part of the Greek's daily life in which Zeus was not involved. He was Zeus Herkeios (protector of the house) and Zeus Ktesios ("the Acquirer"). He was Zeus Hikesios (friend of the fugitive) and Zeus Polieus (guardian of the city). His firmly held position as the supreme and high god within the Greek religion has been easily verified by archaeology, including the discovery of the great temple of Zeus. This masterwork stood in the southern part of the precinct of Zeus at Olympia (the Atlis), and exhibited the famous gold and ivory colossus of Zeus by Pheidias (destroyed in A.D. 462), a single masterpiece estimated to be the greatest work of art in all of antiquity, and one of the Seven Wonders of the ancient world.[13]

More important in ritual than in mythology, was the oracle and altar worship that developed throughout Asia Minor in response to the popularity of Zeus. In Pergamum, perpetual sacrifices were offered to the deity upon the towering and famous 40-foot-high altar of Zeus, the same artifact that now stands inside the Berlin Museum. Some scholars believe that Antipas, the first leader and martyr of the early Christian church in Pergamum, was slain for resisting the altar worship of Zeus in Pergamum. Tradition holds that Antipas was slowly roasted to death inside the statue of a bull, the symbol and companion of Zeus, and some claim that the passage in Revelation 2: 13 is a reference to the cult worship of Zeus at Pergamum. We read: "I know thy works, and where thou dwellest, even where Satan's seat is...wherein Antipas was my faithful martyr, who was slain among you, where Satan dwelleth." Others believe this passage refers to Caesar worship, while still others (me included) contend that the phrase in Revelation 2: 13 is a reference to the cult worship of Asclepius, the Greek god of healing. But the argument could be made for a Pergamum connection between Zeus and the biblical Satan, as both were considered gods of thunder, Zeus in antiquity and Satan in modern times. Zeus was also known as the king or "prince" of the air, as was Satan. (See Eph. 2:2)

Lastly, altars have been discovered near Pergamum which were dedicated to Zeus Kataibates, which most accurately means "Zeus who descends" (in thunder and lightning), and, of course, Jesus said of Satan, "I beheld Satan as lightning fall [descend] from heaven" (Luke 10:18, brackets added). In any case, the fact that Zeus was a powerful presence in ancient cult and ritual is undisputed. His principal oracle was at Dodona, the chief city of Epirus and the "land of the oak trees," where a shrine to Zeus had existed since the second millennium B.C. For a while, the oracle at Dodona rivaled Apollo's famous oracle at Delphi, as consultations with Zeus grew in popularity. At Dodona, Zeus provided the inquiring mortals with divine guidance by whispering through the leaves of a sacred oak tree attended to by barefooted priests called Selloi.[14] At other times, Zeus communicated through the splashing of water in a nearby sacred spring, or through the cooing of sacred pigeons. Eventually, his answers were simplified and divination came through the casting of lots or by interpreting the echo of a gong. But it was the oak tree oracle at Dodona that claimed to be the oldest in Greece and the "father of gods and men." The connection between Zeus and the tree oracles probably began with certain prehistoric religious ideas from Crete and undoubtedly refers to the earliest marriage of the Dorian Zeus and the Minoan/Cretan willow goddesses. In Hagia Triada, Zeus was called Zeus Welkhanos, which means the "god of the willow-tree."[15] He was also known by the name Welkhanos at Gortyna and at Phaistus where he was somehow ritually associated with his lover Leto. The cult worship of Zeus and Leto in Phaistus was curious in its own right, because it connected the ancient elements of earth worship (the children of Gaia conversing through various nature manifestations, i.e., the willow-tree) and transsexualism. In fact, the worship of Zeus was sometimes overshadowed in Phaistus by the cult of Leto, as the Cretan youths cast off their boyish garments during their initiation into manhood. The festival was called the *Ekdysai* ("Casting off") and was associated with the

Aphrodite, by Brooke Townsend

myth of Leucippus, a peculiar legend in which a baby girl (Leucippus) was born to a woman named Galatea who preferred instead to have a son, so she persuaded Leto to let the girl change her sex into a boy when she grew up. During the Cretan initiation, the young men apparently lay down beside a statue of Leucippus in the temple of Leto where the blessings of growth and fertility could be invoked. Comparable traces of sexual deviancy and witchcraft were incorporated into various other goddess myths and will be considered later in this book.

Apollo and the Pythians

According to the Greeks, the greatest outcome of the love affair between Zeus and Leto was the birth of the most beloved of the oracle gods, Apollo. More than any other god in classical Greece, Apollo inspired the nobler passions of poetry, painting, and music. He was the god of prophecy, music, archery, and healing. But the primitive deity whose myth grew into the Olympian Apollo was probably of a much lower original stature as some histories suggest that Apollo started out as a Hittite wolf god who was venerated by shepherds and who protected the flocks against the ravages of wild animals. The Hittite people called him Apulunas or Appaliunaas. The more liberal Greek scholars agreed with the pre-Olympian origin of Apollo, and some even claimed that he had been the god of the Hyperboreans, an ancient and legendary people to the north. Herodotus claimed that the Hyperboreans continued in their worship of Apollo even after his induction into the Greek pantheon, and that they made an annual pilgrimage to the land of Delos where they participated in the famous Greek festivals of Apollo.

Lycia, a small country in southwest Turkey, also had an early connection with Apollo, and he was known there as Lykeios, which some have adjoined to the Greek Lykos or "wolf," thus, the ancient title: "the wolf slayer." But, in the end, it was the mythology of the Greeks that secured Apollo's place in history. Apollo, with his twin sister Artemis, was said by the Greeks to have been born in the land of Delos, the children of Zeus and of the Titaness Leto. Appropriately, an important oracle existed at Delos and played a significant role in the festivals of the god.

While the Delos oracle was important, it was nevertheless the famous oracle at Delphi that became the popular mouthpiece of the Olympian. Located on the mainland of Greece, the omphalos of Delphi (the stone which the Greeks believed marked the center of the earth) can still be found among the ruins of Apollo's Delphic temple. On a singular column were carved the three maxims: "Know thyself," "Nothing in excess," and "Go surety, and ruin is at hand." So important was Apollo's oracle at Delphi that wherever Hellenism existed, its citizens and kings, including some from as far away as Spain, ordered their lives, colonies, and wars, by its sacred communications.

Apollo, by Brooke Townsend

At Delphi, the Olympian gods spoke to mortal men through a priesthood, which interpreted the trance-induced utterances of the Pythoness or Pythia. She was a middle-aged woman who sat on a copper-and-gold tripod, or, much earlier, on the "rock of the sibyl" (medium), and crouched over a fire while inhaling the smoke of burning laurel leaves, barley, marijuana, and oil, until a sufficient intoxication for her prophecies had been produced. While the use of the laurel leaves may have referred to the nymph Daphne (Greek for Laurel), who escaped from Apollo's sexual intentions by transforming herself into a laurel tree, the leaves also served the practical purpose of supplying the necessary amounts of hydrocyanic acid and complex alkaloids which, when combined with hemp, created cerebral and powerful hallucinogenic visions.

An alternative version of the Oracle myth claims that the pythia sat over a fissure breathing in magic vapors that rose up from a deep crevice within the earth. The vapors "became magic" as they were mingled with the smells of the rotting carcass of the dragon Python, which had been slain and thrown down into the crevice by Apollo as a youth. The former version is obviously the truth, and, in either case, it was under the spell of such drugs (and spiritual forces?) that the Pythia prophesied in an unfamiliar voice thought to be that of Apollo himself. During the pythian trance, the medium's personality often changed, becoming melancholic, defiant, or animal-like. This psychosis may have been a source for the origin of the werewolf myth, or lycanthropy, as the Pythia reacted to an encounter with Apollo/Lykeios, the wolf god. In either case, the Delphic "women of python" prophesied in this way for nearly a thousand years and were considered to be a vital part of the religious order, and of the local economy, of every Hellenistic community. An interesting example of this is found in the New Testament Book of Acts:

> And it came to pass, as we went to prayer, a certain damsel possessed with a spirit of divination [of python, a seeress of Delphi] met us, which brought her masters much gain by soothsaying: The same followed Paul and us, and cried, saying, These men are the servants of the most high God, which shew unto us the way of salvation. And this did she many days. But Paul, being grieved, turned and said to the spirit, I command thee in the name of Jesus Christ to come out of her. And he came out the same hour. And when her masters saw that the hope of their gains was gone, they caught Paul and Silas.... And brought them to the magistrates, saying, These men, being Jews, do exceedingly trouble our city. (Acts 16:16–20, brackets added)

The story in Acts is interesting because it illustrates the level of culture and economy that had been built around the oracle worship of Apollo. It cost the average Athenian more than two days' wages for an oracular inquiry, and a lawmaker or military official seeking important State information was charged ten times that rate. That's one reason the actions of the woman in Acts are difficult to understand. She undoubtedly understood the damage that Paul's preaching could do to her industry.

Furthermore, the Pythia of Delphi had a historically unfriendly relationship with the Jews and was considered an enemy of the truth and a pawn of demonic power by both the Jews and the Christians. Quoting again from *Spiritual Warfare: The Invisible Invasion*,

> Delphi with its surrounding area, in which the famous oracle ordained and approved the worship of Asclepius, was earlier known by the name Pytho, a chief city of Phocis. In Greek mythology, Python, the namesake of the city of Pytho, was the great serpent or demon who dwelt in the mountains of Parnassus, menacing the area as the chief guardian of the famous oracle at Delphi.... In Acts 16:16, the demonic woman who troubled Paul was possessed with a spirit of divination. In Greek this means a spirit of python (a seeress of Delphi, a pythoness)... [and] reflects...the accepted Jewish belief...that the worship of Asclepius [Apollo's son] and other such idolatries were, as Paul would later articulate in 1 Corinthians 10:20, the worship of demons.[16] (brackets added)

It could be said that the Pythia of Acts 16 simply prophesied the inevitable. That is, the spirit that possessed her may have known that the time of Apollo's darkness was coming to an end, and the spread of Christianity would ultimately lead to the demise of the Delphic oracle. This is possible. Demons are sometimes aware of changing dispensations (compare the pleas of the demons in Matthew 8:29, "What have we to do with thee, Jesus, thou Son of God? art thou come hither to torment us before the time?").

Perhaps the ancient spirit of Delphi understood the dispensation timing and power of the Gospel Paul was preaching? The last recorded utterance of the oracle at Delphi seems to indicate the spirit of the Olympians understood time for domination was over. From *Man, Myth & Magic,* we read:

> Apollo…delivered his last oracle in the year 362 A.D., to the physician of the Emperor Julian, the Byzantine ruler who tried to restore paganism after Christianity had become the official religion of the Byzantine Empire. "Tell the King," said the oracle, "that the curiously built temple has fallen to the ground, that bright Apollo no longer has a roof over his head, or prophetic laurel, or babbling spring. Yes, even the murmuring water has dried up."[17]

As the oracle at Delphi slowly diminished, Apollo secured his final and most durable characterization through the influence of his favorite son, Asclepius. Beginning at Thessaly and spreading throughout the whole of Asia Minor, the cult of Asclepius, the Greek god of healing, became the chief competitor of early Christianity. Asclepius was even believed by many pagan converts of Christianity to be a living (evil?) presence who possessed the power of healing. Major shrines were erected to Asclepius at Epida urus and at Pergamum, and for a long time he enjoyed a strong cult following in Rome where he was known as Aesculapius. Usually depicted in Greek and Roman art as carrying a sacred snake wound around a pole, Asclepius was often accompanied by Telesphoros, the Greek god of convalescence. He was credited with healing a variety of incurable diseases, including raising a man from the dead, a miracle that later caused Hades to complain to Zeus, who responded by killing Asclepius with a thunderbolt. When Apollo argued that his son had done nothing worthy of death, Zeus repented and restored Asclepius to life, immortalizing him as the god of medicine.

Because the snake was sacred to Asclepius and played a vital role in the healing rituals at his shrines (hospitals), some claim the healing cult of Asclepius began with the biblical story of Moses and the brazen serpent. We read: "And the Lord said unto Moses, Make thee a fiery serpent, and set it upon a pole: and it shall come to pass, that every one that is bitten, when he looketh upon it, shall live [be healed]" (Num. 21:8, brackets added). In 2 Kings 18:4, the children of Israel developed a cult following of the brazen serpent and worshipped the image as a healing oracle. Some scholars believe the Greeks borrowed from this history in formulating the myth of Asclepius. Either way, Asclepius represented the last popular cult of the Olympian Apollo myths and was one of the most durable challenges to Christianity by the ancient pagan's who dominated Asia Minor for more than 4,000 years. So popular had the iconography of Asclepius become that, to this day, the sacred snakes of the healing god can be found adorning the entry doors and halls of hospitals in cities around the world.

Facts about Dionysus (Bacchus)— The Mystery God

Dionysus, the Thirteenth God of the Greeks, was the divine son of Zeus and of the mortal Semele. He was often depicted as the inventor of wine, abandon, and revelry, but this description seems inadequate in that it refers only to the basic elements of intoxication and enthusiasm, which were used by the Bacchae (the female participants of the Dionystic mysteries; also known as Maenads and Bacchantes) in their rituals to experience Dionysus, the intoxicating god of unbridled human desire. Followers of Dionysus considered him to be much more than the inventor of wine. He was the presence that is otherwise defined as the craving within man that longs to "let itself go" and to give itself over to the baser earthly desires. What a Christian might resist as the lustful desires of the carnal man, the followers of Dionysus embraced as the incarnate power that would, in the next life, liberate the souls of mankind from the constraints of this present world, and from the customs that sought to define respectability through a person's obedience to moral law.

Until that liberating (?) day arrived, the worshippers of Dionysus attempted to bring themselves into union with the god through a ritual casting off of the bonds of sexual denial and primal constraint by seeking to attain a higher state of ecstasy. The uninhibited rituals of ecstasy (Greek for "outside the body") supposedly brought the followers of Dionysus into a supernatural condition that enabled them to escape the temporary limitations of the body and mind, and to achieve a state of enthousiasmos, or, "outside the body and inside the god." In this sense, Dionysus represented a dichotomy within the Greek religion, as the primary maxim of the Greek culture was one of moderation, or, "nothing too extreme." But Dionysus embodied the absolute extreme in that he sought to inflame the forbidden passions of human desire. Interestingly, as most students of psychology will understand, this gave Dionysus a stronger allure among the Greeks who otherwise tried in so many ways to suppress and control the wild and secret lusts of the human heart. But Dionysus resisted every such effort, and, according to myth, visited a terrible madness upon those who tried to deny him his free expression. The Dionystic idea of mental disease resulting from the suppression of secret inner desires, especially aberrant sexual desires, was later reflected in the atheistic teachings of Sigmund Freud. Thus, Freudianism might be called the grandchild of the cult of Dionysus.

Conversely, the person who gave himself over to the will of Dionysus was rewarded with unlimited psychological and physical delights. Such mythical systems of mental punishments and physical rewards based on resistance and/or submission to Dionysus, were both symbolically and literally illustrated in the cult rituals of the Bacchae, as the Bacchae women (married and unmarried Greek women had the "right" to participate in the mysteries of Dionysus) migrated in frenzied hillside groups, dressed transvestite in fawn skins and accompanied by screaming, music, dancing, and licentious behavior. When, for instance, a baby animal was too young and lacking in instinct to sense the danger and run away from the revelers, it was picked up and suckled by nursing mothers who participated in the hillside rituals. But when older animals sought to escape the marauding Bacchae, they were considered "resistant" to the will of Dionysus and were torn apart and eaten alive as a part of the fevered ritual.

Human participants were sometimes subjected to the same orgiastic cruelty, as the rule of the cult was "anything goes," including bestiality. Later versions of the ritual (Bacchanalia) expanded to include pedophilia and male revelers, and perversions of sexual behavior were often worse between men than they were between men and women. Any creature (sometimes a child) that dared to resist such perversion of Dionysus was subjected to sparagmos ("torn apart') and omophagia ("consumed raw"). In 410 B.C., Euripides wrote of the bloody rituals of the Bacchae in his famous play, *The Bacchantes*:

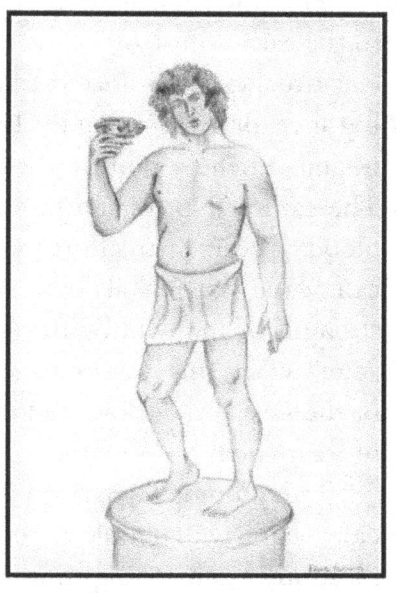

Dionysus, by Brooke Townsend

> The Bacchantes...with hands that bore no weapon of steel, attack our cattle as they browsed. Then wouldst thou have seen Agave mastering some sleek lowing calf, while others rent the heifers limb from limb. Before thy eyes there would have been hurling of ribs and hoofs this way and that, and strips of flesh, all blood be-dabbled, dripped as they hung from the pine branches. Wild bulls, that glared but now with rage along their horns, found themselves tripped up, dragged down to earth by countless maidens hands.[18]

Euripedes went on to describe how Pentheus, the King of Thebes, was torn apart and eaten alive by his own mother as, according to the play, she fell under the spell of Dionysus.

The tearing apart and eating alive of a sacrificial victim may refer to the earliest history of the cult of Dionysus. An ancient and violent cult ritual existing since the dawn of paganism stipulated that, by eating alive, or by drinking the blood, of an enemy or an animal, a person might somehow capture the essence or "soul-strength" of the victim. The earliest Norwegian huntsmen believed this, and they drank the blood of bears in an effort to capture their physical strength. East African Masai warriors also practiced omophagia, and sought to gain the strength of the wild by drinking the blood of lions. Human victims were treated this way by Arabs before Mohammed, and head-hunters of the East Indies practiced omophagia, trying to capture the essence of their enemies.

Today, omophagia is practiced by certain Voodoo sects as well as by cult Satanists. It should be pointed out that such modern omophagia illustrates a continuing effort on the part of Satan to distort the original revelations of God. Eating human flesh and drinking human blood as an attempt to "become one" with the devoured is, in many cases, a demonization of the Eucharist, or Holy Communion. But sparagmos and omophagia, as practiced by the followers of Dionysus, was not an attempt of transubstantiation (as in the Catholic Eucharist), nor of consubstantiation (as in the Lutheran communion), nor yet of a symbolic ordinance (as in the fundamentalist denomination), all of which have as a common goal—the elevating of the worshipper into a sacramental communion with God. The goal of the Bacchae was the opposite: the frenzied dance, the thunderous song, the licentious behavior, the tearing apart and eating alive, all were efforts on the part of the Bacchae to capture the essence of the god (Dionysus) and bring him down into an incarnated rage within man. The idea was not one of holy communion, but of possession by the spirit of Dionysus. When one recalls the horrific rituals of the followers of Dionysus, it's easy to believe that a demonic possession actually occurred. A Christian should find this idea as plausible, and, it would seem, so did the Hebrews.

The Hebrew people considered Hades (the Greek god of the underworld) to be equal with Hell and/or the Devil, and many ancient writers likewise saw no difference between Hades (in this sense the Devil) and Dionysus. Euripedes echoed this sentiment in the Hecuba, and referred to the followers of Dionysus as the "Bacchants of Hades."[19] In Syracuse, Dionysus was known as Dionysus Morychos ("the dark one") a fiendish creature; roughly equivalent to the biblical Satan, who wore goatskins and dwelt in the regions of the underworld.[20] In the scholarly book, *Dionysus Myth and Cult,* Walter F. Otto connected Dionysus with the prince of the underworld. He wrote:

> The similarity and relationship which Dionysus has with the prince of the underworld (and this is revealed by a large number of comparisons) is not only confirmed by an authority of the first rank, but he says the two deities are actually the same. Heraclitus says, "Hades and Dionysus, for whom they go mad and rage, are one and the same."[21]

But the Hebrews considered the magic (witchcraft) of the Bacchae to be the best evidence of Dionysus' Satanic connection, and, while most of the details are no longer available because Dionysus was a mystery god and his rituals were revealed to the initiated only, the Hebrew prophet Ezekiel described the "magic bands" (kesatot) of the Bacchae, which, as in the omophagia, were used to capture (magically imprison) the souls of men. We read,

> Therefore, thus says the Lord GOD, "Behold I am against your magic bands [kesatot] by which you hunt lives [souls] there as birds, and I will tear them off your arms; and I will let them go, even those lives [souls] whom you hunt as birds." (Ezek. 13:20, NAS; brackets added)

In Acts 17:34, we read of a soul liberated from the control of Dionysus: "Howbeit certain men clave unto [Paul], and believed: among the which was Dionysius the Areopagite" (brackets added). To carry the name of Dionysus usually meant one of two things: 1) the parents were devotees of Dionysus and thus the child was "predestined" to be a follower of the god; or 2) the individual was under the spell of the kesatot. The kesatot was a magic arm band used in connection with a container called the kiste.

Wherever the kiste is inscribed on sarcophagi and on Bacchic scenes, it is depicted as a sacred vessel (a soul prison?) with a snake peering through an open lid. How the magic worked and in what way a soul was imprisoned is still a mystery. Pan, the half-man/half-goat god (later relegated to devildom) is sometimes pictured as kicking the lid open and letting the snake (soul?) out. Such loose snakes were then depicted as being enslaved around the limbs, and bound in the hair, of the Bacchae women. Such imagery of Pan, the serpents, the imprisoned souls, and the magic Kesatot and Kiste, have not been adequately explained by any available authority, and the interpretation of them as a method for producing zombies is thus subject to ongoing scrutiny. Since the prophet Ezekiel spoke of the efforts of the Bacchae to mystically imprison the souls of men through the magic bands of Dionysus, and since Pan was most beloved of Dionysus, because of his pandemonium ("all the devils") which struck sudden panic in the hearts of men and beasts, and as the serpent was universally accepted by the Hebrews as a symbol of occult devotion, it can be easily surmised that the iconography of Dionysus represented the most tenacious effort on the part of the Bacchae to embrace the will of evil supernaturalism.

Facts about Demeter— The Mystery Goddess

While the mysteries of Dionysus were closely associated with those of Demeter (some very ancient histories suggest that Dionysus, Demeter, and Persephone were a type of unholy trinity), the rituals of Demeter, the goddess of agriculture and fertility, were different in that they were observed by married women only (participation was mandatory for all wives of Greek citizens), and, unlike the rituals of the Bacchae, chastity was strictly enforced. The Thesmophoria was the most popular of the fertility festivals held in honor of Demeter, and it drew the largest crowds at Athens and Eleusis for nearly 2,000 years. Demeter's celebrations also boasted the most protected cult secrets of the mystery religions because her rituals were performed inside the inner sanctum of the Temple of Demeter (the Telesterion) and were so well-guarded by the Temple devotees that little has survived to enlighten us as to what actually occurred there. Only those portions of the Thesmophoria held outside of the Temple were publicly recorded (sparsely) and provide us with a partial historical record.

What is known is that the rituals of the Thesmophoria were based on the mythology of the abduction and rape of Persephone (Proserpina), and of Demeter's (Persephone's mother) subsequent actions in searching for her daughter. The cult's rituals are, therefore, interpreted according to the Demeter myth. The myth claimed that Hades, the dark god of the underworld, fell in love with beautiful Persephone. One day, as she plucked flowers in a grassy meadow, Hades swooped down in his chariot and dragged Persephone down into the underworld, where he forced her to become his bride. Above ground, Demeter was distraught by her daughter's disappearance, and she searched the earth in vain to find her. With the help of Helios and Hecate, Demeter finally discovered the truth of what happened, and, in her fury, she demanded that Hades release her daughter. When Hades refused, Demeter sent a horrific famine upon the earth. Plants dried up; Seeds refused to sprout, and the gods began to suffer from a lack of sacrifices. Finally, Zeus dispatched Hermes to intercede with the lord of the underworld, and, after a great debate, Hades agreed to release Persephone if she would eat a pomegranate seed.

What Persephone did not understand was that by eating the pomegranate seed in the mystical location of the underworld, a sort of divine symmetry was created that bonded Persephone with Hades. This ensured that the goddess would automatically return to the underworld for a third part of each year (in the winter), during which time the seeds of the ground would not grow. Persephone thus became the upperworld goddess of youth and happiness, and the underworld queen of the dead; a dual role depicting her as both good and evil. On earth, she was the goddess of the young and the friend of the nymphs who appeared in the blooming of the spring flowers (symbolizing her annual return from Hades), and in the underworld she was the dreaded wife of Hades and the Queen of the Darkness who controlled the fates of deceased men. The reenactment of such myths, the abduction and rape of Persephone, was central to the rituals of the Thesmophoria, and, as such, were key to interpreting the bits of information that are known. The festival of the Thesmophoria, sometimes called the Eleusinian Mysteries, lasted from three to ten days. Each day of the festival had a different name and included specific rituals. A highlight of the festival was a procession from Athens to Eleusis which was led by a crowd of children known as Ephebi. The Ephebi assisted in carrying the hiera (sacred objects), and in pulling a statue of Dionysus as a boy (Iacchos), and finally in the ceremonial cleansing of the initiates (candidates of the mystery religion) in the sea. Upon arriving at Eleusis, the women organized the first day of the celebration (Anodos) by building temporary shelters and electing the leaders of the camp. On the second day (Nesteia), they initiated the Greater Mysteries which, according to myth, produced the cult's magical requests (a fertile harvest). Such mysteries included a parody of the abduction and rape of Persephone, and the positioning of the female devotees upon the ground weeping (in the role of Demeter for her daughter) and fasting for the return of Persephone (the return of spring). The setting upon the ground and fasting were also intended to mystically transfer the "energies" of the women into the ground, and thus into the fall seeds.

Not surprisingly, the festival was held during the time of the fall planting, so as to nearly guarantee a positive response to the cult's magic. On the fifth day of the festival, the participants drank a special grain mixture called *kykeon* (a symbol of Persephone) in an attempt to assimilate the spirit of the goddess. The idea was to produce a blessing of fertility, both of the crops and of children. About this same time, certain women, called *Antleriai,* were cleansed in the sea and then sent down into the mountainside trenches to recover the sacrificial piglets and various other sacred objects that had been thrown down into the hillside canyons several days earlier. The sacred objects included dough replicas of snakes and of genitalia, which were burned, with the piglets and a grain-seed-mixture, as an offering to Demeter.

The reason for the casting of the piglets into the mountainside cliffs has been thoroughly debated and no single interpretation has emerged as the absolute authority. While several mystical representations can be made of the symbology, and the dough replicas are obviously fertility symbols, pigs' blood was sacred to the gods and, thus, the piglets are key to understanding the ritual. Greeks venerated pigs because of their uncanny ability to find, and unearth, underground items (roots, etc.). Some scholars conclude from this that the ritual casting of the pigs "into the deep" was a form of imitative magic based on the underworld myth of Persephone and Hades. That is to say, casting the piglets into the deep canyon trenches, and fetching them out again, represented the descent of Persephone into the underworld and her subsequent ascension back up to the surface of the earth. The piglets in the trenches may have also served the practical purpose of supplying a host (body) for Persephone to hide in until the *antleriai* could assist her (by retrieving the piglets) in her annual escape from the underworld. Burning the piglets later that night would, according to an ancient religious idea that fire passes the soul from one location to another, free the spirit of Persephone into the upperworld (compare the children sacrificed to Baal who "passed through the fire" from the physical world into the spiritual). This interpretation sounds reasonable and is considered by some to be true.

Since the New Testament informs us that pagan rituals, such as those performed in the Thesmophoria, were the worship of demons,

"The things which the Gentiles sacrifice, they sacrifice to devils…" (1 Cor. 10:20), one wonders if a connection between the ritual casting of the piglets down into the deep canyon trenches (representing a descent into hell), and the biblical story of the Gadarene demoniac, existed.

In Luke, chapter Eight, we read:

> And they arrived at the country of the Gadarenes…. And when he [Jesus] went forth to land, there met him out of the city a certain man, which had devils…. When he [the demoniac] saw Jesus, he cried out, and fell down before him, and with a loud voice said, "What have I to do with thee, Jesus, thou Son of God most high? I beseech thee, torment me not"…. And Jesus asked him, saying, "What is thy name?" And he said, "Legion:" because many devils were entered into him. And they besought him that he would not command them to go out into the deep. And there was there an herd of swine feeding on the mountain: and they besought him that he would suffer them to enter into them. And he suffered them. Then went the devils out of the man, and entered into the swine: and the herd ran violently down a steep place into the sea, and were choked. (Luke 8:26–33, brackets added)

The word *deep* in this text *is Abussos* (the Abyss), and refers to the underworld, Bottomless Pit. Since the principle elements of the sea, the swine, and the deep were employed; and since the Abyss (part of the underworld) was central to the narrative; and since the cult rituals of the Thesmophoria were well known throughout Asia Minor and were considered by the Hebrews to be an activity of the devil (the inhabitants of Hades were known as "Demeter's people," and Hecate, the goddess of witchcraft, was Persephone's unde1world guide during the rituals); one could easily surmise that Jesus was mocking the Thesmophoria. It is possible Jesus was revealing, to His followers and the neighboring communities, that Dionysus and Demeter were, in fact, devils. It may be a stretch to suggest an interpretation of the biblical story in this way, but clearly the similarities and historical proximities are startling, especially since the demons requested an entry into the swine.

Why would demons make such a plea? There are two possible connections with the Thesmophoria: 1) the demons believed that by entering the swine they could escape the underworld deep (as in the magical Persephone escape ritual described above); and 2) Jesus, by granting the request of the devils, was illustrating that the Thesmophoria ritual of casting the piglets into the deep was inherently demonic. Obviously, there are other possible interpretations of the narrative in Luke 8. But since this is the only record of Jesus granting the petition of demons, it seems possible that a powerful social commentary on a popular pagan idea, like that of the Thesmophoria of Demeter, was being made by the Master.

DEMETER AND THE MOTHER EARTH SPIRIT

While much is still unknown about the mysteries of Demeter, the basis of her popularity was almost certainly rooted in her divinity as a mother-earth goddess. Demeter (De or Da "earth", and meter "mother") actually means "earth mother." As earth mother, Demeter was the giver of generosity and grace and the controller of the awesome forces of nature. She was loved as the giver of food and fertility and was feared as the taker of life. She could open her womb with blessings and abundance and could enclose the dead in her soil. Either way, at all times, she commanded absolute reverence.

Without a doubt, the worship of the earth's "spirit" as a mother, and the incarnation of the earth's fertility forces within specific goddesses, was one of the oldest and most widespread forms of paganism recorded in antiquity. Whether it was Inanna of the Sumerians, Ishtar of the Babylonians, or Fortuna of the Romans, every civilization had a sect of religion based on the embodiment of the earth's spirit as a mother-goddess. The Egyptians worshipped Hathor in this way, as did the Chinese, Shingmoo. The Germans worshipped Hertha as the great

Earth Mother, and the apostate Jews idolized "the queen of heaven." In Greece, the queen of the Olympian goddesses and wife of Zeus was Hera, the benevolent earth mother. Before her was Gaia (Gaea, the Greek creator-mother earth) and beneath her were many other Greek earth goddesses, including Demeter, Artemis, Aphrodite, and Hecate.

The principal idea was, and evidently still is among New Age devotees, that the earth is a living entity. The ancient and universally accepted idea that the "living earth" was also a fertile mother was conceptualized in different ways and in various goddess myths and images throughout the ancient world. In *The Golden Asse*, by second-century Roman philosopher Lucius Apuleius, evidence reveals that the spirit of the earth was perceived as a feminine force, and that such force incarnated itself at various times, and to different people, within the goddess mothers. Note how Lucius prays to the earth spirit:

> O blessed Queene of Heaven, whether thou be the Dame Ceres [Demeter] which art the original and motherly source of all fruitful things in earth, who after the finding of thy daughter Proserpina [Persephone], through thy great joy which thou diddest presently conceive, madest barrain and unfruitful ground to be plowed and sowne, and now thou inhabitest in the land of Eleusie [Eleusis]; or whether thou be the celestiall Venus...[or] horrible Proserpina...thou hast the power to stoppe and put away the invasion of the hags and ghoasts which appeare unto men, and to keep them downe in the closures [womb] of the earth; thou which nourishest all the fruits of the world by thy vigor and force; with whatsoever name is or fashion it is lawful to call upon thee, I pray thee, to end my great travaile. (brackets added)

The earth spirit responds to Lucius:

> Behold Lucius I am come, thy weeping and prayers hath mooved me to succour thee. I am she that is the natural mother of all

things, mistresse and governesse of all the elements, the initial progeny of worlds, chiefe of powers divine, Queene of heaven, the principall of the Gods celestiall, the light of the goddesses: at my will the planets of the ayre [air], the wholesome winds of the Seas, and the silence of hell be disposed; my name, my divinity is adored throughout all the world in divers manners, in variable customes and in many names, for the Phrygians call me the mother of the Gods: the Athenians, Minerva: the Cyprians, Venus: the Candians, Diana: the Sicilians, Proserpina: the Eleusians, Ceres: some Juno, other Bellona, other Hecate: and principally the aethiopians...Queene Isis.[22] (brackets added)

One could assume, based on such texts, that a single spiritual source (or realm) energized the many goddess myths. Likewise, in the ancient hymn, "To Earth, the Mother of All," Homer illustrates how the earth-spirit was universally involved in the affairs and lives of nations. Through Homer's dedication to the earth we discover how far-reaching and omnipresent the mother-earth spirit was thought to be:

I will sing of well founded Earth, mother of all, eldest of all beings. She feeds all creatures that are in the world, all that go upon the goodly land, and all that are in the paths of the seas, and all that fly: all these are fed by her store. Through you, O queen, men are blessed in their children and blessed in their harvests, and to you it belongs to give means of life to mortal men and to take it away. Happy is the man whom you delight to honour! He hath all things abundantly: his fruitful land is laden with corn, his pastures are covered with cattle, and his house is filled with good things. Such men rule orderly in their cities of fair women: great riches and wealth follow them: their sons exult with ever-fresh delight, and their daughters in flower-laden bands play and skip merrily over the soft flowers of the field. Thus it is with those whom you honour O holy goddess, bountiful spirit. Hail, mother of the gods, wife of starry Heaven; freely bestow upon me for this my song substance that cheers the heart! And now I will remember you and another song also.[23]

From these and other ancient records, it is obvious that the earth was more than an agricultural or herbaceous facility to the pagans, she was the personable and "eldest of all beings," the "holy goddess," the "bountiful spirit," the all nourishing mother of men who manifested herself within the popular idols of the mother goddesses.

Christian theologians also believe the physical earth contains spiritual forces. In Revelation 9:14, we read of "the four angels which are bound in the great river Euphrates." Likewise, in Job 26:5, we find "Dead things are formed from under the waters." The literal Hebrew translation says, "The Rafa (fallen angels) are made to writhe from beneath the waters." Additional biblical references indicate the earth is a kind of holding tank, or prison, where God has bound certain fallen entities (2 Pet. 2:4; Jude 6). That such fallen spirits seek to communicate with, or participate in, the affairs of humanity, is described in Scripture. The Hebrew people were warned of spirits who seek regular communion with men (Deut. 18:11), and, when the witch of Endor communicated with the same spirits, they ascended up from "out of the earth" (1 Sam. 28:13). It would seem, based on such scriptures, that the dynamic or energy behind the earth-goddess-spirits is indeed real, and, according to the Christian doctrine, is identical with the legions of fallen spiritual forces that are bound within the earth and that seek association with men. Such conclusions can be made because of the obvious and physical location of the biblical demons within the body of the earth, and also because of the nature of the manifestations, or attributes, of the goddesses. As previously noted, the myths and rituals behind the earth-goddess-mothers, Isis, Demeter, and Persephone, were openly connected with the evil spirits of the underworld.

The Earth-Mother Hecate

Hecate, the Titan earth-mother of the wizards and witches, illustrates, perhaps better than any other goddess, the connection between the earth goddesses and the realm of evil supernaturalism. As the daughter of Perses and Asteria, Hecate (Hekate) was the only one of the Titans to remain free under Zeus. She was the mother of the wizard, Circe, and of the witch, Medea, and was considered to be the underworld sorceress of all that is demonic. This was because Hecate characterized the unknown night-terrors that roamed the abandoned and desolate highways. She was often depicted as a young maiden with three faces, each pointing in a different direction, a role in which she was the earth-spirit that haunted wherever three paths joined together. As the "goddess of three forms" she was Luna (the moon) in heaven, Diana (Artemis) on earth, and Hecate in the underworld. At times of evil magic, she appeared with hideous serpents, spreading demons, encouraging criminal activity, and revealing enigmatic secrets to the crones. At other times, she roamed the night with the souls of the dead, visible only to dogs, who howled as she approached. When the moon was covered in darkness, and the hellhounds accompanied her to the path-beaten crossways, Hecate came suddenly upon the food offerings and dead bodies of murders and suicides that had been left for her by the fear-stricken commonfolk. Her hounds bayed, the ghost torches lit up the night, and the river nymphs shrieked as Hecate carried away the mangled souls of the suicides into the underworld caverns of Thanatos (Death), where the shrill cries of such damned ones were known to occupy her presence. As the dark goddess of witchcraft, Hecate, like

Isis, was worshiped with impure rites and magical incantations. Her name was probably derived from the ancient Egyptian word *Heka* ("sorcery" or "magical"), which may explain her association with the Egyptian frog goddess of the same name. This may also explain the affiliation of frogs with witchcraft, and the various potions of frog-wart and "hecateis" (Hecate's hallucinogenic plant, also called Aconite), which supposedly sprouted from the spittle of Cerberus (Hade's three-headed guard dog), which fell to the ground when Hercules forced him up to the surface of the earth.

Because her devotees practiced such magic wherever three paths joined, Hecate became known to the Romans as *Trivia* (tri "three," and via "roads"). Later, when the Latin church fathers compared the magic of the goddess Trivia with the power of the Gospel, they found it to be inferior, and the pursuit of Hecate's knowledge became known as Trivial Pursuit, or inconsequential. But the fact that Hecate's followers sincerely believed in, and feared, her magic and presence, was legendary. We find an example of such belief in the *Argonautica*, (Jason and the Argonauts) by Apollonius Rhodius, when the sorceress Medea provided a spell for Jason to use in winning Hecate's assistance:

> Take heed now, that I may devise help for thee. When at thy coming my father has given thee the deadly teeth from the dragon's jaws for sowing, then watch for the time when the night is parted in twain, then bathe in the stream of the tireless river, and alone, apart from others, clad in dusky raiment, dig a rounded pit; and therein slay a ewe, and sacrifice it whole, heaping high the pyre on the very edge of the pit. And propitiate only-begotten Hecate, daughter of Perses, pouring from a goblet the hive-stored labour of bees.
>
> And then, when thou hast heedfully sought the grace of the goddess, retreat from the pyre; and let neither the sound of feet drive thee to turn back, nor the baying of hounds, lest haply thou shouldst maim all the rites and thyself fail to return duly to thy comrads."...[and] Jason...bathed his tender body reverently in the sacred river; and round him he placed a dark robe...and...he cut the throat of the sheep, and duly placed the carcase above; and he kindled the logs placing fire beneath, and poured over them mingled libations, calling on Hecate Brimo [the Mighty One] to aid him in the contests.

And when he had called on her he drew back; and she heard him, the dread goddess, from the uttermost depths and came to the sacrifice of Aeson's son [Jason]; and round her horrible serpents twined themselves among the oak boughs; and there was a gleam of countless torches; and sharply howled around her the hounds of hell. All the meadows trembled at her step; and the nymphs that haunt the marsh and the river shrieked, all who dance around that mead of Amarantian Phasis. And fear seized Aeson's son, but not even so did he turn round as his feet bore him forth, till he came back to his comrades.[24] (brackets added)

Such magic, as illustrated in the fiction above, was employed by fearful men to appease Hecate. The appeasement of the dark goddess in this way was primarily because of her role as the sorceress of the afterlife, but true believers also feared Hecate's ability to afflict the mind with madness (as in the Dionystic curses), as well as her influence over the night creatures. That is to say, offerings were made to Hecate because she was thought to govern haunted places where evil or murderous activity occurred. Such areas where violence or lechery had a history were believed to be magnets of malevolent spirits, something like "haunted houses," and if one wanted to get along with the resident apparitions they needed to make oblations to the ruler of the darkness, Hecate. The acceptance of the oblations was announced by Hecate's familiar (the night owl), and the spooky sound of the creature was perceived as a good omen by those who gathered on the eve of the full moon. Statues of the goddess bearing the triple face of a dog, a snake, and a horse, overshadowed the dark rituals when they were performed at the crossing of three roads. At midnight, Hecate's devotees left food offerings at the intersection for the goddess ("Hecate's Supper"), and, once deposited, quickly exited without turning around or looking back.

Sometimes the offerings consisted of honey cakes and chicken hearts, at other times puppies, honey, and female black lambs were slaughtered for the goddess and her strigae. The strigae were deformed and vicious owl-like affiliates of Hecate who flew through the night feeding on the bodies of unattended babies. During the day the strigae appeared as simple old women, and such folklore may account for the history of flying witches. The same strigae hid amidst the leaves of the trees during the annual festival of Hecate (held on August 13), when Hecate's followers offered up the highest praise of the goddess. Hecate's devotees celebrated such festivals near Lake Averna in Campania where the sacred willow groves of the goddess stood, and they communed with the tree spirits (earth spirits, including Hecate, were thought to inhabit trees) and summoned the souls of the dead from the mouths of nearby caves. It was here that Hecate was known as Hecate Chthonia ("Hecate of the earth"), a depiction in which she most clearly embodied the popular earth-mother-spirit, which conversed through the cave-stones and sacred willow trees.

Whereas Hecate was known elsewhere as Hecate-Propylaia, "the one before the gate," a role in which she guarded the entrances of homes and temples from nefarious outside evils (talk about Satan casting out Satan!); and whereas she was also known as Hecate-Propolos, "the one who leads," as in the underworld guide of Persephone and of those who inhabit graveyards; and finally she was known as Hecate-Phosphoros, "the light bearer," her most sacred title and one which recalls another powerful underworld spirit, Satan, whose original name was Lucifer ("the light bearer"); it was nevertheless her role as the feminist earth goddess-spirit Hecate-Chthonia that popularized her divinity and commanded such reverence from common people.

Such popular religious concepts of earth-spirits inhabiting trees, soliciting incantation and ritual, and revealing abstruse secrets, is an idea familiar to students of eastern mythology. The following chapter will discuss the revival of such paganistic notions, and, more importantly, will attempt to answer the disturbing question: Do the ancient spirits of the gods and goddesses converse with modern man?

Important Notes Regarding the Gods of Greece

The following notes on the Greek deities are important and relate to the remaining chapters of the book.

From the example of Gaia we learn: 1) Gaia was the original Greek "mother earth"; 2) she was worshipped as a literal spirit; 3) her body (the planet earth) was made to contain the elder spirits of the Titans; and 4) such spirits were known to communicate through trees, streams (etc.), and various idols.

From the example of Zeus we learn: 1) Zeus, among other things, was the king or "prince of the air" and the "god of thunder," titles biblically and historically associated with Satan; 2) his altar at Pergamum may have been the "throne of Satan" mentioned in Revelation 2:13; 3) he was an oracle spirit and communicated through trees, streams, and other nature devices; and 4) he was ritually associated with transsexualism through his lover Leto.

From the example of Apollo we learn: 1) Apollo was the most important oracle god in Greece; 2) his oracle at Delphi was the most famous in antiquity; 3) his pythian prophetesses popularized the social status of mediums (psychics); 4) natural hallucinogens used as instruments of paranormal communication was a part of his spirituality; 5) his gospel was humanistic: "know yourself," "do nothing in excess," and "don't get in a hurry," were the basic rules; 6) unlike the Hebrew prophets, the Delphic "psychics" commercialized the prophetic gifts and charged for their services; and 7) Apollo's son, Asclepius, combined earth elements, spirit-guide animals (especially serpents), energy channeling, incantation, and psychic dreams, with healing.

From the example of Dionysus we learn: 1) the uses of wine, sensuality, song, and revelry, were combined with having a "religious experience"; 2) Dionysus' feminist devotees, the Bacchae, challenged the traditional roles of women by dressing transvestite, behaving violently masculine, and disregarding virtuous sexuality; 3) the Bacchae embraced physical pleasures including the drink, the dance, the song, and sexual perversion, at the expense of their children; 4) the Bacchae practiced magic, embraced evil, destroyed children, and profaned the sacred, in the name of women's rights; and 5) they manipulated others (magically imprisoned their souls) for personal gain.

From the example of Demeter we learn: 1) Demeter was the popular goddess of the environment; 2) her rituals and rewards taught people to tune in with, and care for, the planet; 3) her doctrines involved an amalgam of human energy, superstition, and mystical earth forces; 4) she, along with Gaia, Hera, Artemis, Hecate, and others, incarnated the earth's fertility forces within the goddess images; 5) the Bible reveals that such forces are demonic and seek communion with mankind; and 6) this was illustrated in the myths, behaviors, and rituals of the goddesses, especially of Hecate.

— *Chapter Four* —

THE OLD GODS OF THE NEW AGE

"The kind of events that once took place
will by reason of human nature take place again."
—Thucydides

A few years ago during the Christmas season, my wife, Nita, and I walked through a local mall. As we perused the different shops, we came across a New Age bookstore conducting a "Grand Opening." In a derisive tone, I said to my wife, "Can you believe the lack of intelligence of some people?" I strolled casually into the store, and without hesitation, snatched a book from the shelf and began offering a sarcastic commentary as I read from the pages. When I noticed that Nita was growing uncomfortable; I placed the book back on the shelf and proceeded out of the store. Suddenly, a dull sensation hit me. It began in my stomach and shot upward through my cranium, impacting my equilibrium. As I stepped outside onto the main mall walkway, my head started to spin, my hands began to shake, and I felt as if I were going to faint. It was literally as if an invisible terror had "jumped" on me, and was somehow injecting powerful feelings of nausea and anxiety throughout my entire body. I tried to shake it off, but couldn't. I attempted to walk it off, and failed. At last, feigning interest in something, I moved away from my wife and began to pray. I asked the Lord to forgive me for my sarcastic attitude, for my lack of caution, and for my want of concern for the lost. I prayed for deliverance from evil and for a healing of the body and mind. After several hours of such walking and praying, I was finally restored. I discovered a valuable lesson that day: while it's true that a Christian cannot be demon possessed, it's equally true that the "princes" of this world are powerful, and we should enter their arena only after prayer, and at the prompting of the Lord. I also learned the mystical forces of the New Age movement are genuine (and willing to protect their territory!), and that much of what is currently published under the guise of New Age "enlightenment," is nothing less than Old Age doctrines of nefarious, invisible hosts.

As in antiquity, so in modern times, those who practice paganism are guilty of worshipping "devils" (Rev. 9:20). The dogma, which were once embraced (and still are, through the New Age Movement) as the wisdom of the gods, are defined in the scriptures as the "doctrines of devils." The Apostle Paul declared: "The things which the Gentiles sacrifice, they sacrifice to devils" (l Cor. 10:20). In Acts 7:41–42 (Jerusalem Bible), we find that those who worship idols are joined to the "army of heaven" [stratas, the "fallen angel army"], and Psalm 96:5 concludes that "all the gods of the nations are idols" (elilim, LXX *daimonia* [demons]). Thus, pagan images, such as represented the ancient gods and goddesses, were elilim (empty, nothing, vanity), but behind the empty idols were the living dynamics of idolatry, and spiritual objects of heathen adoration, the daimonia (demons) of the Bible.

Since the Bible clearly defines idolatry as the worship of demons, and since demons are eternal personalities that desire the worship of men, it is fair to conclude the characterization of such deities as "Zeus," "Amun-Ra," "Demeter," and "Isis," were simply the classical names attributed to specific fallen spirits. In other words, Apollo was a real personality; Osiris was a genuine underworld fiend; Hecate actually lived, and still does! One also concludes that the images of the gods (falcon-headed statues, animal forms, etc.) served the purposes of such spirits by providing a point of focus, and by revealing the "nature" of the particular spirit existing within the god. The iconographies, myths, and rituals of each deity exhibited the specific characteristics (nature, gender, underworld authority, etc.) of that particular entity. Thus, the myths and images of Zeus, according to such theory, were the physical manifestations of a literal demon of air, while statues of the goddess Demeter represented an earth spirit. It is my assertion, and the claim of this book, that the same spirits of antiquity, including Zeus, Athene, Dionysus, and others, continue to express themselves within modern paganism. Dr. Jones agrees, asserting that the connection between the New Age Movement and the gods of mythology is strong. "Nothing has changed in Satan's game plan," says Jones, 'just the names of the players, and, in some instances, even the names are the same."

Paganism in America is exploding as we approach the new millennium. Throughout Hollywood, government, cyberspace, and even the church, people rush to embrace the religious philosophies of the New Age of Aquarius. As a modernistic process by which the old gods are worshipped, the New Age Movement emerged in the United States during the 1960s, and has experienced a steady growth ever since. The broad appeal of the New Age Movement as a Western phenomenon can be explained to some degree as the result of a changing culture. Americans have gradually abandoned the fundamental precepts of Christianity (prayer in school, Bible in courts, etc.), which provided the cornerstone of civil life and jurisprudence in American society for more than 200 years. As a generation of baby-boomers has focused on human potential and the "god within us all," Eastern philosophies of Monism, Pantheism, Hinduism, and self-realization, continue to provide Americans, and even some Christians, with an alluring opportunity to throw off the "outdated ideas" of fundamental Christianity and to espouse a more "enlightened" world view of God and reality.

Some of the most notable celebrities have joined the political ambitions of the New Age Movement (goals include a United Nation's sponsored Environmental Sabbath for the Goddess Earth), including Shirley MacLaine, Dick Gregory, Lindsay Wagner, Dennis Weaver, Dirk Benedict, Cloris Leachman, Richard Gere, Ally Sheedy, and the late John Denver. Many mainstream "Christian" denominations have also annexed the New Age ideas, and believers who once held strong doctrinal positions of the supremacy of Christ, have abandoned those views in exchange for a New Age universal philosophy.

Examples include a witch who teaches principles of goddess worship at a Roman Catholic college in California, and United Methodist pastors who propose replacing the name of Jesus with Sophia (Goddess of Wisdom) when reading about the crucifixion. Such persons claim we should join the efforts of New Agers and be sympathetic to "Goddess-minded Christians." Former New Age devotee Judy Vorfeld re-discovered the real Jesus after embracing such ideas. She became involved in freelance writing as a result of experiencing the dangers involved in participating in the New Age Movement. For many years she actively avoided anything to do with the Christianity of her childhood. When she was in her early forties, a neighborhood minister said he was starting a new church, and she thought the time might be right to look at Christianity again. Judy writes:

> For a time I was involved in a fellowship that worshipped a different deity than the God of the Bible.... I joined a church that evolved from ecumenism to religious syncretism.... Six months after I became part of the fellowship, fundamental Christianity was retired in favor of a universal religious system, one designed to be inoffensive to people of any theological persuasion. The fellowship then put together a creed that would be acceptable for any visitors coming to worship with us. Jews, Hindus, Muslims, and Buddhists were welcome, as were Theosophists, Rosicrucians, and Hare Krishnas.... Our minister brought a popular seminar, advertised a self-improvement course into our church. Most of us were impressed with the professional manner of the leaders and their sophisticated system of teaching self-realization.... The organization's format, we were told, held the answers to all our problems.... Church leadership eagerly blended the organization's ideas into

an agenda that became a part of our church curriculum. Eastern meditation, Psychic healing, and guided imagery were all practiced.[25]

Judy Vorfeld is a friend of mine and has provided me with guidance on the New Age Movement. In recent correspondence, she described modern Druids, and spoke of their methods of magic healing through "visualization." She confessed:

> Tom.... When we were involved in Silva Mind Control [through her local church], we did the same thing [visualized healing]. At that time, I thought God was behind all this stuff. I 'saw' people in my mind's eye who had various diseases, and I sent energy to heal them. In groups like this, the leader often has a list of people who are sick. This gives them a way to follow through and see who was healed. I have no doubt some people were healed, but since we were invoking a power other than that of the real God, what were we doing?"

What indeed?

An amazing component of the New Age Movement (as verified by such examples as my friend, Judy's) is its capacity to adapt to a variety of religious, even Christian, ideas. Consequently, many of the popular "Christian" doctrines advocated today are nothing more than the cultic propositions of Eastern mysticism and ancient paganism. These include concepts of psychic healing, self-realization, emotional experiences, rules of success, breathing techniques, positive confession, name it and claim it, environmental theology, the ecumenical movement, visualization, hypnosis by clergy, mind manipulation, and so on. At times, and I say this with caution, even the activity within the "fundamental" church, including certain physical phenomena we sometimes embrace as the miraculous evidence of "revival," is a modern form of magic and opens the door for "old gods" and their mysticism to invade the church. The line between a true manifestation of God, and human orchestration, is often blurred. Sincere people, in a quest to experience God, frequently mimic the doctrinal and physical activity of others. Some physical phenomena (crawling on the church floor and making animal sounds, etc.) are extrabiblical in nature (not everything that is extrabiblical is unbiblical, however) and therefore undefined by New Testament teachings.

As a result, some Christians have been drawn to mystical experiences rather than concentrating on God and His Word. Even sermons preached by well-meaning ministers have tempted Christians to pursue "supernatural" encounters with God, rather than instructing them to live by faith. The danger of such undisciplined sincerity is that human nature rarely limits its opportunity for experience. If the Bible has no clear guidelines of conduct and order, and the activity is being promoted by church authorities as a way of experiencing God, then the person seeking the experience may have trouble defining what is, and what isn't acceptable, and thus go too far. For emotional people, the experience may be expressed by a physical reaction, while academics tend to interpret mystical experiences with God as divine revelations or imparted knowledge. The dangerous consequences of such conduct often lead to religious behavior more reminiscent of Dionysus or Apollo worship than of New Testament Christianity. As a result, people like Judy Vorfeld start out in a Christian church and wind up in the New Age movement.

The dangers of mysticism, such as those inherent with emphasizing experiences over doctrine, were soundly illustrated in a recent report by Samantha Smith. She writes:

> I became strongly concerned about this movement after observing a "service" at a south Denver Vineyard church... [a woman] stood in the middle of a group of people who ran their hands over her body (within an inch or so of the clothing), then kept swooshing some invisible thing toward

her heart area. Saddened, I walked toward the door, where a church member said, "You should come back on Sunday night. That's when they levitate."...[another group] in Seattle...sit in circles, clucking, flapping their tucked arms and visualizing themselves hatching the "Man Child Company," a heretical Manifested Sons of God concept. In Kansas City, a pastor watched in horror as men and women lay on the floor with their knees up and legs spread apart, trying to birth the same thing I tape-recorded a group of Episcopalians howling at the moon, like wolves, giving a "Howl-le-lu-ia Chorus" for Earth Day. It gets worse. There are reports of "holy vomiting" (seance ectoplasm?) and of Christians becoming demonized by being "slain in the spirit." How can this be?[26] (brackets added)

I share Samantha Smith's concerns. Recently I was approached by a young man during a Sunday morning service (at a church that stresses supernatural "experiences" as a test of one's spirituality) and was told how, he, and other members of the "intercessory prayer group," were experiencing temporary possessions (?) of evil spirits. When I asked him what he meant, he stated that evil spirits were "coming out of people, and, as they do, they are going into us [the people in the prayer room] and then speaking out loud." When I asked for clarification, he repeated that evil "spirits" were audibly conversing through him and other members of the prayer group during the Sunday morning church services! I warned him of the dangers of mysticism and reminded him that the Jews were forbidden to communicate with spirits. I strongly advised him not to allow any spirit (other than the Holy Spirit) to speak through him, and showed him how Michael the archangel did not discourse with the devil, but said, "The Lord rebuke thee" (Jude 9). I'm unsure if the young man followed my instruction, but the episode illustrates how a church environment emphasizing supernatural experiences over sound biblical doctrine can create an atmosphere conducive to New Age mysticism, mediumism, spiritism, and paganism. I believe the young man was earnest, and it's my understanding that the "medium" practices at the church have ended.

Gaia, Hathor, and Demeter Live! New Age Earth Worship

The majority of New Age mysticism and other forms of modern paganism (the ongoing worship of the gods and goddesses) is unquestionably occurring outside of the fundamentalist church. Expressions of neo-paganism ranging from self-help organizations working with large corporations to offer stress management symposiums to their employees using the principles of the New Age Movement to produce positive harmony, prosperity, and overall business success, to other not-so-subtle forms of paganism, such as those practiced by WICCA and the Women's Spirituality Movement, account for more than 600,000 women nationwide participating in the invocation of ancient earth-goddesses, including Demeter, Aphrodite, and Isis.

Retail stores springing up in faddish malls across the United States supply replica idols of the popular female deities, and marketing of the occultic paraphernalia used in venerating the goddesses (crystals, candles, books of spells, etc.) has become a multimillion-dollar industry. Dimly lit "occult" bookstores that once inhabited shabby old buildings have been replaced with trendy New Age shops located amidst the most fashionable strip malls in the nicest areas of town. One such store, Necromance, is located at stylish Melrose Avenue in Los Angeles, and business is booming with sales of "human fingers on a leather cord, necklaces of human teeth, bone beads, human skulls, and even a tiny fetal one."[27] The Necromance, and similar New Age businesses, are attentively supported by a growing population of neo-pagans and teachers of the arcane rites. Store owners are generally New Agers or practicing witches, and many have been publicly embraced by politicians, religious leaders, and Hollywood entertainers. Not long ago, one such witch claimed to be a temple prostitute of the goddess Astarte and performed sequential ritual earth-magic sex with 251 men at the University of Southern California.

In her book, *Goddess Earth,* Samantha Smith connected the pagan agenda of the Earth Summit, the Environmental Movement, and the current mix of politics and public education, with the New Age Movement's goals of a revival of Mother Earth worship under a united World Order. After attending a lecture by Miriam Starhawk (a teacher of the "ancient craft") at the University of Denver, she wrote:

> Miriam Starhawk, who calls herself "a goddess-worshipping pagan witch," appeared at the University of Denver to lecture... about her concerns on "Magic, Sex and Politics."...There was a time, she said, thousands of years ago, when people lived in harmony with the earth and each other. They practiced magic and used the art of evoking power from within, trancing, and became one with the balance of things. When they turned from the goddess, all havoc broke loose. Men ruled over women and other men. They waged endless wars. People splintered into rich and poor, free and slave, powerful and powerless. The witch (goddesses) were battered, raped, tortured, burned, poisoned, and dismembered. And so, the Earth herself nearly died. But, she was not destroyed! Some continued to practice [earth-centered magic] in secret...[and now] Just at a time when the final destruction of the earth is probable and nearly inevitable, women are remembering the goddess (Mother Earth]. They are crying out against the war and the destruction of the human race. "The reborn are walking the Earth in new forms and the witches arise and dance (skyclad) in the open. The Goddess has not come to save us. It is up to us to save Her [the earth]."[28] (brackets added)

Today, New Agers ask, "If God is our Father, then who is our Mother?", and they happily answer, "Earth!" Not surprisingly, the worship of the earth's "spirit" as a nurturing goddess mother has been revived as a central feature of paganism. Earth Day 1990 celebrated

THE GODS WHO WALK AMONG US

Athene, by Brooke Townsend

the start of the decade by coordinating nearly 200 million people worldwide into a universal effort aimed at saving "our endangered Mother Earth." Christian leaders signed "Green Pledges," and Wiccan witches performed arcane rituals in honor of the Earth Goddess, Gaia. Interest in such contraptions as the sweat lodge, a device used by several ancient religions, including many American Indian tribes, as an apparatus whereby one reenters the womb of the Earth Mother, was celebrated. Such famous personalities as Ted Turner and Jane Fonda built their own private sweat lodges, and were praised for following the primitive and simple pattern of furrowing a womblike "nest" into the surface of the earth and covering it with a dome of natural materials. The entry into Ms. Fonda's lodge was intentionally kept so low as to simulate the birthing experience during exit, and the ground inside was left uncovered so as to allow the inhabitants the opportunity of getting in touch with the all-knowing Earth Spirit.

The sweat lodge method of communing with the sacred Earth Mother, Gaia, as practiced by various ancient religions and New Age devotees, includes sitting in a semicircle around heated stones inside the lodge, and entering into a mystical state of consciousness. As with ancient pythians, the prophetesses of Apollo, the altered mental condition is accomplished through repetitive chanting, drumming, and breathing the fumes of natural stimulants, such as peyote. Spirit animals, called "power animals" by New Agers and American Indians, are called upon to guide the soul through the underworld journey, or "vision quest," and participants are encouraged to "dance their animal" for revelations and healing of the body and mind. Such animal dancing is accomplished by allowing the spirit of the creature to enter into, and take control of, the participant.

Dr. Leslie Gray, a noted University instructor and female shaman (something like a witch doctor), employs such uses of "animal dancing" in the psychiatric (shamanic) treatment of her patients. She described the positive results of animal dancing in the case of one insecure young woman, saying, "I lay down on the ground next to her and put us both into an altered state of consciousness via a tape of drumming. I came back from my 'journey' and blew the spirit of a mountain lion into [her]. I then instructed her to go out into nature and dance her animal...[and when she did] She no longer felt afraid of people."[29] (brackets added)

Such uses of animal images and other natural products in the worship of the Great Earth Mother is by design. New Age pagans, drawing on Eastern philosophies and the occult, believe that, unlike the evil human race, such elements are at one with Gaia. According to them, if it were not for the male-dominated, Styrofoam-producing, beef-eating, gas-guzzling, bulldozer-driving destroyers of the rainforests (human beings), the earth would be a better place. Natural earth-centered resources, such as animals, crystals, and even colors, are thus the products of choice for the students of New Age earth-magic. For instance, light blue is the color of Mother Earth's sky, thus Wiccans burn candles of light blue to acquire her magic tranquility or understanding. Red candles are burned for strength or sexual love, and green candles for financial assistance, etc. Instruments of magic, such as magic wands, are also made of Mother Earth's natural supply, usually of Willow, Oak, or fruit tree branches. Magic potions employed during the witches' Esbats (earth-celebrations held during the new and full moons) also contain the Earth's natural byproducts, including clover, olive oil, grape juice, garlic cloves, and rosebuds. Finally, special ceremonies conducted at the crossing of three earth-paths (remember the triple-path earth-mother, Hecate?) are dedicated to the Mother Earth goddesses, Gaia, Demeter, Persephone, Isis, Aphrodite, Hathor, Hera, Diana, Athene, and Hecate.

While such rituals are gender-inclusive, they are specifically designed to elevate the goddess, or female spirit. In fact, an enlightening component of nearly every form of goddess-earth worship is the absence of male leadership. Goddess deities, especially the ones that exhibit independence of the male presence, are cheerfully exalted during the worship of Gaia. Athene, the manly goddess of Olympus, and Diana (Artemis), the lesbian[30] earth-goddess and patroness of witches, are considered especially important during the contemporary worship of the Earth Goddess. Venerating such "she-devils" is more widespread than ever, and anyone visiting the local university library, the area bookstore, the internet, or Saturday morning cartoons, will undoubtedly discover the presence and deification of Mother Earth. The effect of New Age cartoons on young people is particularly disturbing, as it teaches innocent kids the principles of paganism. Characters such as Captain Planet and the Planeteers tell children to use their "mystical powers" to protect the environment, and to assist Gaia, the motherly earth-spirit, in her quest to join forces with Captain Planet and his "special children" to save the earth from middle-aged capitalist swine (there go those rotten adults again!) who want to destroy the loving Mother Earth. Each episode of Captain Planet ends by encouraging kids to help Gaia and the Planeteers save the earth from evildoers. The new animated Superman, that once proud defender of "truth, justice, and the American way," has also seen the light, and, evidently, converted to New Age mysticism. His girlfriend, Lois Lane, consults the "white Wiccan coven" for information or magic to assist in Superman's task.

Diana, by Brooke Townsend

The Burning Man

For the past ten years such earth-worshipping pagans, and their little cartoon-watching pagans, have migrated from Canada, Brazil, Germany, Russia, and 25 other countries, to an isolated corner of Black Rock Desert in Nevada, where a four-day-long New Age techno-fest known as "The Burning Man" has been conducted. Attendance at the 1997 pagan carnival included an estimated 15,000 Wiccans, Satanists, Goddesses (white witches), nudists, and a consortium of other lost partygoers, who converge on the hot Nevada desert for a Labor Day weekend of "glorious Hell on earth." The number of participants at the Burning Man gala has nearly doubled each year since 1986, and, by the year 2000, organizers hope to break 30,000. The Burning Man is a no-holds-barred New Age "Woodstock" style festival, where neo-pagans, Wiccans, transvestite entertainers, backslidden Christians, and a host of others, go into a trance, perform rituals, burn sacrifices to idols, dance in the nude, engage in sex, and otherwise "express" themselves and become one with Gaia.

Attendees set up theme camps such as "Lost Vegas," "Motel 666," and "Crucifixion with a Celebrity" (where one can purchase a picture of a crucified obese Elvis). Hamburgers are sold by devil-worshipping pagans at the McSatan cafe, and T-shirts are available that proudly proclaim, "Praise the Whore." The Burning Man itself is a forty-foot-high effigy of the "Spirit Cave Man" (sacred to local Indians and New Agers) which is torched, together with just about everything else, at the close of the festivities.

George Otis Jr., president of The Sentinel Group (a Christian research agency), attended the 1996 Burning Man festival with a colleague. He wrote of the experience:

> On Saturday night, the hell-themed 1996 festival reached its crescendo in the form of a drama.... These people were literally celebrating the fact that one day they would enter hell.

To simulate their journey, the camp's center stage was transformed into the "Vestibule of Hell." The guest of honor was none other than "Papa Satan"... As the lecherous Papa Satan bowed in mock chains before a placard reading "Believe in the Lord Jesus Christ and thou shalt be saved," a group called "Idiot Flesh," [supposedly Christians] dressed as hooded executioners, began to play a discordant dirge accompanied by flashing strobes. When the crowd started its torchlight procession toward the Gates of Hell and an eerie, sculpted castle called The City of Dis, I sensed an unmistakable chill in the air. Our march had been joined by unseen, malevolent guests...nudist and a moving sea of devil banners [also] moved around us... At the tri-tower City of Dis, our descent into the Inferno reached a demonic sanctuary... While massive loudspeakers pumped out a hellish bass tone accompanied by tormented screams...people dressed as demonic insects celebrated by copulating with other captured souls. It was a scene that looked as if it had been plucked from a horrific nightmare. Mesmerized by the evocative music, the performers began to chant, "Devil's delight, fire tonight!" Wood piles inside the towers of Dis were ignited, causing orange flames to belch forth from the eyes and mouths of demonic gargoyles built onto the turrets. *As* the heat became more intense, the entourage danced around the towers. Satan had defeated the church.[31] (brackets added)

Otis continued the report by confessing, "I had to remind myself that what I had witnessed at the Burning Man Festival was happening right here in the United States, not in the temples of India or the deserts of Sinai." He also admits that he met many friendly, creative, and intelligent people at the Burning Man festival, and he encourages believers to contend for such lost souls in prayer.

Zeus, Osiris, and Apollo Live!— New Age Oracles

"What advantage then hath the Jew?... Much every way: chiefly, because that unto them were committed the oracles of God" (Rom. 3:1–2). When the apostle Paul wrote to the church at Rome concerning the oracles *(logion,* "divine utterances") that God gave to the Jews, he was referring to the revelations of the Old Testament Law and Prophets. In the Bible, the word "oracle" means supernatural utterance. It can also refer to a device used in the production of divine utterances. The Bible is an oracle, as was the Urim and Thummim (sacred devices) of the Old Testament. When a man or a woman speaks as a true prophet of God, he or she is likewise considered "an oracle of God" (1 Peter 4:11).

New Age pagans, such as those who attend the Burning Man Festival, are extremely interested in such oracular phenomena, and readily accept certain portions of the Bible as divinely oracular (the verses they believe support their ideas of God, reincarnation, spirit communing, and the afterlife). But, in the quest for spiritual knowledge, modern pagans also reach out beyond the "confines" of the Bible into a veiled world of mystical utterances, table-tapping, Ouija boards, psychic phone lines, visualization, channeling, and other esoteric forms of prognostication.

I once preached a sermon on oracles and the "death of the Olympian gods." I boldly proclaimed that Christianity had swept the globe, and that, as far as I knew, not a living person remained on earth that bowed in reverence to Apollo, or consulted at his sacred shrines. The sermon was received with rousing applause by the audience, and I sold some tapes. The only problem was, I was wrong. Apollo's Oracle at Delphi, the most famous oracle of antiquity, is in ruins. But the worship of the Olympian god, and the order of his pythian priestesses, are actively involved in Wiccan and New Age paganism in the 1990s. The fact is, it's unclear if the worship of Apollo or the consulting of his oracles ever ceased.

There is some evidence that generational witches may have continued the worship of Apollo and the secrets of his pythian divination for centuries. Whether or not that's true, the admirers of Apollo number in the tens of thousands today. This is primarily because Apollo is an oracle god, and his disciples are granted a "divine audience." Unlike other underworld spirits, Apollo audibly communicates (at times with amazing accuracy in antiquity) through the vocal cords of the pythoness to his followers. This characteristic originally caused, and apparently continues to cause, a tremendous cult popularity for Apollo. The Greek historian, Herodotus (considered the father of history), wrote of an interesting event. Croesus, the king of Lydia, expressed doubt regarding the accuracy of Apollo's Oracle at Delphi. To test the oracle, Croesus sent messengers to inquire of the pythian prophetess as to what he, the king, was doing on a certain day. The priestess surprised the king's messengers by visualizing the question, and by formulating the answer, before they arrived. A portion of the historian's account reads:

> The moment that the Lydians (the messengers of Croesus) entered the sanctuary, and before they put their questions, the Pythoness thus answered them in hexameter verse: "…Lo! on my sense there striketh the smell of a shell-covered tortoise, Boiling now on a fire, with the flesh of a lamb, in a cauldron. Brass is the vessel below, and brass the cover above it." These words the Lydians wrote down at the mouth of the Pythoness as she prophesied, and then set off on their return to Sardis… [when] Croesus undid the rolls…[he] instantly made an act of adoration…declaring that the Delphic was the only really oracular shrine…For on the departure of his messengers he had set himself to think what was most impossible for any one to conceive of his doing, and then, waiting till the day agreed on came, he acted as he had determined. He took a tortoise and a lamb, and cutting them in pieces with his own hands, boiled them

together in a brazen cauldron, covered over with a lid which was also of brass. (Herodotus, book 1: 47, brackets added)

The demon Apollo established an enormous following through such prophetic trickery, and, evidently, continues to do so. On the Internet, there are numerous Web sites dedicated to the modern worship of Apollo, and some such sites teach the methods and sacred locations of current pythian oracular activity.

Modern pagans are drawn to oracles because oracles ostensibly prove the existence of a spirit world, and because they seemingly provide a method of communicating with such spirits. Besides the pythian, ancient oracles being revived by the participants of New Age paganism include interpreting the flame of candles, the organs of animals, the behavior of water, and the wisping of wind through the leaves of trees. Tree oracles, such as the necromantic oak tree of Zeus at Dodona, were among the most popular oracles of the ancient world. This was due in part to the belief that the root of the tree extended into the lower world, and the tree was thus connected to the underworld dead. Judy Vorfeld admitted communing with tree spirits when she was involved in New Age mysticism. As a biblical endorsement of the activity, New Agers erroneously claim that 2 Samuel 5:24 is a scriptural account of King David consulting with tree oracles, and they point out that Jehovah instructed David to "smite the host of the Philistines" after he heard "the sound of a going in the tops of the mulberry trees."

Angels are another popular oracular entity of New Agers. Literally dozens of New Age books describe methods of communicating with the spirit world through the "assistance" of angels. Such book titles are self-explanatory: *Ask Your Angels: A Practical Guide to Working with the Messengers of Heaven to Empower and Enrich Your Life*, and, *The Angels Within Us: A Spiritual Guide to the Twenty-two Angels that Govern Our Lives*. In one publication, we discover the interesting "identity" of such governing spirits as the author describes an encounter with his angel-oracle:

The swirling fog began to dissipate, and I could see the flicker of a light ahead—a darting, pulsating glow resembling a firefly. I paused for a moment to observe, and the tiny flare expanded in size and appeared as a small full moon touching the earth. As I moved closer to the radiance, it suddenly changed into a vertical beam, a pillar of transparent light.

"Are you the angel I am seeking?" I asked. The soft yet powerful feminine voice replied,

"I am the Angel of Creative Wisdom."

"Do you have a name?"

"Some have called me Isis," she said, and with those words the pillar of light slowly materialized to reveal the face and form of a beautiful woman wearing a flowing white robe trimmed in gold.[32]

Can you believe it? "Isis" is identified as a New Age angel! Satan is clever. While such angel-oracles are undoubtedly popular among New Age devotees, the most curious form of oracular activity reinvigorated by pagans today is the "psychomanteum": a simple, yet eerie, idea. A chair, placed in front of a large mirror in a dark room, serves as the oracle. Once positioned on the chair, the occupant stares into the mirror and waits for contact with the ghosts of the departed. In ancient times, the psychomanteum's mirror system of communicating with "spirits" was employed by primitive Greeks in gloomy underground caverns called "halls of visions." Standing in front of a shining metal surface or caldron, grieving ancients saw and spoke with familiar apparitions.

The Sumerians, Egyptians, and Romans employed similar oracles of polished crystal, brass mirrors, and pools of water. Some argue that the Apostle Paul was referring to such mirror-oracles when he said, "For now we see through a glass, darkly; but then face to face: now I know in part; but then shall I know even as also I am known" (1 Cor. 13:12). The New Age psychomanteum is likewise used to facilitate contact with deceased relatives or family members and is increasingly being encouraged by New Age psychiatrists as a method for dealing with grief. Sometimes, under nefarious conditions, the mirror-contact phenomenon spontaneously occurs. As a teenager, my wife was involved in a horrific accident that killed her dad and sister. Following the accident, her eleven-year-old sister "materialized" in the bedroom mirror on two occasions. Since the house she lived in was formerly occupied by gypsies, my wife believes this fact contributed to the spontaneous psychomanteum activity.

In his book, *Reunions,* Raymond Moody promotes the use of the New Age psychomanteum as an oracle. He has documented the experiences of more than three hundred users of the device, and points out that 50 percent claim to have been contacted by a deceased relative or friend during the first try. People interviewed by Moody include physicians, teachers, housewives, business owners, and law enforcement officials. One such witness, an accountant who grieved over his departed mother a year after her death, testified of his experience with the psychomanteum:

> There is no doubt that the person I saw in the mirror was my mother! I don't know where she came from, but I am convinced that what I saw was the real person. She was looking out at me from the mirror. I could tell she was in her late 70s, about the same age as...when she died. However, she looked happier and healthier than she had at the end of her life. Her lips didn't move, but she spoke to me and I clearly heard what she had to say. She said, "I am fine," and smiled.... I stayed as relaxed as I could and just looked at her.... Then I decided to talk to her. I said, "It's good to see you again."
>
> "It's good to see you, too," she replied. That was it. She simply disappeared.[33]

A physician was unexpectedly contacted by a nephew while seated in a psychomanteum:

I suddenly had a very strong sense of the presence of my nephew, who had committed suicide.... I heard his voice very clearly. He greeted me and brought me a very simple message. He said, "Let my mother know that I am fine and that I love her very much." This experience was profound. I know he was there with me.[34]

Although the Bible warns of communicating with "familiar spirits" and of consulting mediums, the revival of ancient oracles, and the experiences being drawn from them, are especially seductive curiosities to the followers of New Age paganism. Communications with the dead, channeling, trancing, near-death experiences, and other forms of mediumship, harmonize a coveted and reassuring New Age theme, "I'm fine now," "All is well," "I'm waiting for you." New Agers and neo-pagans cherish such next-life universalism, and, while they typically reject the Judea-Christian Hell, they willingly embrace the message of the oracle gods, Osiris, Zeus, and Apollo, which tell them that everyone eventually goes to "heaven."

DIONYSUS, ASCLEPIUS, AND HECATE LIVE! NEW AGE MYSTICISM

A spirit of mysticism has been present in the United States for generations. Like an insidious cancer, unseen, patient, deadly, it has grown. Indications of its presence have been felt occasionally, and confirmations of its actuality have been documented from Washington D.C. to Portland, Oregon. By tracing city-name origins, such as Ceres, Alexandria, Mars, Fortuna, and Media, one discovers the early influence of such mysticism within the United States. By looking at sites such as the House of the Temple, the home office of Scottish Rite Freemasonry, one discovers a continuation of the ancient occultism. Located several blocks from the White House on 16th Street in Washington D.C., the House of the Temple contains eight candelabrum fashioned after Hermes, the "god of light," as well as various other artworks reminiscent of the Temple of Dionysus. Statues of the goddesses, Isis and Nephthys, stand hallowed inside.

One can exit the House of the Temple, walk down the street and around the corner, and take pictures of an enormous obelisk (phallic Egyptian symbol of fertility) known as the Washington Monument. From there one can travel across country to Portland, Oregon, where a huge statue ("Portlandia") representing of the goddess Hecate, stands overshadowing the entrance to the City of Portland Office buildings. On the Portland City Seal, "Lady Commerce" holds a trident under a six-pointed star. Both are important instruments of Hecatian witchcraft.

To the South, in California, Athene (Minerva), the manly goddess of war, greets humans from a prominent position on the Great Seal of the State of California. Other states boasting similar Great Seals and goddesses include New York (Liberty and Justice); Oklahoma (Themis); New Jersey (Ceres and Liberty); and Florida. Even the Great Seal of the United States depicts an array of equally abstruse symbols, including an unfinished Egyptian pyramid overshadowed by the "All-Seeing Eye" and bearing the cryptic phrase, *NOVUS ORDO SECLORUM*, "A new order of the ages."

As we approach the culmination of the "new order of the ages," cult experts forecast a staggering revival of idolatry and Eastern mysticism. As church attendance declines across the United States, Buddhists, Muslims, Hindus, Theosophists, Christian Scientists, and New Agers, expand to meet the desires and mystical interests of Americans. Tarot card reading is at an all-time high. Psychic phone lines are jammed with over $300 million in calls per year, and celebrities such as LaToya Jackson and Dionne Warwick lend credibility to psychic consultations. Even the US Government has shown interest in such phenomena. During the 1995 budget cuts, the CIA was forced to release a $20 million project ("Operation Stargate") aimed at studying the usefulness of psychics in gathering military secrets from foreign powers.

The wives of two U.S. Presidents, Nancy Reagan and Hillary Clinton, have also been the subject of public examination since it was discovered that they consulted with astrologers and psychics. Hillary Clinton went so far as to channel "conversations" with the spirit of Eleanor Roosevelt. Whether such conversations included a White House psychomanteum, or other oracular device, is unknown, but the obvious widespread interest in such paranormal activity substantiates what Judy Vorfeld has said: "Dabbling in the realm of the occult is currently stylish. Even some Christians seem unable to avoid the attraction of this colorful, seductive world."[35]

The colorful seduction of mysticism is reaching into every fiber of our culture. From public school Environmental Education to faddish television good guys, today's generation is bombarded with a New Age Occultianity (Western Christian beliefs mixed with occultism) that popularizes the supernatural. Beloved comic book heroes such as "Spawn" teach our youth the dangerous Persephonian idea that a person can be in league with the devil, and still be a good person. Such doctrines of "harmonizing duality" are extremely popular (comics of "Spawn" have sold over 100 million copies) and blend nicely with the syncretistic goals of the New Age Movement. Judy Vorfeld continues:

> The mystical, make-believe world of yesteryear, whose delightful stories tickled the imaginations of generations of young people, has evolved into a magical world of pseudo-reality for people of all ages. It's seen as a world of "good" creatures having supernatural powers and using them to stamp out "evil" beings. These popular characters are displayed on such items as cereal boxes, T-shirts, glassware, jewelry, bumper stickers, bedding, school folders, and toothbrushes.... Television paved the way by giving us sympathetic, clever characters like Samantha, Tabitha, Endora, and Jeannie.... Now our culture is surrounded with supernatural cuddly toys, adorable magic elves, pastel-colored unicorns, and extraterrestrial entities who roam earth's atmosphere offering love, justice, comfort, reincarnation, and other types of eternal life.[36]

Christians must realize that powerful and ancient entities are behind such mystical playthings. In the air above and the earth beneath are nefarious progenitors of Old/New Age mysticism. "Gods" to some and "demons" to others, such forces have numerous titles. They can appear in hideous forms or as beautiful angels of light. They are the "wicked spirits" *(poneria:* the collective body of demon soldiers comprising Satan's hordes), "rulers of darkness" *(kosmokrators:* governing spirits of darkness), "powers" *(exousia:* high ranking powers of evil), and "principalities" *(arche:* commanding generals over Satan's fallen army) of Ephesians 6:12. As the gods who walk among us, they live today and encourage mysticism among pagans, witches, New Agers, churchgoers, and the general public, in at least the following ways:

Aphrodite—sensuality, fertility rites, wiccan rituals, sacred prostitution;

Amun-Ra—masturbation, self-realization, environmentalism, Darwinism;

Apis—animal worship, animal rights, animal channeling, occultianity;

Apollo—humanism, oracles, channeling, psychics, drugs, visualization;

Artemis—goddess worship, animal worship, animal rights, debauchery;

Asclepius—holistic medicine, psychic dreaming, spirit-guide animals;

Athene—goddess worship, feminism, the spirituality movement;

Baal—oracles, polytheism, abortion, fertility issues;

Demeter—environmental education, earth worship, goddess worship;

Dionysus—excessive wine, Freudianism, ecstasy, pornography, sexual perversion, abortion;

Eros—eroticism, mystical sex, body worship, body piercing, sacred prostitution;
Gaia—earth worship, environmentalism, paganism, pantheism, sweat lodges;
Geb—environmental movement, animal rights, eco-paganism;
Hades—devil worship, occultism, spiritism, necromancy;
Hathor—goddess worship, earth worship, animal rights, animal worship;
Hecate—witchcraft, necromancy, crystals, spells, druidism, feminism;
Heka—mysticism, demonism, animal rights, environmentalism;
Hypnos—hypnotism, psychic dreaming, prognostication, e.s.p., clairvoyance;
Imhotep—mystic healing, animal dancing, holistic medicine, vision quests;
Isis—Wicca, witchcraft, goddess worship, magic, channeling, visualization;
Min and Qetesh—fertility rites, body worship, sensuality, pornography;
Osiris—occultianity, necromancy, anthropomorphism, occultism, spiritism;
Persephone—animism, Zoroastrianism, dualism, magic, necromancy;
Ptah—universalism, pantheism, mysticism, holistic medicine;
Sekhmet—environmentalism, mystic medicine, animal worship;
Seth—rebellion, earth worship, environmental movement;
Vatchit—devil worship, channeling, trancing, visualization, necromancy;
Zeus—Satanism, transsexualism, pantheism, oracles, animal worship.

By whatever names they may be called, the underworld spirits, historically referred to as gods and goddesses, are gathering the combined efforts of the kingdom of Satan into a conspiracy of apocalyptic proportions. As a consequence, we are experiencing an unprecedented revival of paganism at a time when the United States is considered the most advanced economic and technological power in the world. Why paganism? There's an ominous answer. Billy Graham declares, "Lucifer, our archenemy, controls one of the most powerful and well-oiled war machines in the universe. He controls principalities, powers, and dominions. Every nation, city, village, and individual has felt the hot breath of his evil power. He is already gathering the nations of the world for the last great battle in the war against Christ—Armageddon."[37]

The following chapter will discuss paganism's ultimate contribution to the battle of Armageddon—the resurrection of the Pharaoh spirit, the human god-king.

— *Chapter Five* —

THE NEW AGE OF THE GOD KING

> "Kingship, like the gods, has for most people at most times had an appeal far profounder than its purely practical and political significance would explain: in many parts of the world kings have been reverenced as being sacred, or even divine."
> —*Man, Myth & Magic*

In the near future, a man of superior intelligence, wit, charm, and diplomacy will emerge on the world scene as a savior. He will seemingly possess a transcendent wisdom that enables him to solve problems and offer solutions to many of today's most perplexing issues. His popularity will be widespread, and his fans will include young and old, religious and nonreligious, male and female. Talk show hosts will interview his colleagues, news anchors will cover his movements, scholars will applaud his uncanny ability at resolving what has escaped the rest of us, and the poor will bow down at his table. He will, in every human way, appeal to the best idea of society. But his profound comprehension and irresistible presence will be the result of an invisible network of thousands of years of collective knowledge. He will, like the pharaohs of Egypt, represent the embodiment of a very old and super-intelligent spirit. Just as Jesus Christ was the "seed of the woman" (Gen. 3:15), he will be the "seed of the serpent." Although his arrival in the form of a man was foretold by numerous Scriptures, the broad masses of the world will not recognize him as paganism's ultimate incarnation, the "beast" of Revelation 13:1.

It's been assumed for centuries that a prerequisite for the end-time Pharaoh (the Antichrist) will be a "revived" world order, an umbrella under which national boundaries dissolve, and ethnic groups, ideologies, religions, and economics from around the world, orchestrate a single and dominant sovereignty. Such a system will supposedly be free of religious and political extremes, and membership will tolerate the philosophical and cultural differences of its constituents. Except for minor nonconformities, war, intolerance, and hunger will be a thing of the past. At the head of the utopian administration, a single personality will surface. He will appear to be a man of distinguished character, but will ultimately become "a king of fierce countenance" (Dan. 8:23). With imperious decree, he will facilitate a one-world government, a universal religion, and global socialism. Those who refuse his New World Order will inevitably be imprisoned or destroyed, until at last he exalts himself "above all that is called God, or that is worshiped, so that he, as God, sitteth in the temple of God, showing himself that he is God" (2 Thess. 2:4).

For many years, the idea of an Orwellian society, where a one-world government oversees the smallest details of our lives and where human liberties are abandoned, was considered anathema. The concept that rugged individualism could be sacrificed for an anesthetized universal harmony was repudiated by America's greatest minds. Then, in the 1970s, things began to change. Following a call by Nelson Rockefeller for the creation of a "new world order,"[38] presidential candidate Jimmy Carter campaigned, saying, "We must replace balance of power politics with world order politics."[39] Evidently, he struck a chord with world leaders. During the 1980s, President George Bush continued the one-world dirge by announcing over national television that "a new world order" had arrived. Following the initial broadcast, President Bush addressed Congress and made the additional comment:

> What is at stake is more than one small country [Kuwait], it is a big idea—a new world order, where diverse nations are drawn together in common cause to achieve the universal aspirations

of mankind: peace and security, freedom, and the rule of law. Such is a world worthy of our struggle, and worthy of our childrens' future![40] (brackets added)

Ever since the President's astonishing newscast, a parade of political and religious leaders has discharged a profusion of New Age rhetoric aimed at implementing the goals of the New World Order. Al Gore, in his book *Earth In the Balance,* wrote that "we must all become partners in a bold effort to change the very foundation of our civilization." The director of the United Nations World Health Organization, Brock Chisolm, announced: "To achieve world government, it [will be] necessary to remove from the minds of men their individualism, loyalty to family traditions, national patriotism."[41] (brackets added)

And New Age guru Benjamin Creme hit the nail on the head by admitting: "What is the plan? It includes the installation of a new world government and a new world religion under Maitreia."[42] (Maitreia is a New Age "messiah.")

Concurrent with the political aspects of the New World Order is the syncretistic and spiritual goals of the New Age Movement. The blending of politics and spirituality, such as occurs in New Age mysticism, harmonizes perfectly with the ideas of an end-time marriage of governmental policy and religious creed as was prophesied in the Bible. To that end, the tools necessary for paganism's ultimate incarnation, the god-king of the Great Tribulation (Satan in flesh), are in place. The "gods" have been revived through modern mysticism. The pagan agenda of governing by "divine representation" is being constructed. The governments of the world are uniting beneath a one-world banner, and the earth's masses stand at the brink of a decisive moment in time.

In his book, *The New World Order,* Pat Robertson sees the strategy of the coming world leader played out in the following way:

> It is as if a giant plan is unfolding, everything perfectly on cue. Europe sets the date for its union. Communism collapses. A

hugely popular war is fought in the Middle East. The United Nations is rescued from scorn by an easily swayed public. A new world order is announced. Christianity has been battered in the public arena, and New Age religions are in place in the schools and corporations, and among the elite. Then a financial collapse accelerates the move toward a world money system.

The United States...turns its defense requirements over to the United Nations, along with its sovereignty. The United Nations severely limits property rights and clamps down on all Christian evangelism and Christian distinctives under the Declaration of the Elimination of All Forms of Intolerance and Discrimination Based on Religious Belief already adopted by the General Assembly.... Then the New Age religion of humanity becomes official, and the new world order leaders embrace it. Then they elect a world president with plenary powers who is totally given to the religion of humanity.[43]

Who will be enthroned as the President of the New World Order? Lord Maitreia? United Nations Secretary General Boutros Boutros-Ghali? A resurrected John F. Kennedy? The Pope? A complete unknown? I do not know. But an ancient scheme is unfolding. At the core of the conspiracy, a leader of indescribable brutality is scheduled to appear. He will make the combined depravities of Antiochus Epiphenes, Hitler, Stalin, and Genghis Khan, all of whom were types of the antichrist, look like child's play. He will raise his fist, "speaking great things...in blasphemy against God, to blaspheme his name, and his tabernacle, and them that dwell in heaven" (Rev. 13:5–6). He will champion worship of the "old gods" and "cause that as many as would not worship the image of the beast should be killed" (Rev. 13:15), and he will revive an ancient mystery religion that is "the habitation of devils, and the hold of every foul spirit, and a cage of every unclean and hateful bird" (Rev. 18:2). Such verses are reminiscent of the Mystery religions of Dionysus and Demeter, in which the Greek god Pan, a consort of

Dionysus, was famous for his pandemonium ("all the devils"). The coming world religion will be similar to the Dionysian cult in that those who reject the will of the New Age god-king will be destroyed.

Pandemonium!
The Pagan Gospel of the New Age God King

The Gospel, according to the New Age Movement, is an expansive idea centered around the birth of a new world "consciousness." As a religion of monism (all is one), New Agers hope to accomplish what the builders of the Tower of Babel failed to do: unify the masses of the world under a single religious umbrella, and, at the macro level, harmonically converge the world's energies with the power of Gaia. To promote such goals, New Agers claim that God is pantheistic *(God is all and all is God)* and that humans are divine members of the whole "that God is." According to New Ageism, Jesus came to reveal this pantheistic nature of God and to teach humanity the gospel of Self Realization. After illustrating the divine principle of "God within us all," Jesus ascended to a place of distinction to live among the Masters of the Spiritual Hierarchy, including Buddha and Krishna. Jesus promised that the essence of God would be revealed from time to time, and, thus, New Agers look for the imminent appearing of a World Teacher who will, as Jesus did, illustrate the divine human potential. In this way, New Age theology prepares the world for the coming of the False Prophet and the Antichrist.

Pagans claim such a religion of Self-realization, a belief that will be championed by the Antichrist, is older than Christianity. That's true. The gospel according to the New Age Movement, a gospel of "becoming god," is as old as the fall of man. It began when the serpent said to the woman "ye shall be as gods" (Gen. 3:5), and it will culminate during the reign of the Tribulation god-king. The New Age movement provides the perfect creed for implementing such an end-time religion. It unifies the religions of the world. It consecrates the forces of nature. It provides for human divinity, and it is vogue, postmodern, and politically correct. Tal Brooke, former New Age disciple of Hindu holy man, Sai Baba, confirms that "the New Age movement, and its progeny, Gaia, are spiritually correct for a new world order. Christianity is not."[44] Thus, history repeats itself, and the ancient Egyptian gospel of men becoming "gods" is fashionable again! Consequently, New Age celebrities such as Shirley MacLaine represent themselves as "I AM that I AM" at human potential symposiums around the world, and the Vice President of the United States, Al Gore, describes God in terms of "a constant and holy spiritual presence in all people, all life, and all things."[45] Hillary Clinton channels the spirits of the dead and members of the House of Representatives warn Congress of "increasing evidence of a government-sponsored religion in America…[a] cloudy mixture of New Age mysticism, Native American folklore and primitive earth worship."[46] (brackets added)

For many years, Christians wondered how the Antichrist would deceive the earth's masses. How does one convince millions of people, especially in countries where Christianity exists, to exchange their souls for temporary earthly benefits? Then, the New Age Movement came along with its focus on human-potential and self-empowerment and successfully drew many Christians away from Christ-exalting doctrines. Old-fashioned Gospel preaching was replaced with positive thinking, self-realization, and pop psychology, and mystical experiences which tantalize the flesh, were sanctioned as "the last great revival." As a result, celebrity preachers advance sermons focusing on "the inner self," and Sunday morning services begin with shouts of "Are you ready for God to do great things!?" The implication that God will meet with believers and grant their many requests is touted as dynamic Christianity. The days of unconditional Christian devotion are threatened as contemporary congregations expect God to "manifest" Himself and please the whims of the audience. Although Jesus warned of an "evil and adulterous generation [that] seeketh after a sign," physical and mystical "thrills" have become the benchmark of many popular Christian gathering places. The result is a growing superficiality among some Christians who are preoccupied with mysticism and "me-ism."

As a businessman and ministry leader, I've tasted the bitter results of the "new age" segment of Christianity. Too often, these believers fall, flop, quiver, shake, and gyrate on Sunday, but can't get out of bed and go to work Monday morning. Among such employees, I've found insignificant character differences between religious groups, and "Christians" have been just as likely as nonbelievers to lie, cheat, and steal at my place of business. Perhaps I've been unlucky, or maybe, as I believe, twenty years of popular New Age metaphysical focusing on "self" has so impacted this generation that many "Christians" are willing to dilute their character to acquire what pleases them. Either way, an inward-focusing generation of "religious people" willing to trade their soul for whatever makes them happy is exactly what is necessary for the appearance of Antichrist. "You can stamp my hand if you'll give me what I want" is the required attitude. While many Christians and New Age devotees are sincere, giving people, the lasting result of the New Age Movement is nevertheless demonic, self-absorbed, and paves the way for the coming of paganism's preeminent materialization, the god-king of the Great Tribulation.

New Age Angels and the Chariot of the God King

When I was a child, my father made an amazing discovery while deer hunting in the mountains of Arizona. Several large and perfectly spherical craters, perhaps twenty feet across and eight feet deep, were located in an unexplored section of the range where he was hunting. The mysterious cavities were so precise that it looked as if an enormous white-hot ball had pushed into the rock, and the finish on the walls was such that rainwater filled the orbs. The sides of the holes were slick and each "pool" contained deer that had fallen in and drowned while attempting to drink the water. Dad took pictures of the obscure semi-spherical holes (he showed them to the family and I remember being especially impressed), and led a representative of the Army Corps of Engineers to the location. The origin of the puzzling craters was never determined, and the Corps of Engineers filled the pools with rock to protect the wildlife. A local newspaper ran an article on the baffling holes, reprinted photographs of my father kneeling beside the orbs, and that seemed to be the end of the story.

Then, on 5 November 1975, along the northeastern ridge of an Arizona mountain range, Travis Walton stepped out of his pickup to look at a mysterious glowing object. While a crew of loggers waited nearby, Travis approached the UFO and was jolted by a blast of inexplicable energy. As his companions fled in terror, Travis was taken onboard the alien spacecraft and subjected to a variety of physical examinations. His story, *Fire in the Sky*, is now a motion picture. It reports what's considered to be the best documented account of a UFO abduction ever recorded. Is Travis Walton's story true? Was there a connection between the Walton-UFO and the mysterious mountain holes? Did the experiences of my sister who saw small alien-like creatures around her bed at night for years following the discovery mean anything? I don't know. But the strange phenomenon known as UFO activity is sure to play a part in the coming World Order and in the introduction of the New Age god-king.

As mentioned in chapter one, I believe a portion of UFO activity is demonic. Increasingly, others agree with that opinion. Hal Lindsey states, "I have become thoroughly convinced that UFOs are real.... I believe these beings are not only extraterrestrial but supernatural in origin. To be blunt, I think they are demons."[47] In *Angels Dark and Light*, Gary Kinnaman claims, "I am fairly convinced that...UFO sightings are the manifestations of angels of darkness. My main reason for thinking this is that UFO sightings have never, at least to my knowledge, led a person closer to God. In fact, most UFO experiences have just the opposite effect."[48] UFO celebrity and author of *Communion* (the bestselling book about his alleged alien abduction), Whitley Streiber, describes UFOnauts in terms of demonology.

THE NEW AGE OF THE GOD KING

He writes:

> There are worse things than death, I suspected. And I was beginning to get the distinct impression that one of them had taken an interest in me. So far the word demon had never been spoken among the scientists and doctors who were working with me. And why should it have been? We were beyond such things. We were a group of atheists and agnostics, far too sophisticated to be concerned with such archaic ideas as demons and angels."[49]

Associate professor of psychology Elizabeth L. Hillstrom points out that a growing number of academics support the conclusion that UFOnauts are synonymous with historical demons. In her informative book, *Testing the Spirits,* she writes:

> From a Christian perspective, Vallee's explanation of UFOs is the most striking because of its parallels with demonic activity. UFO investigators have noticed these similarities. Vallee himself, drawing from extrabiblical literature on demonic activities, establishes a number of parallels between UFOnauts and demons.... Pierre Guerin, a UFO researcher and a scientist associated with the French National Council for Scientific Research, is not so cautious: "The modern UFOnauts and the demons of past days are probably identical." Veteran researcher John Keel, who wrote *UFOs: Operation Trojan Horse* and other books on the subject, comes to the same conclusion: "The UFO manifestations seem to be, by and large, mere minor variations of the age-old demonological phenomenon."[50]

It's easy to believe that demons are involved with "flying saucers." Evil spirits can manipulate energy and matter, and the theological terms, "Transmogrification" and "Poltergeist" ("noisy ghost"), imply that spirits can make lights go off and on, doors bang, icons bleed, and saucers fly. But if a portion of "flying saucer" activity is demonic, what nefarious purpose is served by the stealthy nature of UFO phenomena? The answer is diabolical. UFO-ism seems to be aimed at preparing the earth for the coming of Antichrist, i.e., an extraterrestrial "visitation of the gods," and, more importantly, at changing our religious beliefs. This occurs in two ways: First, from a technological standpoint, UFO sightings challenge the claim of human superiority and dispute our unique role in the universe. We are made to feel shallow, undeveloped, unenlightened. Second, from a religious point of view, extraterrestrials bring a message (as reported in hundreds of abduction cases) of easy universalism and New Age mysticism including dialogue of humans "on the verge of extraordinary telepathic and technological growth." Benevolent ETs profess to watch over us and promise to appear at the appropriate time to assist in our next big evolutionary, spiritual, and technological step forward. To prepare us for their coming, popular movies, bestselling books, cultural trends, and religious ideas, focus the earth's masses on "help from above," and New Agers smile and explain "It's okay, they've been here before" and "Don't worry, ancient men simply described flying saucers in terms of demons, angels, and gods, because they didn't understand what they were seeing."

In other words, New Agers believe that space vehicles manipulating laws of physics (suddenly appearing and disappearing, operating anti-gravitationally, etc.) were assigned "god" or "angel" status by sincere but ignorant prophets, and that Ezekiel's living creatures will return someday in wheels "in the middle of a wheel" providing explanations of our origin and solutions to our problems. Such New Age claims of extraterrestrials visiting the earth in ancient times and interacting with men is biblically and historically true. Where Christians differ from New Agers is in the definition of who these creatures were and what they were doing. In the *Interlinear Hebrew Bible*, we read:

> The benei Elohim saw the daughters of Adam, that they were fit extensions. And they took wives for themselves from all those that they chose... The Nephelim were in the earth in those days, and even afterwards when the benei Elohim came in to the daughters of Adam, and they bore to them—they were Powerful Ones which existed from ancient times, the men of name. (Gen. 6:2, 4)

As noted in the first two chapters of this book, the benei Elohim were "extraterrestrial" angelic creatures also known as "watchers," "sons of God," and "rephaim." They visited the earth during antiquity and used the daughters of Adam as "fit extensions" or instruments through which they extended themselves into the physical world. They sought to corrupt the bloodline of Adam, to deceive the human race, and to prevent the birth of the Messiah. They represented themselves as "gods," and their offspring, the Nephilim ("fallen ones"), attempted to exterminate the people of Yahweh. In what may be a prophecy of end-time UFOs, Isaiah connected the benei Elohim to "fiery flying seraph." We read, "Do not rejoice O Philistia, all of you, for the rod of your striking is broken, because a viper (Antichrist) comes forth from the root of the snake (Satan) and his fruit is the fiery flying seraph" (Isa. 14:29). The seraph (seraphim) were powerful angels known for their brilliance. If, as we suspect, some of the seraphim followed Lucifer in the fall, it could be that such "fiery flying seraph" are the source of UFOs today. As previously noted; the "air" above the earth was considered by ancient Hebrew scholars to be the dwelling place of fallen angels. An interesting point of this is made by J. N. Schofield in *Man, Myth & Magic*:

> The warm interest of angels in mans' welfare is vividly expressed in the saying of Jesus that there is joy before the angels of God over one sinner who repents' (Luke 15), and that children have their guardian angels standing as favoured envoys near

God Himself (Matthew 18). It was through Jewish Christians that angeology, based on the Old Testament and other Jewish writings, entered the teaching of the Church. Angels were set over the life of Nature, and over human communities. God was Israel's portion but Michael was her protector, taught her Hebrew and gave the law on Sinai. Every individual had his guardian angel and babies exposed or aborted were cared for by guardian angels. There continued to be angelic intercessors and messengers of revelation or warning, but further functions were more specialized. There was an Angel of Repentance who brought to man consciousness of sin and the promise of forgiveness, and an Angel of Peace received the soul as it left the body and bore it to paradise. The Angel of Death in Sheol was a good angel and guardian of souls.

Angelic rank was associated with speculation about the universe, which increased to the three heavens known to St. Paul. All these were thought to be above the firmament [the kosmos] where fallen angels were imprisoned, and all were inhabited exclusively by angels, the lower heavens by those in charge of human affairs, the upper by Angels of the Presence. According to some speculation, these heavens (the *Hajoth Hakados*) were successive stages through which souls must pass, encountering their guardian angels to whom account must be given.

If it's true that fallen angels inhabit the earth's atmosphere and that, historically, they conducted genetic experiments on the daughters of Adam and thereby produced the mutant Nephilim, does the prophecy of Jesus in Luke 17:26 indicate such activity would reoccur before the Rapture? Does recent UFO abduction activity point to genetic engineering of a new race of anti-God warriors (Nephilim) as we approach the Great Tribulation? Will UFOs provide the grand entry of the ultimate cross-mutation of angelic and human species, the god-king of the New World Order? Time will tell. Until then:

> The mystery of iniquity doth already work: only he who now letteth will let, until he be taken out of the way. And then shall that wicked be revealed, whom the Lord shall consume with the spirit of his mouth, and shall destroy with the brightness of his coming: Even him, whose coming is after the working of Satan with all power and signs and lying wonders. (2 Thess. 2:7–9)

THE REAL WAR OF THE WORLDS

In a popular New Age book on angels we read:

> Even in this day and age, films like *The Omen*, *Rosemary's Baby*, and *The Seventh Sign* evoke horror, because they tap into the possibility that we may be influenced in some way by universal messengers of evil. However, according to our angelic informants [?], the situation, thank God, is not like that at all... Slowly, surely, we are collectively emerging from this *illusion of evil*.... Many contemporary Christians have begun to abandon the concept that there is a real devil, recognizing once again that there is only one omnipotent force in the universe.[51] (emphasis and brackets added)

Whereas some pagans profess a belief in Karma or Zoroastrianism (opposing forces of good and evil), the idea of personal evil spirits such as Satan and his angels is rejected by New Agers. The concepts of Hell and a future Great Judgment are also disregarded. But the reality of Hell and the doom of Satan's followers is nevertheless described in the Bible. The "old gods" of the underworld, including Zeus, Apollo, Demeter, Isis, and others, will be judged by Yahweh. "The Lord will be terrible unto them: for he will famish all the gods of the earth" (Zeph. 2:11). "The Lord of hosts, the God of Israel, saith; Behold, I will punish the...gods" (Jer. 46:25). Yahweh will also punish the leader of the gods, that old serpent, called the Devil, and his human followers. In Isaiah we read:

Come, my people, enter thou into thy chambers, and shut thy doors about thee: hide thyself as it were for a little moment, until the indignation be overpast. For, behold, the Lord cometh out of his place to punish the inhabitants of the earth for their iniquity: the earth also shall disclose her blood, and shall no more cover her slain. In that day the Lord with his sore and great and strong sword shall punish Leviathan the piercing serpent, even Leviathan that crooked serpent; and he shall slay the dragon that is in the sea. (Isa. 26:20–27:1)

However futile, the gods will retaliate, and a war of indescribable intensity will occur in the future. It will be fought on land and sea, in the heavens above, and in the earth below, in the physical and spiritual worlds. It will include "Michael and his angels [fighting] against the dragon; and the dragon [fighting] and his angels" (Rev. 12:7, brackets added). Heretics will join the battle and call upon "idols of gold, and silver, and brass, and stone, and of wood" (Rev. 9:20) to convene their evil powers against the Christian God, and New Agers will unite with "unclean spirits like frogs…the spirits of devils [the frog goddesses Heka or Hekate?] working miracles, which go forth unto the kings of the earth…to gather them to the battle of that great day…[to] a place called in the Hebrew tongue Armageddon ["Mount Megiddo"]" (Rev. 16:13–14; 16, brackets added). There, in the valley of Megiddo, the omnipotent Christ will utterly repel the forces of darkness and destroy the New World army. Blood will flow like rivers, and the fowl of the air will "eat the flesh of the mighty, and drink the blood of the princes of the earth." Tim LaHaye says, "As far back as the time of Napoleon, that great valley was claimed to be the most natural battleground of the whole earth."[52] Besides Armageddon, battles will be fought in the Valley of Jehoshaphat and in the city of Jerusalem. But the battle of Armageddon will climax the hostility between God Almighty and the lower gods of the underworld. Once before, Satan and his "god" spirits challenged Yahweh at Megiddo. They lost. On Mount Carmel, overlooking the Valley of Armageddon, the prophets of the demon-god Baal dared the Hebrew God to answer by fire. He did and He will again. When He does, where will you be? Will you join forces with the gods of the underworld and trust in the armies of the New Age/New World Order? If so, here is your future:

> And I saw the beast, and the kings of the earth, and their armies, gathered together to make war against him that sat on the horse [Jesus], and against his army [Christians and angels of God]. And the beast was taken, and with him the false prophet that wrought miracles before him, with which he deceived them that had received the mark of the beast, and them that worshipped his image. These both were cast alive into a lake of fire burning with brimstone. And the remnant were slain with the sword of him that sat upon the horse, which sword proceeded out of his mouth: and all the fowls were filled with their flesh.... And I saw a great white throne, and him that sat on it, from whose face the earth and the heaven fled away: and there was found no place [to hide]. And I saw the dead, small and great; stand before God; and the books were opened: and another book was opened, which is the book of life: and the dead were judged out of those things which were written in the books, according to their works... And whosoever was not found written in the book of life was cast into the lake of fire. (Rev.19:19–21; 20:11–12, 15, brackets added)

If you repent of your sins and believe on the Lord Jesus Christ you will experience a different destiny at the battle of Armageddon:

> And I saw heaven opened, and behold a white horse; and he that sat upon him was called Faithful and True [Jesus], and in righteousness he doth judge and make war. His eyes were as a flame of fire, and on his head were many crowns; and

he had a name written, that no man knew, but he himself. And he was clothed with a vesture dipped in blood: and his name is called The Word of God. And the armies which were in heaven [Christians and angels of God] followed him upon white horses, clothed in fine linen, white and clean. And out of his mouth goeth a sharp sword, that with it he should smite the nations: and he shall rule them with a rod of iron: and he treadeth the winepress of the fierceness and wrath of Almighty God. And he hath on his thigh a name written, KING OF KINGS, AND LORD OF LORDS... And I saw a new heaven and a new earth: for the first heaven and the first earth were passed away; and...I heard a great voice out of heaven saying, Behold, the tabernacle of God is with men.... And God shall wipe away all tears from their eyes; and there shall be no more death, neither sorrow, nor crying, neither shall there be any more pain: for the former things are passed away. And he that sat upon the throne said...I will give unto him that is a thirst of the fountain of the water of life freely. He that overcometh shall inherit all things; and I will be his God, and he shall be my son [or daughter] (Rev. 19:11–16; 20:1–7, brackets added).

Preceding such apocalypse, the year 2000 will undoubtedly herald the unprecedented changes of a final millennium. As the gods of the underworld work to establish dominion over mankind and within a new world order, the god-king (Antichrist) of the Great Tribulation will prepare for his appearance. Such is a time for Christians worldwide to unite in common cause. What can believers do about the spread of paganism and the goals of a New World Order?

First, Christians must resist the temptation to squander their time and energy pursuing silly mystical experiences and religious entertainment and wholly commit to the vocal community declaration of the Gospel of Jesus Christ. It is the preaching of the Gospel that embodies the power of God unto salvation; both of nations and of individuals.

Second, we must be willing to intercede in prayer and fasting for our nation and its leaders. The lower gods of the underworld and their impact on society have historically been overcome by heavenly activity generated by righteous men and women on bended knees.

Third, political representatives need to hear about Christian concerns. A single call or letter is considered by most congressmen to represent the will of many thousands of other Americans.

Fourth, let's prepare for the coming of Christ! Believers in this age need to draw close to God and to His Word and live righteously. As R.L. Brandt said in the foreword, "We are at the end of the age. The coming of our Lord is near. Let us sound the trumpet in Zion!"

A Word from Ex New-Ager Judy Vorfeld

"Everything is about power," says a character in a best-selling novel. This certainly appears to be the key theme of the Bible. God the Father, God the Son, and God the Holy Spirit, from the beginning, have all power, and, in their holiness, are worthy of the highest form of worship.

Early in the Bible we see Satan working relentlessly to become the only object of worship on Planet Earth. Fully aware of the nature and purposes of Jesus, Satan still tried to manipulate Him into worshipping him. Matthew 4:8 reveals that Satan "took Him to a very high mountain, and showed Him all the kingdoms of the world, and their glory; and he said to Him, 'All these things will I give You, if You fall down and worship me.'"

Through the centuries, the enemy downplays God's power and the work of the Cross. He continues to work vigorously to make Jesus an equal of Buddha, Mohammed, the Dalai Lama, and other wise ones. He often succeeds. But Christians know that Jesus came to Earth to die, not to teach platitudes or become politically correct. God didn't plan that Jesus would be on the *All-time List of the World's Greatest Teachers* or become *Time* magazine's Person of the Year.

Many people we love have fallen under the influence of deceived teachers and deceptive philosophies. Their doctrines, often graced with biblical words and phrases, undermine God's authority, ability, promises and power. These people cling to religion, hoping for peace, happiness, and meaning for their lives. They honestly believe that religious practices will accomplish this. At one time, so did I, ignorant of the fact that Satan offers a highway to happiness paved with empty promises and cheap glitter. Some of the road signs say, *This Way to a God Who Won't Embarrass You* (subtitle: Forget This "Born Again" Nonsense), *Turn Left For The God Of Your Design*, and *Two Miles To An Intellectually Stimulating God*. Countless souls struggle on this wide, but crowded, road.

God offers a slim, straight highway of simple faith, paved with the blood of Jesus, and ending at Calvary. Christianity offers a spiritual life based on what Christ did 2,000 years ago. Beyond the requirement of belief, God offers something quite different than all other religions: relationship.

I grew up thinking that Christianity required good works and constant church attendance. I also thought God was watching me with a lightning bolt in one hand and a sledgehammer in the other, waiting to get me if I misbehaved. After moving from Humanism to the New Age Movement to Christianity, I discovered that going to church was a choice and a privilege, but my eternal destiny wasn't based on how many times a week I attended church. Relationship with God, not religion, is everything.

Part of a healthy relationship comes from listening well, and I'm not always the best listener. God's voice is soft and gentle. I've learned that He loves me deeply and passionately. He shows it many times each day in tiny, precious ways. His delight in me helps me see myself through His eyes as one who is lovable. I've always been able to see the value and beauty in others, but not in myself.

How has He revealed Himself to me? Perhaps the best example is in filling a basic need, of having a loving relationship with my father. For most of my life, my father and I were strangers, and I had a hole in my soul. My parents divorced when I was a teen. I've been close to my mother most of my life; she's a friend and a delight. But by the time Dad reached 90, I figured things would always be the same. I loved him, but didn't know him. Several years ago, his family, converging from many parts of the country, and including many great-grandchildren, threw a surprise 90th birthday party for him. I believe this activated something deep inside him. The following year, I flew up from Arizona to visit him in Washington. For a solid week, we lugged cameras, maps, and sack lunches, hiking to many breathtaking locations. Actually, I hiked. Sometimes Dad (who has Congestive Heart Failure) crawled. We laughed a lot.

This visit triggered something in both of us, and our relationship began to change. Most of our contact since then has been via telephone. How can I express my feelings when my 94-year-old father says "I love you" as our conversations come to a close? His voice seems coated with honey. My heart bubbles with joy. I always hang up the phone in awe of a Heavenly Father who allowed this to happen. Would I have loved God as much if Dad had died before our special reconciliation? Absolutely. But God gave me a special gift, a just-for-Judy gift, another taste of his grace.

Christians, are any of your loved ones traveling the highway of futility? Are they trapped in paganism? Do you feel frustrated in your inability to share Jesus with them? Here are a few things you can do that may help them see the truth: Intercede. Ask God to help you see them from His perspective, to feel what He feels toward them. Be willing to have your heart broken with love as you experience God's deep, powerful love for them. Never stop praying for them. My family and Christian friends lifted me up before the Lord (some, for years) before I accepted Him.

Separate the believer from the belief, but be willing to be totally honest in discussing those beliefs, if God makes an opening.

Resist shooting them with "Bible Bullets," but know your Bible well, and be prepared to share the truth when the opening comes. If you are not a Christian, I ask one thing: on your own, begin reading the Bible, with the understanding that it may be more than an ordinary book and more than mere words. Consider reading, each day, about six chapters in the Old Testament to two in the New Testament, starting with Genesis and Matthew. Read it with this in mind: *does it reveal Jesus Christ as God's Son, and does it show how He made a way for you to have a deeply intimate relationship with Him?* Surely you can take time to read this book and see if it has truth and consistency running through it.

There is much truth in the statement that everything is about power. We humans constantly look for it in our lives. Anything we can understand, we can control (to one extent or another). This is why it is important for so many to have a god they can figure out. Many sincere people search in vain for a magic blueprint for happiness and meaning to life. One road offers any kind of a god you want. Pick from the gods of the past, the gods of the New Age, or go the create-a-god route: choose size, shape, age, race, gender, and composition.

The other road is just wide enough for one person at a time. At the end is Jesus. His open arms reach toward the traveler. All He offers is two nail-scarred hands.

NOTES

Spiritual Warfare

1. Smith, Dr. William, *Dictionary of the Bible* (New York: S. S. Scranton Company, 1903), 173.
2. Barnes, Albert, *Barnes Notes on the New Testament* (Grand Rapids, Mich.: Baker Book House, 1979), Corinthians, Introduction, IV, v.
3. *Empires Ascendant-Time Frame 400 BC–AD 200*, ed. George Constable (Alexandria, VA.: Time Life Books, 1987), 32.
4. Webster, David Hutton, Ph.D., *Ancient History* (New York: D. C. Heath & Co., Publishers, 1913), 293.
5. Fox, Robin Lane, *Pagans and Christians* (New York: Knopf, 1987), 245.
6. *The Illustrated Columbia Encyclopedia*, 4th ed., s.v. "Asclepius."
7. Durant, Will, *The Story of Civilization* (New York: Simon and Schuster, 1966), vol. II, 96.
8. Ibid.
9. Ibid., vol. III, 62.
10. Smith, *Dictionary of the Bible*, 723.
11. Fox, *Pagans*, 153.
12. Ibid.
13. Brown Ph.D., James D., *Jesus' Letter to the Church at Pergamus*, a presentation delivered at First Assembly of God in New Orleans, La., on December 14, 1986.
14. Unger, Merril F., *Biblical Demonology* (Wheaton, IL: Scripture Press Publishers, 1952), 140.
15. Tenney, Merril C., *New Testament Survey* (Grand Rapids, Mich.: Eredmans Publishing Co., 1961), 2.
16. *The Illustrated Columbia Encyclopedia*, 4th ed., s.v. "Caduceus."
17. Smith, *Dictionary of the Bible*, 724.
18. Woodrow, Ralph, *Babylon Mystery Religion* (Riverside, Calif.: Ralph Woodrow Evangelistic Association, Inc., 1966), 9–10.
19. 1 Maccabees 3:10–13.
20. 1 Maccabees 15:15–24.
21. *The International Standard Bible Encyclopedia*, s.v. "Gadara."
22. *The Works of Josephus*, Section on Wars (Chicago: John C. Winston Co., 1942), IV, VII, 1–4.
23. Pfeiffer, Charles F., *Bakers Bible Atlas* (Grand Rapids, Mich.: Baker Book House, 1979), 178.
24. Grant, Michael, *Herod the Great* (New York: American Heritage Press, 1971), 96–97.

NOTES

25 Ibid.
26 *Josephus*, Ant., XV, x, 3.
27 Gross, William J., *Herod the Great* (Baltimore: Helicon Press, 1962), 236–237.
28 Ibid.
29 Wuest, Kenneth S., *Word Studies in the Greek New Testament* (Grand Rapids, Mich.: Eredmans Publishing Co., 1966), vol. 1, 103.
30 Smith, *Dictionary of the Bible*, 276.
31 Russell, D. S., *The Jews from Alexander to Herod* (London: Oxford University Press, 1967), 24.
32 *International Bible Dictionary*, s.v. "Diana."
33 *The Broadman Bible Commentary* (Nashville: Broadman Press, 1972), vol. 12, 263.
34 Bruce, F. F., *The Book of Acts* (Grand Rapids, Mich.: Eredmans Publishing Company, 1977), 398.
35 *Comptons Pictured Encyclopedia and Fact Index*, s.v. "Diana."
36 *International Bible Dictionary*, s.v. "Diana."
37 *Encyclopedia of Occultism*, s.v. "Hecate."
38 Woodrow, *Babylon Mystery*, 17.
39 Goldman, Ari L., *The Oregonian* (April 13, 1991): Sec. C, 1.
40 *The Oregon Forward* (July/August Edition): vol. 89, issue 4, 14.
41 Rubenstein, Sura, *The Oregonian* (June 10, 1991).
42 Frank, Gerry, *The Oregonian* (December 2, 1988).
43 O'Neil, Patrick, *The Oregonian* (August 4, 1989).
44 Bella, Rick, *The Oregonian* (October 14, 1988).
45 Oliver, Gordon, *The Oregonian* (December 27, 1990): front page, vol. 139.
46 Aldrich, Dr. Joe, The Arise Conference, Multnomah School of the Bible, Portland, Oregon, October 26, 1988.
47 Seyl, Susan, *Origin and Brief History of the Seal of the City of Portland* (Portland, Oreg.: Oregon Historical Society, May 1981): l.
48 *Comptons Pictured Encyclopedia and Fact Index*, s.v. "Hecate."
49 *The Pentecostal Evangel* (January 30, 1994): 26.
50 Koch, Kurt E., *Christian Counseling and Occultism* (Grand Rapids, Mich.: Kregel Publications, 1972), 162.
51 Unger, Merril F., *Biblical Demonology* (Wheaton: Scripture Press Publishers, 1952), 193.
52 *Encyclopedia of Occultism*, s.v. "Litanies."
53 Cho, Dr. Paul, derived from a sermon he delivered at New Hope Community Church in Milwaukee, Oregon, October 8, 1986, evening service.
54 Buckingham, Jamie, *Charisma & Christian Life* (January 1990): 69.
55 Bureau of the Census, Statistical Abstract of the U.S., 1989.
56 *Oklahoma City Times* (June 28, 1982).
57 S.T.O.P., a project of the National Coalition Against Pornography, 800 Compton Rd., Cincinnati, Ohio.
58 Ibid.
59 Kennedy, Ph. D., James D., *Witches, Satanists, and the Occult* (Ft. Lauderdale, Fla.: Coral Ridge Ministries, n.d.), 1.

NOTES

60 Weintraub, Judith, *The Oregonian* (May 11, 1991): C-10.
61 Unger, *Demonology*, 60.
62 Interl' Inc. Times, New York (September 8, 1987): 1.
63 Ibid.
64 *Time* (June 12, 1986): 52.
65 *Journal of Epidemiology* (April 1989): 651.
66 *Charisma & Christian Life* (January 1991): 62.
67 *Charisma & Christian Life* (January 1990): 70.
68 Lutzer, Erwin, "America Today: A Nation Adrift," *The Rebirth of America*, Section Two (Philadelphia: Arthur S. DeMoss Foundation, 1986), 90.
69 Abraham Lincoln, April 30, 1863 (Rebirth of America), 151.
70 Ibid., 183.
71 Silvoso, Ed, Prayer Power, Global Church Growth, 1987 (July-August-September edition): 5.
72 Needham, Mrs. George C., *Angels and Demons* (Chicago: Moody Press Chicago), 70-71.
73 Marshall, Peter (Rebirth of America), 205.
74 Price, John, "America Tomorrow: A Nation Reborn," *The Rebirth of America*, Section Three (Philadelphia: Arthur S. DeMoss Foundation, 1986), 155.
75 Gordon, S. D., "America Tomorrow: A Nation Reborn," *The Rebirth of America*, Section Three (Philadelphia: Arthur S. DeMoss Foundation, 1986), 191.

THE GOD'S WHO WALK AMONG US

1 von Daniken, Erich, *Chariots of the Gods* (G.P. Putnam's Sons, New York, 1970), 10.
2 Ibid., 26.
3 McManus, Jason, *The UFO Phenomenon: Mysteries of the Unknown* (Time Life Books, Alexandria, VA, 1987), 12.
4 The Hollywood Reporter, *The Oregonian* (9 August 1996), Arts & Entertainment Guide, 26.
5 Wilford, John Noble, *The Oregonian* (7 August 1996), front page.
6 Kennedy, Ph. D., James, *The Real Meaning of the Zodiac* (TCRM Publishing, Ft. Lauderdale, FL, 1993), 6-8.
7 Horn, Thomas R., *Spiritual Warfare: The Invisible Invasion* (Lafayette, IA: Huntington House Publishers, 1998), 21–22.
8 Ibid., 24.
9 Durant, Will, *The Story of Civilization* (New York: Simon and Shuster, 1996), vol. 1, 199.
10 Cavendish, Richard, *Man, Myth & Magic* (Italy: B.P.C. Publishing Ltd., 1970), vol. 2, 237.
11 Jones, Horace Leonard, *The Geography of Strabo* (Cambridge, MA: Harvard University Press, 1967) vol. 8, 2453.
12 Fairservis, Jr., Walter A., *Egypt, Gift of the Nile* (New York: The Macmillan Company), 115.

NOTES

13 Cavendish, Richard, *Man, Myth & Magic,* s.v. "Zeus."
14 Ibid.
15 Ibid.
16 Horn, Thomas R., *Spiritual Warfare: The Invisible Invasion* (Lafayette, LA: Huntington House Publishers, 1998), 23–24.
17 Cavendish, Richard, *Man, Myth & Magic,* s.v. "Apollo."
18 Euripides, *The Bacchantes,* Dramatis Personare (Messenger to Pentheus concerning the Bacchantes), 410 B.C.
19 Otto, Walter F., *Dionysus Myth and Cult* (Indianapolis, IN: Indiana University Press, 1965), 114.
20 Ibid., 169.
21 Ibid., 116.
22 Lucius Apuleius, *The Golden Asse,* Book Eleven, 1566.
23 *The Hymns of Homer, XXX,* Chapter 11: 1–19.
24 Rhodius, Apollonius, *Argonautica,* translated by R.C. Seaton (Cambridge MA: Harvard University Press, 1912), 1026–1062; 1191–1224.
25 Vorfeld, Judy, *Joyful Woman* (July/August 1988), 15.
26 Smith, Samantha, *The Eagle Forum* (Fall/Winter 1997), 20.
27 Lindsey, Hal, *Planet Earth-2000 A.D.* (Palos Verdes, CA: Western Front, Ltd., 1994), 24.
28 Smith, Samantha, *Goddess Earth* (Lafayette, LA: Huntington House Publishers, 1994), 80–81.
29 Carolyn R. Staffer, *Shaman's Drum* (Fall 1987), 25.
30 Cavendish, Richard, *Man, Myth & Magic,* s.v. "Diana."
31 Otis Jr., George, *Charisma & Christian Life* (March 1997), 54–56.
32 Price, Randolf, *The Angels Within Us: A Spiritual Guide to the Twenty-Two Angels that Govern Our Lives* (New York, NY: Fawcett/Columbine/Ballantine, 1993), 2–3.
33 Moody, Raymond, with Paul Perry, *Reunions* (New York, NY: Villard Books, 1993), 54–62.
34 Ibid.
35 Vorfeld, Judy, *Light and Life* (June 1989), 17.
36 Ibid., 17–18.
37 Graham, Billy, *Angels: God's Secret Agents* (Waco, TX: Word Books, 1995), 250–251.
38 Robertson, Pat, *The New World Order* (Dallas, TX: Word Publishing, 1991), 5.
39 Ibid., 6.
40 Ibid., 14.
41 Ibid., 7.
42 Ibid., 6.
43 Ibid., 176–177.
44 Ibid., 167–168.
45 Gore, Al, *Earth In the Balance* (Boston, MA: Houghton Mifflin Company, 1992), 368.
46 Schindler, Jayne, *The Eagle Forum* (Fall/Winter 1997), 16.
47 Lindsey, *Planet Earth 2000 A.D.,* 68.
48 Kinnaman, Gary, *Angels Dark and Light* (Ann Arbor, MI: Servant Publications, 1994), 132–133.

NOTES

49 Streiber, Whitley, *Cornrnunion* (William Morrow, NY: Beech Tree Books, 1987).
50 Elizabeth L. Hillstrom, Elizabeth L., *Testing the Spirits* (Downers Grove, IL: InterVarsity Press, 1995) 207–208.
51 Daniel, Alma, with Timothy Wyllie, and Andrew Ramer, *Ask Your Angels: A Practical Guide to Working with the Messengers f Heaven to Empower and Enrich Your Life* (New York: Ballantine Books, 1992), 39–40.
52 LaHaye, Tim, *Revelation Illustrated and Made Plain* (Zondervan Publishing House, Grand Rapids, MI, 1975), 267.

www.ingramcontent.com/pod-product-compliance
Lightning Source LLC
Chambersburg PA
CBHW010315090526
44586CB00039B/2588